DEVELOPMENT CENTRE SEMINARS

DEVELOPMENT STRATEGY, EMPLOYMENT AND MIGRATION
Country Experiences

Edited by
David O'Connor
and Leila Farsakh

ORGANISATION FOR ECONOMIC CO-OPERATION AND DEVELOPMENT

ORGANISATION FOR ECONOMIC CO-OPERATION AND DEVELOPMENT

Pursuant to Article 1 of the Convention signed in Paris on 14th December 1960, and which came into force on 30th September 1961, the Organisation for Economic Co-operation and Development (OECD) shall promote policies designed:
- to achieve the highest sustainable economic growth and employment and a rising standard of living in Member countries, while maintaining financial stability, and thus to contribute to the development of the world economy;
- to contribute to sound economic expansion in Member as well as non-member countries in the process of economic development; and
- to contribute to the expansion of world trade on a multilateral, non-discriminatory basis in accordance with international obligations.

The original Member countries of the OECD are Austria, Belgium, Canada, Denmark, France, Germany, Greece, Iceland, Ireland, Italy, Luxembourg, the Netherlands, Norway, Portugal, Spain, Sweden, Switzerland, Turkey, the United Kingdom and the United States. The following countries became Members subsequently through accession at the dates indicated hereafter: Japan (28th April 1964), Finland (28th January 1969), Australia (7th June 1971), New Zealand (29th May 1973), Mexico (18th May 1994) and the Czech Republic (21st December 1995). The Commission of the European Communities takes part in the work of the OECD (Article 13 of the OECD Convention).

The Development Centre of the Organisation for Economic Co-operation and Development was established by decision of the OECD Council on 23rd October 1962 and comprises twenty-two Member countries of the OECD: Austria, Belgium, Canada, the Czech Republic, Denmark, Finland, France, Germany, Greece, Iceland, Ireland, Italy, Japan, Luxembourg, Mexico, the Netherlands, Norway, Portugal, the United States, Spain, Sweden and Switzerland, as well as the Republic of Korea since April 1992 and Argentina and Brazil from March 1994. The Commission of the European Communities also takes part in the Centre's Advisory Board.

The purpose of the Centre is to bring together the knowledge and experience available in Member countries of both economic development and the formulation and execution of general economic policies; to adapt such knowledge and experience to the actual needs of countries or regions in the process of development and to put the results at the disposal of the countries by appropriate means.

The Centre has a special and autonomous position within the OECD which enables it to enjoy scientific independence in the execution of its task. Nevertheless, the Centre can draw upon the experience and knowledge available in the OECD in the development field.

Publié en français sous le titre :

STRATÉGIES DU DÉVELOPPEMENT, DE L'EMPLOI ET DES MIGRATIONS

Évaluation par pays

THE OPINIONS EXPRESSED AND ARGUMENTS EMPLOYED IN THIS PUBLICATION ARE THE SOLE RESPONSIBILITY OF THE AUTHOR AND DO NOT NECESSARILY REFLECT THOSE OF THE OECD OR OF THE GOVERNMENTS OF ITS MEMBER COUNTRIES.

© OECD 1996
Applications for permission to reproduce or translate all or part
of this publication should be made to:
Head of Publications Service, OECD
2, rue André-Pascal, 75775 PARIS CEDEX 16, France.

Foreword

This volume is one of two publications based on the papers and discussions at a Workshop held from 11th to 13th July 1994 at the Development Centre entitled "Development Strategies, Employment and International Migration". The companion volume is being published under the title: *Development Strategy, Employment and Migration: Insights from Models.* Financial support from the Government of the Netherlands is gratefully acknowledged.

Table of Contents

Preface 7

Introduction: Development and Migration - An Overview
    by David O'Connor and Leila Farsakh 9

Part I. Growth, Structural Change, and Labour Market Adjustment

Structural Change and Labour Migration in East Asia
    by Manolo Abella and Hiromi Mori 35

    Malaysia and Chinese Taipei: Labour Market and Migration Experiences Compared
    by Pang Eng Fong 63

Part II. Labour Market and Migration Transitions

Thailand: Development Strategies and Their Impacts on Labour Markets and Migration
    by Chalongphob Sussangkarn and Yongyuth Chalamwong 91

Indonesia: Notes on Employment, Earnings and International Migration
    by Martin Godfrey 127

Part III. Migration, Remittances and Return: Macro and Micro Impacts

Remittances, Inequality and Asset Accumulation: The Case of Rural Pakistan
    by Richard H. Adams, Jr.. 149

International Return Migration and Remittances in the Philippines
    by Edgard R. Rodriguez and Susan Horton 171

Labour Migration from South Asia: Patterns and Economic Implications
    by Beatrice Knerr... 203

Part IV. Trade Liberalisation, Economic Growth and Migration Humps

Trade and Migration: The Case of NAFTA
    by Philip Martin.. 231

Preface

Rising concern about international migration appears increasingly in international discussion of development issues. Concern stems both from the perception of it as a threat to social stability in some migrant-receiving countries and from the sense that migratory pressures are more likely to increase than to decrease in the coming years. The latter reflects a view that persistent migratory outflows from some developing countries stem at least in part from the sense of insecurity based on a perceived dearth of productive employment opportunities and low and sometimes declining incomes. As a good deal of recent work at the Development Centre and elsewhere has emphasised, a chronic failure to generate sufficient new productive employment for the rapidly growing labour force is a very serious problem in many developing countries. This is a continuing challenge. For the foreseeable future, close to 90 per cent of people making an entry into the world's labour market will have been born in a developing country. For example, by the year 2015, sub-Saharan Africa alone will add annually to the world's labour force more than *three times* as many new workers and work seekers as the OECD countries, Eastern Europe and the former Soviet Union combined.

Although migratory pressures and domestic conditions relating to employment and income are closely linked, the specialists working on these questions continue to form two rather distinct groups — development and labour economists on the one hand and migration specialists on the other. Thus, while a rapidly growing body of literature addresses either trade and employment or international migration, rarely are they considered in relation to one another. In bringing the two groups together at the OECD Development Centre's 1994 Workshop the hope was that new insights into a variety of migration-related issues might emerge and a new impetus be created for work in this area. The central purpose is to begin to integrate policy-relevant research on trade, employment and migration in a way that will be useful to a policy audience.

Many of the papers in this volume deal with the experience of countries, mostly located in East Asia, that achieved sustained, rapid growth. In some instances, labour exporting countries have become labour importing ones over a relatively short period of time. The papers shed light on the development strategies and policies that have enabled these countries to create abundant opportunities for productive employment at rising real wages. What lessons can they offer the numerous other countries whose governments are committed to reform programmes designed to restore macroeconomic stability and lay the foundations for sustained, employment-generating growth? Policies exist that could help to change abundant labour from a curse into a blessing. However, their adoption will require profound changes in a wide range of current practice within the developing countries, much support from the developed countries and a change of heart on their part in guaranteeing greater freedom of market access through trade.

Another set of essays examines the economic significance of migration for certain high migration countries and regions (e.g. the Philippines and South Asia). Some developing economies have become heavily dependent on migrants' remittances for foreign exchange earnings, and those remittances can also have a significant impact on such variables as income distribution and investment in productive assets. The notion that remittance income is overwhelmingly consumed rather than saved is contradicted by much country evidence. A policy dilemma is posed, however, by the apparent tradeoff — at least in some settings — between the positive effects of international remittances on investment and their negative distributional effects.

Other policy dilemmas arises in connection with the so-called "migration hump" — a situation wherein accelerated growth in a migrant sending country tends to augment migrant outflows in the short run before reducing them in the long run. In this volume, the migration hump argument is illustrated with regard to the effect of trade liberalisation on Mexican migration to the United States, though the hump phenomenon may be of wider relevance. How significant such humps are in practice remains a topic for research, but their possibility means that advocates of free trade as an effective means of reducing migration have a more difficult task of persuasion.

For the OECD countries, which have sought increasingly to restrict immigration in recent years, the policy message emerging from these studies is an increasingly complex one. First, whatever short-term control measures may accomplish, the only satisfactory long-term answer to the problem of economically-induced migration is to support the implementation of development strategies that generate productive employment and steadily rising real incomes in the migrant sending countries. Whether or not higher migration in the short term does materialise would seem to depend on a range of conditions — market failures, labour market rigidities and others — raising questions about the sequencing of reforms and the possibility of programmes which support reform while acting to dampen a possible migratory response. The work described in this and the sister volume entitled *Development Strategy, Employment and Migration: Insights from Models* throws some light on these issues, but it is also clear that there is still much room for additional research.

Jean Bonvin
President
OECD Development Centre
January 1996

Introduction: Development and Migration — An Overview

by David O'Connor and Leila Farsakh

In recent years, international migration has become a sensitive political issue in many OECD countries. There is a perception, particularly in Europe, that migration pressures from poorer countries to the South and East are intensifying and that OECD labour markets cannot accommodate new immigrants at a time of persistently high domestic unemployment. Thus, there is a keen interest among OECD governments in finding ways to promote rapid growth of productive employment in migrant sending countries. Several of the countries examined in this volume have achieved a remarkable transformation in the space of roughly a generation, from having large numbers of people working in low productivity jobs — and in some cases sending sizeable numbers of their citizens to work abroad — to having tight labour markets and relying increasingly on immigrant labour to relieve labour shortages. How have they managed this feat? A number of the essays address this question. The general consensus is that policies ensuring macroeconomic stability, favouring high rates of savings and investment, encouraging private entrepreneurship, and stressing competition in export markets have been central to the rapid growth and transformation of these economies.

Migration has a variety of motivations, but the desire to improve economic prospects clearly weighs heavily. The simplest economic explanation for international migration is the existence of differential returns to labour in different countries and the expectation that, even after financing migration, the net rewards to work abroad exceed those obtainable in the domestic labour market. While this provides a general rationale for economic migration, it is far from an adequate explanation for the levels and patterns of migration actually observed. A number of other factors — economic and non-economic — intervene. For one, not all those who might be willing to migrate in search of work are able to afford the costs of migration. Even if they could, the probability of their finding a job would be very low since the number of unskilled jobs in high-income countries is tiny in relation to the potential supply of immigrant workers from low-income countries. Moreover, legal immigration into high income countries is strictly limited and there are significant uncertainties and risks associated with illegal immigration. Also, some low income countries with large populations have in the past exercised strict controls on emigration. Historical and cultural factors may also influence particular patterns of migration. Once a migratory process has been set in motion, the formation of migration networks (including via family ties) can help sustain the process even after economic conditions have improved markedly in the sending country.

Return migration is discussed in a few of the country studies. While migrant return may in some cases be involuntary (e.g., a result of illness, deportation, war, etc.), where it is a voluntary decision by the individual migrant there are two sorts of questions that arise. One is what factors influence the timing of the individual migrant's decision to return home. The other is what conditions in the home country might prove sufficiently attractive to induce large numbers of nationals resident abroad to return home, a question of particular relevance in the case of skilled migrants. In the last decade, for example, Korea, Chinese Taipei and other East Asian countries have begun to witness a significant return flow of professionals, many of whom had resided abroad for many years and usually had the option of doing so permanently.

Migration has economic impacts on both sending and receiving countries. Several of the essays discuss these. For the sending country, the most important impacts arise from the remittances migrants send home. At the macro level, they can be a major source of foreign exchange earnings and, in some cases, contribute a sizeable share of GNP. At the micro level, they can augment household income and savings, facilitate purchases of consumer durables and investments in productive assets, and alter the local income distribution. In receiving countries, migrant inflows can ease labour shortages, both of the highly skilled and of the unskilled. In the case of unskilled immigrant workers, a question which sometimes arises is whether their willingness to work at low wages has a depressing effect on the wages of native workers. There is little evidence to support this view in the countries studied here, though admittedly these are not among the major migrant receiving countries.

Development Strategy and Employment

A major objective of development strategy is to create opportunities for productive employment for all those willing and able to work. Sustained increases in the productivity of labour are essential for steady improvements in living standards. Measured by this criterion, performance varies widely across developing countries. A few countries — mostly in East Asia — stand out for their high growth rates of per capita income sustained over a number of decades. During the 1980s, a few more countries — also mostly in Asia — moved onto a high growth path. Encouraged by their example if not forced by economic crisis, many more countries are now undertaking sweeping economic reforms aimed at establishing conditions for accelerating their own growth. The elements of most reforms are broadly similar: macroeconomic stabilisation through tightening of fiscal and monetary controls, maintenance of stable and competitive exchange rates, trade liberalisation and institutional reform, particularly of the financial sector and state-owned enterprises. For the many developing countries endowed with an abundance of labour, trade liberalisation is expected to encourage greater specialisation in labour-intensive production both for the domestic market and for export. In effect, the countries pursuing such reforms are hoping not only to achieve East Asian growth rates but also to emulate East Asia in spreading widely the benefits of growth.

The countries studied in this volume are overwhelmingly Asian — Mexico being the only exception. Several are among the high-growth Asian economies which have already been the object of extensive analysis, a notable recent example being the World Bank's *The East Asian Miracle* (World Bank 1993). The essays in this volume seek to shed light on only one aspect — albeit an important one — of the East Asian experience, viz., what has happened to employment and real earnings over the decades of rapid growth. While even moderate growth, sustained sufficiently long, should eventually yield full employment, what is noteworthy about the East Asian experience is how early real wages began a steep and sustained climb, how broadly spread was the advance in real earnings across the skill distribution, and how quickly full employment was attained. Advances in labour productivity have clearly been central to sustained real wage growth, and these in turn owe much to the adoption of development strategies and policies which have exposed domestic producers to the demands of competing in the international market. Could a reorientation of development strategy in other developing countries along East Asian lines be expected to yield similar employment and earnings gains?

The countries of South Asia and the Philippines provide a study in contrasts to the East Asian experience: their governments have until fairly recently adhered to a highly protectionist set of trade and industrial policies which minimised domestic producers' exposure to international market forces and often reduced domestic competition as well. Despite this, the countries of South Asia have managed fairly steady if modest gains in per capita income, helped by a relatively stable macroeconomic environment[1] and by improvements in agricultural productivity, notably through the application of green revolution technologies. Light manufactured exports also contributed to growth in some South Asian economies if not in India. The Philippines has until very recently been plagued not only by macroeconomic instability but by considerable political uncertainty. For the Philippines, as for Mexico, the 1980s were a lost decade when per capita incomes actually fell. Both countries are now embarked on a programme of macroeconomic stabilisation and trade policy reform aimed at promoting a more efficient allocation of resources and a stronger dynamic of technical change. The reform process is far from complete and, as the recent Mexican experience suggests, further painful adjustments may be needed before being able to move onto a sustainable high growth path.

Certain of the high growth economies of East Asia were sizeable sources of international migrants in an earlier period. Korea, for instance, sent large numbers of contract workers to the Middle East in the 1970s and early 1980s (almost 200 000 at the 1982 peak). Others continue to send migrant workers abroad, though in most cases their numbers have been diminishing. With the exception of Indonesia, the other East Asian economies studied here have become net importers of labour (or, in the case of Thailand, achieved a rough balance between imports and exports), reflecting worsening domestic labour shortages. Indeed, a growing proportion of migrants from the lower wage countries of Asia (South Asia, Burma, China, Laos, the Philippines) seek work in higher income economies of East Asia. (Meanwhile, demand has stagnated in the Middle East labour market.)

The countries discussed in this volume can be divided roughly into four groups, each with its own set of labour market and migration challenges:

1) *countries of full employment*: Japan, Korea, Chinese Taipei and, more recently, Malaysia have experienced growth-induced labour shortages[2] and been confronted with the question of how far to rely on immigrant labour to relieve shortages;

2) *countries undergoing rapid structural transformation*: Thailand and Indonesia have begun to face skilled labour shortages with the rapid growth of their manufacturing and service sectors, even though they both still have large numbers of unskilled workers in agriculture;

3) *countries reorienting development strategy*: the countries of South Asia have achieved moderate GDP growth rates over the last decade, but have done less well in raising per capita incomes due to relatively rapid population growth; new jobs have been created but normally at low levels of productivity.

4) *countries seeking to restore stability and growth*: two of the countries discussed in this volume — the Philippines and Mexico — experienced negative per capita income growth over the last decade; they are also two countries with very high rates of labour force growth and the highest rates of international migration.

The first two groups have followed broadly similar development strategies in recent years, with the main difference between them lying in the shorter duration of the high growth period in the latter than the former. Thailand and Indonesia remain much more heavily rural economies, especially in terms of employment structure, than any of those in the first group. The third group are also heavily rural, but a major difference with the second is the inward-oriented development strategy which until very recently the South Asian countries (possibly excepting Sri Lanka) have pursued. The fourth group has pursued a more outward-oriented strategy than in South Asia, but one heavily financed by external borrowing, which has made them more vulnerable to macroeconomic instability. Another characteristic shared by Mexico and the Philippines has been the very low productivity growth of their agricultural sectors.

Tightening Labour Markets and Growing Immigration

The first group of countries has resolved the classic employment problem in the sense of having reduced unemployment to very low (frictional) levels while achieving rapid improvements in living standards for their populations. Thus, the problems they currently face could be viewed as the problems of success, the most striking of which is a growing difficulty in finding native workers to fill jobs at the bottom end of the skills and earnings distribution.

Abella and Mori examine the development experiences of Japan, Korea and Chinese Taipei from the perspective of labour market dynamics. Pang Eng Fong compares the Taiwanese and Malaysian experiences. In broad terms, these countries have all undergone a similar process of structural transformation, from agricultural economies to industrial and service economies. While Japan had already achieved a high level of industrial development prior to the second world war, the transfer of workers from agriculture continued during the post-war boom, with some 7 million people leaving agriculture during the 1960s and 1970s. In Korea and Chinese Taipei the farm population began declining in the mid-1960s, falling in the Korean case by 10 million people from 1966 to 1991. In Malaysia, agricultural employment has only begun to decline in absolute terms since the late 1980s. By the early 1990s, the ratio of agricultural to total employment had fallen to 7 per cent in Japan, 12 per cent in Chinese Taipei, 17 per cent in Korea, and 25 per cent in Malaysia. By that time, all four economies were operating very close to full employment. In Japan and Chinese Taipei, labour markets have been tight since the 1960s, with unemployment never rising above 3 per cent during recession years. By contrast, Korea and Malaysia had both registered fairly high unemployment rates (around 7 per cent) at the onset of their industrialisation drives, which by the early 1990s had fallen to 2 per cent and 3 per cent respectively.

In all four countries, expansion of labour demand has more than kept pace with what have been — with the exception of Japan — fairly rapid labour force growth rates. While the shift of workers from agriculture to industry served to boost overall labour productivity, agriculture itself has enjoyed sizeable productivity gains in these countries. As a result, agricultural real wages have risen along with (in some instances in advance of) those in manufacturing. Real agricultural wages began to post marked increases already in the 1950s in the case of Chinese Taipei and in the 1970s in the case of Malaysia — i.e. well before absolute employment levels in agriculture began to decline. In Chinese Taipei, real farm wages increased by over 3 per cent per year between 1953 and 1968 (Turnham 1993), with the rate of increase accelerating towards the end of the period. In Malaysia, real earnings of rubber plantation workers rose by approximately 2 per cent per year between 1972 and 1987, while the real earnings of construction workers rose even faster, at 2.7 per cent per year (Richardson and Soon 1990). Korea also witnessed a rise in farm workers' earnings dating from the mid-1960s; in the early 1970s, the real wages of unskilled industrial workers began a steep ascent even as agricultural wages continued their gradual one (Ranis 1993). In short, the evidence would seem to suggest that rapid, labour-intensive growth has yielded improvements in real incomes quite early in the industrialisation process, even at the lower end of the wage distribution.

The rapid growth in urban labour demand in these countries was met through a combination of growth in numbers of school leavers, migration out of agriculture, and an increase in female participation rates. An additional source of wage workers was the shift from self-employment or family employment outside agriculture (e.g. in the urban informal sector). Ongoing changes in the structures of these economies and of their labour forces are altering the sources and patterns of labour supply drastically. First, reserves of agricultural labour have been largely exhausted in some countries and will soon be in others. Second, while female participation rates may continue to increase for some time, they are likely to level off below male rates. Third, declining population growth has already begun to translate into smaller cohorts of school leavers in some countries (Japan and Chinese Taipei) and will do so before long in Korea. Fourth, and finally, young people are remaining in school longer, thereby reducing the number of young workers. Moreover, the rising educational levels of new school leavers normally lead them to expect (demand) not only higher paying but higher quality jobs; in short, they are increasingly reluctant to accept jobs offering few benefits, little job security and few opportunities for skills development as well as those of the 3D-type (dirty, dangerous and degrading).

Labour force growth is already very low in Japan, has slowed significantly in Chinese Taipei since the mid-1970s, and should do so soon in Korea (though in Malaysia it will remain high longer due to a continued high population growth rate). The labour forces in these countries are ageing and new entrants are better and better educated. Thus, the shift towards a more skill-intensive employment structure will need to be sustained or even accelerated if the young are to realise the expected returns on their investments in education. In any case, it is likely that education-related wage differentials will narrow with rising average educational levels of the workforce. The effect of economic restructuring on the employment elasticity of GDP growth is ambiguous: while manufacturing employment elasticity seems likely to fall, this could be more than offset by a rapid expansion of service sector jobs, as appears to be happening in Japan. Even if virtually all incremental labour demand is for skilled workers, some proportion of low-skill, low-productivity jobs is almost certain to remain. These include jobs in the non-tradeables sector (restaurants, hotels, janitorial services, construction, retail trade) as well as some manufacturing jobs which are complementary to high-skilled ones. Policy makers are coming to accept (however reluctantly) that, if such jobs are to be filled at prevailing wages, they will increasingly have to be filled by immigrant workers.

Already in all four countries immigrant labour has begun to assume importance in certain sectors of the economy. Malaysia has by far the largest number of immigrant workers, primarily from Indonesia and primarily in the plantation and construction sectors. In the others, immigrants are heavily represented in construction, in certain low-skill services, and in 3D manufacturing activities. Many of these workers are illegal, though Malaysia has permitted a sizeable number of Indonesian workers to regularise their status while Chinese Taipei has begun to permit some legal contract worker immigration. In Japan and Korea, government policy has thus far consisted largely of a refusal to allow the legal employment of immigrant workers, except in strictly limited numbers in the context of company-sponsored training programmes. In Korea, for example, such a programme is managed by the federation of small businesses, with most of the imported workers employed in textiles and other labour-intensive manufacturing industries. The fact that those same workers can earn much higher wages in the underground economy suggests that the programme falls far short of alleviating the country's unskilled labour shortages. While restructuring towards more skill-intensive industries may reduce somewhat the shortages, it is doubtful whether this will happen very quickly. Meanwhile, governments of these high growth economies are faced with the choice of either devising more coherent policies on immigrant labour or causing sizeable numbers of domestic enterprises to close down[3].

Rapid Structural Transformation

A second group of countries — represented in this volume by Thailand and Indonesia — are undergoing rapid structural transformation but are still at a relatively early stage of industrial development. Though Thailand is considerably more advanced than Indonesia (with a per capita income roughly three times higher), both still have a very sizeable proportion of their labour forces employed in agriculture. In the Thai case, while the contribution of agriculture to GDP has been more than halved over the last two decades, its contribution to employment has declined by less than one-fourth. As Chalongphob and Chalamwong point out, the high proportion of the labour force still engaged in agriculture probably owes something to the sizeable numbers of farmers who cultivate land without legal title and who thus risk its loss without compensation in the event they cease to occupy it.

The high rates of industrial growth in Thailand, especially in the last decade, have given rise to scarcities of certain types of skilled labour (notably engineers and technicians), which have contributed to a widening of education-related wage differentials and of income inequalities. In Indonesia, such wage differentials narrowed significantly between the mid-1970s and the mid-1980s; more recently, they have continued to narrow but at a much reduced rate. The contrast between Indonesia and Thailand in this regard may owe something to differences in the educational profile of their labour forces. One possibility is that Indonesia's labour force, with its higher proportion of those with secondary education, is able to adapt more quickly to growing demand for skilled workers as a consequence of rapid expansion of manufacturing and services. Another is simply that, given Indonesia's lower level of development, the demand for educated labour is not increasing as rapidly as in Thailand.

A measure of how widely the benefits of growth have diffused in these economies is what has happened to the real wages of the least skilled workers normally proxied by wages of agricultural labourers or of construction workers. Given the limited historical reach of wage series, it is possible to trace wage trends only since the late 1970s in Thailand and the early 1980s in Indonesia. In the former, as Chalongphob and Chalamwong show, real wages of those with primary education or less rose by 2 per cent per year from 1978 to 1984, then slowed to 1.2 per cent annual growth from 1984 to 1992 and, in the latter period, rural workers with only basic education experienced a slight fall in real earnings. The causes of this drop are not entirely clear; one hypothesis is that the growing numbers of unskilled immigrant workers is depressing rural wages, but this has yet to be tested. In any case, while income disparities between agricultural and non-agricultural households have widened over the last two decades, poverty incidence has also fallen markedly.

In the Indonesian case, real earnings data are available from the mid-1970s. Godfrey (1991) presents data on real wages in agriculture which suggest some rise from the mid-1970s to the mid-1980s in east and west (but not in central) Java, after which they were roughly constant through 1991 (see Godfrey's contribution to this volume). This period of flat real wages was also one of rapid growth in wage employment, averaging almost 5 per cent per year between 1986 and 1990. Then, in 1991, there was a sharp upturn in real agricultural wages, which lagged by one year a similar upturn in construction wages. Whether these wage increases reflect merely a temporary tightness in unskilled labour markets induced by Indonesia's construction boom or the onset of the transition to a phase of sustained real wage increases is unclear, though the latter seems doubtful in view of the large numbers of people still employed in agriculture and the relative immaturity of the country's industrial transformation.

Both Thailand and Indonesia are sizeable sources of international migrants, though recent migration trends differ between the two. In the former case, the number of migrants peaked in 1989 and has declined steeply since (following a political row between Saudi Arabia and Thailand), while in the latter case the number has continued to increase, with a growing proportion of Indonesian migrant workers destined for Malaysia. Even though Thailand still sends some migrants abroad, it is becoming a host to growing numbers of migrants from low income neighbouring countries, particularly in agriculture, construction and services. Virtually all of the unskilled immigration into Thailand is illegal, while the government permits sizeable numbers of foreigner professionals to work in the country as a way of relieving the skills constraints noted above. Thailand is approaching the status of a net labour importer. Policy makers are concerned that immigrant workers may be competing directly with poorly educated Thai workers not able to shift into higher wage employments.

A Shift in Development Strategy: South Asia

The South Asian countries examined in this volume (Bangladesh, India, Pakistan and Sri Lanka) have recorded moderate growth over the last few decades, but have enjoyed only modest per capita income gains due to relatively rapid population growth (although fertility rates have fallen significantly in all but Pakistan): average annual GDP growth rates (1981-91) ranged from 4.3 per cent to 6.8 per cent, while population growth rates (1980-92) varied from a low of 1.4 per cent per annum in Sri Lanka to a high of 3.1 per cent in Pakistan. All four South Asian countries are migrant sending countries but on a modest scale: in the early 1990s, their combined migrant outflow was lower than that from the Philippines alone.

With the partial exception of Sri Lanka, until recently these South Asian countries have followed highly protectionist and statist development policies. The lack of exposure to international competition has resulted in an inefficient utilisation of scarce investment capital, especially evident in Bangladesh and India. The problem of low capital productivity is exacerbated by low savings and investment: on a per capita basis, investment ranges from a low of $20 in Bangladesh to a high of $90 in Sri Lanka; by comparison, per capita investment in Indonesia is $170 and in Thailand $580. The initiation of fundamental reforms in India in 1991 and the gradual dismantling of protectionist policies in other countries should improve growth prospects. There remain uncertainties, however, about the sustainability of reforms.

Labour markets in South Asia would appear to be more highly segmented than those in East Asia, hindering the transfer of workers from agriculture to industry and from informal to formal sector employment. Possible reasons for this may be the skewed distribution of educational opportunities and the legacy of import substituting policies which has offered opportunities for a minority of workers in the protected industries — often organised into unions — to lay claim to a share of the rents. Where labour-intensive manufacturing has been encouraged, excessive regulation and protection — e.g. of the Indian textile industry — have discouraged technological innovation and quality improvements necessary to compete in international markets. Bangladesh and Sri Lanka's clothing industries are exceptions, but their expansion has been hamstrung by protectionism in major OECD markets.

From Economic Stagnation to Renewed Growth?

Two countries discussed in this volume, Mexico and the Philippines, saw growth stagnate in the 1980s; on a per capita basis, income actually fell. Mexico[4] faced a debt crisis followed by a political crisis and the Philippines the reverse, but in both countries the situation was exacerbated by high labour force growth, 3.2 per cent a year (1981-91) in Mexico and 2.5 per cent in the Philippines. The two countries are the largest sources of international migrants in the world. Poor economic performance is only a part — but a rather important one — of the explanation for their high rates of outmigration. Mexico was a major source of migrant labour to the United States even before its recent economic difficulties, and (as Martin notes in this volume) the networks that have sustained large inflows were already well in place by the onset of the debt crisis in 1982. As Rodriguez and Horton note, the Philippines also has a long history of migration, particularly to the United States, and sent large numbers to the Middle East beginning in the mid-1970s, but the onset of the economic crisis in the early 1980s has led to an upsurge in outmigration, with a growing number heading for new destinations like Europe and the higher income countries of Asia and the Pacific (notably Australia, Japan, Hong Kong and Singapore).

The characteristics of migrants appear to be quite different between Mexico and the Philippines. Whereas in the former most migrants come from rural areas and have only a primary education or less, in the latter migrants are more likely to come from urban areas and have a better than average level of education. Why Philippine migrants should be better educated than the average Filipino is not clear, especially in view of the fact that a high proportion of recent migrants are working in low-skilled service sector jobs. One hypothesis is that many Filipino women migrants are employed as nurse maids where language skills and other skills or character traits acquired through education may be valued by employers.

Given the extensive overseas networks both countries' migrants have established, even a return to more rapid, labour-absorbing domestic growth would not have a noticeable short-run effect on migration flows. Indeed, for reasons discussed by Martin and Taylor (see the companion volume, Taylor, ed., 1995), the short-run effect of accelerated growth might well be to cause a migration hump before flows begin to trend downwards. In the case of Mexico, a plausible scenario giving rise to a hump is one where trade liberalisation with the United States causes a major contraction of subsistence agriculture, particularly maize cultivation, displacing large numbers of rural workers, some of whom will cross the northern border in search of work. In the case of the Philippines, dislocations associated with economic reform could also contribute to increased migration flows. In addition, the costs of international migration are substantially higher than in Mexico, in which case one impact of higher income growth could be to augment the ranks of those would-be migrants actually able to finance migration. Though faster growth should eventually begin to reduce the incentive to migrate, the time lag could be quite long, depending on the size of the initial earnings gap and people's expectations about whether high growth can be sustained. Thus, demand-side considerations and the height of entry barriers to foreign labour markets are likely to be the operative constraints on both Mexican and Filipino migration for some time to come.

Assuming a return to macroeconomic and political stability, both Mexico and the Philippines have reasonably good prospects of accelerating export-oriented growth. In Mexico, foreign direct investment (FDI) in labour-intensive export industries is expected to increase in the aftermath of NAFTA, while the Philippines has the advantage of being located in the most dynamic region, where outward FDI in labour-intensive manufacturing has been expanding very rapidly in the last several years. Infrastructure constraints may deter some investment, but the extensive port facilities left by the US Navy at Subic Bay have already lured a number of investors to the neighbouring export processing zone. In the past, a highly politicised labour movement has acted as a discouragement to FDI. The steep rise in real wages since the mid-1980s may be a one-time reaction to their steep erosion over the preceding 15 years, not unlike the wage adjustments which occurred in Korea after the onset of democratic government (though the latter were designed to catch up with productivity rather than with inflation).

By Way of Summary

In terms of development strategies and policies, most developing countries would resemble those in either group 3 or group 4: either reforming gradually in the hope of moving from moderate to rapid growth, or reforming more urgently in the face of economic crisis and falling living standards. In either case, the lessons from the development strategies pursued by the high growth economies of groups 1 and 2 would seem to apply. Taking macroeconomic and political stability as a precondition, policies which expose producers to greater competition — whether in the domestic market or in international markets — are crucial. For many countries, the resulting specialisation and reallocation of resources will favour more labour-intensive activities, though with differing mixes of skilled and unskilled labour. A dynamic agricultural sector facilitates the transfer of resources and of workers to manufacturing and service while sustaining improvements in agricultural incomes and thereby securing essential political stability. A dynamic non-farm rural economy can also contribute significantly to rural employment and incomes, slowing the migration of population to cities in advance of the expansion of productive employment opportunities. A broad spread of primary and secondary education should enhance labour force mobility, reduce tendencies towards labour market segmentation and inhibit the emergence of gross inequalities in the distribution of income.

The Effects of Migration on Development

Just as development can affect migration, migration in turn can affect the development process in migrant sending countries. International migration permits some fraction of the labour force to earn substantially higher returns than it could have in the domestic market. At the same time, depending on the degree of slack in the domestic labour market and the numbers migrating, migration should raise the returns to labour of those remaining at home above what they would otherwise have been. Once working abroad, migrants normally remit a sizeable share of their earnings to their home country. The size, distribution and use of these remittances are among the most significant economic variables associated with migration[5]. For the national economy of the sending country, their main significance is as a source of foreign exchange in some cases larger even than foreign exchange earnings from merchandise exports. For the individual migrant household, remittances can constitute a sizeable share of income — one which does not co-vary with agricultural or other income. The size of remittances is clearly influenced by the earnings potential of migrants (a function principally of education and skill levels). Macroeconomic conditions in the sending country can influence both the volume and the channels of remittances. The institutional and policy environment in the sending country can have a major impact on how remittances are used — whether for productive investment and entrepreneurship or for consumption. Type of use also depends on the income level and other characteristics of remittance receiving households.

While many Asian migrants still head towards countries of the Middle East and countries of permanent immigration such as the USA and Canada, in recent years Middle East migration has tended to stagnate while flows towards new destinations — Japan and dynamic Asian economies like Hong Kong, Korea, Singapore and Chinese Taipei — have increased. In those countries, the worsening labour shortages, particularly in certain low skill occupations, have been a major pull factor. As with Middle East migration, most intra-Asian labour migration is temporary in nature; legislation in receiving countries generally does not allow permanent settlement. While unskilled workers predominate, there are also significant movements of highly skilled professionals, and immigration laws tend to be more accommodating for the latter.

Labour Market Implications

In formal terms, the labour market implications of migrant outflows depend on how large a shift they cause in the relevant labour supply curve. Rarely are the numbers involved sufficiently large to have a marked effect on labour availability at a national level. This is especially so with unskilled labour migration. Nevertheless, within a country, there may be some regions or localities which send a disproportionate number of migrants abroad. There, outmigration — whether to the city or overseas — could significantly alter local labour market conditions. Referring to results from CGE-based models of direct and indirect effects of international migration on sending villages in Mexico, Java and Kenya, Taylor (1995, companion volume) finds that migration results in a reduction in household labour inputs, causing a fall in local production, particularly in the more labour-intensive sectors. However, to the extent that expenditure of remittance income creates demand for non-tradeables (e.g. construction) or investment in productive assets, the longer term effect would be to raise local output and employment. The migration-induced increase in local labour costs tends to favour more capital-intensive methods and activities (e.g., livestock raising). Knerr observes that, in the migrant sending areas of India and Pakistan, employment grew during the migration boom period, particularly in agriculture and construction sectors, though this growth clearly cannot be entirely attributed to the effect of remittances.

Viewed from the perspective of the national labour market, the number of migrants is normally small in relation to total active population but also quite variable (ranging from 0.8 per cent in India to 6.2 per cent in Mexico), but in some countries and in some years labour outflows can be equivalent to the total increase in the labour force (e.g., Pakistan, Philippines, Mexico), suggesting that migration can act as an important employment outlet in periods of economic stagnation. Migrants do not, however, always represent a net reduction in the domestic labour force — e.g. by one estimate (Rodrigo and Jayatissa 1989) half of the women migrants from Sri Lanka (who represent more than 60 per cent of all migrants) were not in the labour force prior to migration. Where skilled labour is in short supply, large-scale migration can create serious shortages. Knerr finds, for example, that the outflow of semi-skilled construction workers in Pakistan led to shortages and pushed up wages. The departure of doctors in the 1970s from Bangladesh and Pakistan was associated with a deterioration of health services.

The effects of migration on real wages at the national level are probably small in most countries. There is some evidence suggesting a connection between migration and wages in those sectors in which remittance expenditures tend to be concentrated. In Pakistan for example, Knerr finds that real wages on average increased by almost 25 per cent between 1978-83 (the migration boom period), and in the construction sector they increased by 41 per cent. Labour outflows can also have a knock-on effect, stimulating internal migration. In Kerala, for example, the outflow of migrants towards the Gulf encouraged in-migration by workers from neighbouring regions to replace those who left, thereby dampening any localised wage pressures.

Migration may affect the structure of labour markets and of relative wages. For instance, if demand for migrants is biased towards the educated or highly skilled, their withdrawal from the domestic labour market could serve to increase education-/skill-related wage differentials. Rodriguez and Horton suggest that this may have happened in the Philippines. In other cases, migrants may be drawn more heavily from the ranks of the uneducated, in which case a large enough demand might contribute to a narrowing of wage differentials. Countries where migrants are drawn heavily from poor households include Egypt, Mexico and Sri Lanka, but effects on relative earnings have not been adequately studied. Studies of the effects of migration on household income distribution (e.g., Adams' contribution to this volume) suggest that, where poor households provide most migrants, post-migration income distribution improves.

The Role of Remittances

The impact of remittances on the migrant-sending countries' economies is probably the most important dimension of migration. Migration is above all a household decision, frequently involving the pooling of household savings to finance the costs of migration. The remittances from the migrant's earnings (net of any decline in domestic income associated with migration) could thus be interpreted as the expected return on that investment. The size and frequency of remittances vary with migrant's age, education, and position in the household (head of family or not). The duration of the migration period also has an important influence on the propensity to remit: while the propensity to remit increases initially with the duration of migration and the approach of expected return, after the point where the probability of return falls off so does the propensity to remit. In effect, migrant's ties to relatives back home weaken. The type of migration involved (contract or permanent) is also a consideration, but it is not always the case that temporary migrants remit more than permanent migrants, since the latter are often higher income earners than the former[6]. Rodriguez and Horton find that Filipino migrants to the Middle East have a lower probability of remitting than those working elsewhere since their disposable income is more limited[7]. Whether migrants remit regularly through official channels depends on such factors as the availability of efficient mechanisms for funds transfer through the banking system, and government tax and exchange rate policy *vis-à-vis* remittances. Even if migrants do not remit regularly, the amount of money that they bring home upon return can be large.

How remittance income is used depends in part on the level of pre-remittance income and wealth of the recipient households. Where remittance income is earned principally by poor households, it may well go to supplement basic consumption expenditures, although the distinction between consumption and investment may not be very meaningful where consumption expenditures include human capital investments, e.g. health, nutrition and education. Consumption expenditures by lower income households may have a higher multiplier effect on local incomes than comparable expenditures by wealthy households which often have a higher propensity to "import" goods from outside the local economy.

Stark, Taylor and others have interpreted migration and associated remittances as part of a strategy for diversifying risks and raising capital on the part of rural households, especially poor landless households without access to local capital markets. Migrants are found in general to have a higher propensity to save and invest than non-migrants. The remittances may be invested in physical assets or in human capital (e.g. children's education), the allocation being a function in part of the household's wealth and of the expected returns to different sorts of investment. Adams argues that in Pakistan, international remittances positively affect asset accumulation, particularly through the renting-in of additional land and the purchase of livestock. Taylor (1995) finds similar evidence on livestock acquisition in rural villages in Kenya, Mexico and the island of Java in Indonesia. The effective productive contribution of remittances, however, remains dependent on the kind of institutional and policy framework in place. If migrant households are found to prefer to invest in consumption or in speculative activities rather than in productive assets, the reason often lies in an uncertain inflationary environment which makes long-term investment expensive and risky. It could also be due to the effect of certain sectoral or macroeconomic policies that discriminate against agricultural or small-scale production activities in which migrants are usually involved.

What impact do remittances have on income distribution? The studies in this volume suggest that international migration may widen income inequalities, while domestic migration tends to have the reverse effect. Using household survey data from a few poor localities in rural Pakistan, Adams finds statistical evidence for such opposing distributional effects. This derives in no small measure from the fact that it is the wealthier households that can afford to send a member abroad while poorer households can more easily finance migration for work or job search in an urban centre or another part of Pakistan. Rodriguez and Horton report similar findings for the Philippines: viz., that remittances of foreign income contribute to widening income disparities (as measured by the Gini coefficient), both nationally and within the urban areas. As in Pakistan, costs of migration are thought to be one reason for bias towards wealthier households. The nature of demand in overseas labour markets may also explain why, in both Pakistan and the Philippines, international migrants tend to be more educated than non-migrants.

The contribution of remittances at the macro level is difficult to assess since only a small proportion of these flows actually go through official channels. While in some countries governments offer tax or financial incentives to encourage migrants to remit their earnings through the banking system, these are often insufficient in the face of grossly overvalued official exchange rates. Nevertheless, in some cases official remittances represent a very significant source of scarce foreign exchange[8]. In Bangladesh, for example, they have hovered around 50 per cent of merchandise export earnings while in Pakistan (from the mid-1970s to the mid-1980s) they consistently exceeded the value of merchandise exports. While in theory a very large upsurge in remittance flows could cause a real appreciation of a country's currency and associated "dutch disease" symptoms (a shift of resources from tradeables to non-tradeables production), in practice there is little evidence of such effects. The highly elastic supply of labour in most migrant-sending countries implies that expansion of the non-tradeables sector need not adversely affect the supply of tradeables.

Using regression analysis to assess the impact of remittances on macroeconomic aggregates, Knerr confirms that lagged remittances have a positive and statistically significant effect on GDP growth in South Asian countries. In some cases however, regional GNP per capita is seen to have grown faster than GDP per capita, reflecting the fact that a significant portion of remittances are spent on imports from other regions (the case of Kerala in India). While remittances may stimulate agriculture in situations where low initial incomes imply a high income elasticity of demand for food, the construction and service sectors are the most directly and strongly affected. Manufacturing requires larger and longer-term investments which may have low profitability in the face of imports from other regions or countries. Macroeconomic stability and appropriate policies and institutions (e.g., rural banks) can contribute to channelling a larger share of migrant remittances into long-term productive investment.

Returning Migrants

A sizeable percentage of international migrants eventually return to their country of origin, especially as people derive utility from living in their culture and with their families. Yet, little is known about the optimal timing for ending the migration period. Various exogenous factors, such as deportation, sickness, or war in the host country can force migrants to return sooner than they would like. Voluntary decisions to return are often related to the initial motivation for migration. If the aim of migration was to increase individual consumption capacity, then the duration of stay will depend on the tradeoff between the marginal utility of additional consumption and the marginal disutility of additional time abroad. If the migrant is a target saver, then return would occur when a certain net asset position has been achieved. Stark (1994) suggests another explanation: if migration is considered a form of income insurance, then it may permit the migrant-sending household to undertake a high-risk, high-return investment which it would otherwise not have considered. If the investment pays off, then the need for insurance vanishes and the migrant can return. Rodriguez and Horton find for the Philippines that the migrant position in the household has a significant effect on likelihood of return, with returnees more likely to be heads of household or their spouses.

Conditions in the home country, particularly the level of unemployment in the local or national economy, also have a significant impact on the decision to return. Rodriguez and Horton find, for the Philippines, a significant negative correlation between the rate of return to a particular region and the regional unemployment rate. The impressive record of Chinese Taipei, Korea and Singapore in generating productive employment and high incomes has begun to attract sizeable numbers of skilled nationals to return home either temporarily or permanently. In 1991, some 10 000 emigrants returned to Singapore and Malaysia (Pang, 1993).

Returning migrants normally bring with them their foreign-earned savings and a work and living experience that could be potentially enriching in terms of exposure to new ideas and ways of doing things. However, if skills are acquired abroad, they are not necessarily well matched to local needs. Various studies on return migrants suggest that they do not fare very well in the labour market. In many cases, their unemployment rate is higher than non-migrants, though perhaps the more relevant comparison is with unemployment among new labour force entrants or with their own employment status prior to migration. In Kerala, 46 per cent of returning migrants were unemployed compared with 38 per cent before migration. Return migrants may be able to use their accumulated savings to finance a spell of unemployment while searching for a suitable job. This is borne out by evidence that those returnees with higher levels of education, skills and financial savings tend to have higher rates of unemployment than others.

In summary, the principal macroeconomic contribution of migration to sending countries lies in remittances' contribution to foreign exchange earnings and GDP growth, though in a few cases outmigration has also noticeably ameliorated domestic employment problems. Though not adequately documented here, in some cases the loss of skilled labour and perhaps of certain public goods associated with a professional community (civic leadership, role models) could be a significant cost of "brain drain" migration. In recent years and for a few countries, reverse brain drain has begun to play a positive role. At the micro level, remittances can be a valuable source of income and of risk diversification for the household, and can provide investment capital to those without access to domestic capital markets. Incentives for their productive investment are provided in the first instance by the broader institutional and policy environment, which matters more than any special government policies to encourage such investment. Distributional effects of international remittances vary across countries, but in the few cases where such effects have been measured in this volume, income disparities appear to have been exacerbated.

The Implications of Migration for Receiving Countries

While not a major focus of the essays in this volume, the impact of migration on receiving countries merits some discussion. The bulk of international migrants are unskilled or semi-skilled workers who find jobs in low-wage occupations, often in agriculture but also in construction, tourism and other services and, to a lesser degree, in manufacturing. Oftentimes, employers in these sectors face difficulties finding native workers willing to accept the low wages and difficult working conditions associated with such jobs. This would suggest that immigrants are usually not in direct competition with native workers. Such competition might occur, however, where immigrant workers were relatively free to move from these 3-D type jobs into other sectors or occupations. The degree of immigrant labour mobility is a topic warranting further research, particularly in those Asian countries which have only recently begun to experience sizeable immigration.

Another issue of some concern to those countries is whether the ready availability of low-skilled immigrant labour could slow the structural transformation of the economy towards higher-skill activities. There is little firm evidence, however, that unskilled immigrants delay restructuring or depress wages. Indeed, there is some reason to expect the reverse viz., that low-skill immigrant workers complement higher-skilled native workers and that, as a result, the latter might have lower incomes in their absence. For example, low-cost domestic help provided by immigrants in places like Hong Kong and Singapore allows sizeable numbers of educated, middle-class women to join the labour force. More generally, in countries characterised by rapid growth, high employment elasticities and low unemployment, migrants are likely to play a valuable role in helping to avert employment bottlenecks that could slow growth. In this sense, the dynamic Asian economies do not find themselves in the same situation as many OECD countries, where the immigrants enter economies characterised by low growth, very low employment elasticities and high unemployment.

Looking at the larger developed East Asian economies (Japan, Chinese Taipei, and Korea), foreign workers today (including illegals) represent less than 1 per cent of the total labour force. Governments have generally sought to discourage immigration flows, but with continued tightening of labour markets, it has been very difficult to prevent illegal immigration. Service sector firms as well as small-scale manufacturing establishments unable to automate or relocate their production are the principal employers of unskilled immigrant labour. In Tokyo, 10.7 per cent of small industries were reported to be employing some foreign labour in 1990. Recently, governments have begun to redefine their policies on unskilled immigrants as well, in recognition of the need to discourage illegality and to appease the numerous small-scale enterprises whose survival is seen to depend on employing immigrants. Government policies have been considerably more lenient towards skilled immigrant workers. In Thailand, for example, skilled workers account for 60 per cent of officially admitted migrants. Throughout the region, skilled immigrants are often employed by foreign firms unable to find qualified local candidates.

Some countries in Asia have quite a long history of reliance on immigrant labour, notably Singapore and Malaysia. Thailand, too, has relatively large numbers of immigrant workers from neighbouring countries, even as sizeable numbers of unskilled or semi-skilled Thais continue to find work abroad. If the estimate for the number of immigrants in Malaysia is correct, foreign workers (including illegals) could constitute up to 17 per cent of the labour force. In Singapore, in 1990, there were 300 000 foreigners in the country (not all in the labour force), compared to a native population of only 2.7 million (Pang, 1993). In 1980 (the last year for which such figures are available), foreigners represented about 10 per cent of the labour force. About one-third of those were permanent residents (mainly skilled workers) and the rest (mostly unskilled) were non-residents.

Migration flows within Asia are not likely to subside in the near future. Demand for unskilled labour is seldom entirely eliminated, even at very high levels of development. Hotel maids, restaurant dishwashers, janitorial services, sanitation services, and domestic help are examples of low skill occupations and activities for which demand tends to be rather income-elastic. The increasing educational and skill profile of the domestic labour force makes it ever more difficult to fill such jobs with natives. As Abella and Mori note, the presence of foreign workers in Japan and Chinese Taipei is partly attributable to the mismatch between the relatively highly educated labour force and a persistent demand for unskilled labour. Labour shortages may well become more rather than less acute in future. Not only have domestic sources of new labour force entrants been depleted (e.g. as female participation rates plateau), but the changing age profile of the population points in coming decades to a rising dependency ratio as more and more elderly people look for support to a slow-growing working age population. The focus of policy will need to reflect the changing demographic and economic realities, i.e. to shift from what is likely to prove a futile effort to stop immigration to a policy of managing flows in co-operation with major sending countries.

Directions for Future Policy Research

The essays in this volume raise a number of questions and policy paradoxes which point to the need for further research. Several possible lines of research are discussed here under the broad themes of employment and development strategy, and migration policies.

Employment and Development Strategy

A number of the successful East Asian economies have achieved virtual full employment of the domestic labour force in a matter of a generation. Labour shortages have become acute in countries like Japan, Korea, Chinese Taipei, Hong Kong, Singapore and even Malaysia. While the last three have relatively accommodating policies towards immigrant labour, the first three have quite restrictive policies. One topic which immediately suggests itself for research is whether the difference in policy approaches has made any difference to these countries' economic performance and if so how. How has a more liberal policy affected domestic labour markets for unskilled workers? Are immigrant workers competitors for low-wage jobs with native workers? Are immigrant workers complements to more highly skilled native workers? How do the returns to such labour differ between those countries with easy access to such complementary inputs and those without? Policy makers in both groups of countries would benefit from answers to these questions as they seek to formulate coherent immigration policies consistent with economic realities. Another question is whether access to low-cost immigrant labour significantly affects savings and capital investment. Where labour scarcities cannot be relieved through labour imports, is there a tendency towards a more capital-intensive economic structure and/or a less efficient utilisation of capital?

A second line of research would investigate the problem of duality in the labour markets of certain developing countries, which is reflected in a widening gap between the real earnings of the skilled and the unskilled, the educated and the uneducated. While such a widening of differentials could be expected as a transitional phenomenon associated with rapid structural transformation from an agricultural to an industrial and service economy, the duration of the "wage transition" may vary between countries, perhaps as a function of the initial educational profile of the workforce. Its duration may be of some political importance if a protracted widening of wage disparities creates social discontent which in turn threatens to slow growth. Thailand is mentioned in this volume as one country where education-related wage differentials have been widening recently. What lies behind this trend? One hypothesis, yet to be tested, is that it reflects a major restructuring in the skill composition of labour demand in Thai industry and a resultant mismatch with the educational/skill profile of the labour force. Further research is needed to shed light on this, not only for Thailand but for certain other developing countries with similar labour force characteristics facing similar sorts of economic transformation. Brazil and Indonesia are two large countries which suggest themselves for comparison. In both, mean years of schooling of the adult populations are virtually identical with Thailand's (3.8 years), though in Indonesia secondary school enrolment rates are significantly higher.

A third line of research relates to what might be called "migrant-dependent" economies like Mexico and the Philippines. In the case of the Philippines and other countries where migrants tend to be highly educated, there is the familiar problem of "brain drain" on the domestic economy. How do opportunities for skilled labour migration affect levels and patterns of investment in human capital? To what extent are scarce public resources being allocated to educating and training potential migrants and what are the opportunity costs of those resources? The long-run social implications of investing resources in preparing labour for migration depend critically on whether those migrants are temporary or permanent. This distinction could be expected to matter not only for the obvious reason that the skills of permanent migrants are lost once-and-for-all to the sending country, but also because permanent migrants appear to have a lower propensity to remit their earnings than temporary migrants. The essay in this volume on the Philippines suggests such a difference in remittance behaviour, but there is scope for similar research along these lines in other countries. Another issue of interest regarding "brain drain" migration is what impact it has on intangible aspects of development, e.g., on the presence of educated community leaders and role models who can contribute to maintaining social cohesion and social dynamism. It is not a simple matter, however, to quantify this aspect of the "brain drain" for analytical purposes.

East Asia has begun to experience a significant "reverse brain drain". The contribution which highly skilled returnees make to the home economy, in terms of entrepreneurship, technological upgrading, etc., warrants further research. That contribution may depend in part on the timing of return, i.e. whether the domestic technological capabilities and other complementary assets are in place to make effective use of the returnees' expertise. To the extent this is so, government policies which succeed in inducing a "premature" reverse brain drain may yield only small returns.

In the case of Mexico and other countries where unskilled labour makes up the bulk of migration, "brain drain" is not a central issue. Still, there is a question of the degree to which large-scale migration of unskilled workers may have distorted domestic factor markets, promoting a more capital-intensive investment pattern than would be warranted by relative factor availabilities (in the absence of migration). Whether this matters depends on whether migrant outflows are vulnerable to sudden large-scale reversals and how quickly domestic factor markets might be expected to adjust to such reversals. Certain developing countries have had to cope with the reabsorption of sizeable numbers of returning migrants, including Vietnam when its special economic relationship with the CMEA countries ended and the Philippines in the immediate aftermath of the Gulf war.

The Mexican case also suggests another area for research, viz., what kind of empirical support exists for the "migration hump" hypothesis. While this has been posited in the context of NAFTA-induced trade liberalisation in North America, there are other examples of structural adjustment in "migration-dependent" developing economies which might lend themselves to an investigation of the hump phenomenon[9]. The Philippines is one case in point. Since the early 1990s there appears to have been a marked increase in migrant outflows from that country. To what extent can these be explained by structural adjustments occurring in the context of the Philippine government's attempts to achieve macroeconomic stability, to de-regulate industry and to open the economy more widely to international trade and investment? Interestingly in the Philippine case, migrant networks would appear to play only a limited role in this upsurge, since the destinations of recent migrants differ quite markedly from those of earlier generations. Research on recent Philippine migration experience could shed more light on the question of "migration pathways".

Migration Policies

A number of papers in this volume argue that international migration is an option open principally to the better-off members of society, in part because of the high costs of entry into the international labour market at least from certain countries. One question for research is how far the cost of migration can explain differences between actual and potential migration, especially given the large the pool of unemployed unskilled workers in many developing countries? In some cases, financial arrangements have evolved to address capital market imperfections, allowing migrants to borrow against future earnings to finance migration. More research is warranted on how far such arrangements may overcome selection bias among potential migrants. Where governments are seeking to promote greater migration of the unskilled, perhaps as part of a broader strategy to address domestic unemployment problems, does the government need to provide incentives to encourage the development of such financing arrangements? Put differently, are there reasons why private institutions would not emerge to provide such financing without government encouragement?

On the other hand, governments may be interested in reducing people's incentive to emigrate. While in the longer term, policies conducive to generation of productive employment are apt to be most effective, the new microeconomics of migration suggests that reducing migration may call for interventions in other markets than the labour market. If migration is part of a household income risk diversification strategy or a means of gaining access to capital for productive investment, then interventions to remedy imperfections in local insurance or capital markets may be called for. Empirical research informed by the insights from this literature is still in its early stages.

Another area that would need to be tackled in understanding migration flows is the relation between internal and international migration. Often the cohort of internal migrants is different from that of international migrants, due to differences in the migration costs and in the nature of demand for labour in internal and international markets. Yet, internal migrants often become international migrants. What are the factors at work that encourage or discourage such a transformation? What impact do such phenonema have on income distribution and what role can government policies play in this respect, if any?

Remittances are among the most valuable contributions that migration can make, both to the household and the economy as a whole. However, their macroeconomic consequences are not yet fully understood. While econometric work reported in this volume suggests a significant effect of remittance inflows on aggregate demand and growth, there is need for further model-based analysis in a general equilibrium framework[10], taking into account simultaneous impacts of remittance inflows and labour outflows. More econometric work, particularly using pooled time series for a number of migrant-sending countries, could also be useful. There are several countries for which migration has been occurring on a sizeable scale for at least two decades (i.e. from the onset of the first oil boom), so time-series analysis should be able to shed light on what difference migration has made to their growth, to income distribution, or to other relevant variables. What structural or policy variables may explain differences in the net benefits from migration across countries?

While remittances increase household income, yet the impact of remittances on expenditure patterns is still inadequately researched. Migrants' socio-economic status, the domestic policy environment, and local institutional factors may all influence migrant household expenditures. To shed light on patterns of remittance expenditure, expenditure functions could be estimated for samples of remittance-receiving and non-remittance-receiving households, assuming household income and expenditure survey data provide a sufficiently detailed breakdown of expenditures, including investments in productive assets. The question of savings out of remittance income and the productive investment of those savings raises broader policy questions about how far government policy can encourage higher rates of savings and whether existing financial institutions are effective in mobilising and channeling savings into productive uses.

There is some evidence to suggest that returnees often become self-employed, using savings out of foreign-earned income to start up small businesses[11]. However, there is not much evidence on how successful they are as entrepreneurs relative to other self-employed individuals. Is there any evidence that returned migrants make more successful entrepreneurs and, if so, what explains this? Is it the savings migrants are able to accumulate, the skills and/or contacts they acquire abroad, etc.? Answers to these questions should clearly be of interest to policy makers in migrant sending countries.

Evidence on the effect which international migrant remittances have on domestic income distribution is mixed. What factors explain why in some cases remittances widen disparities and in others they reduce them? Also, what effect do remittances have on the position of individual households in the income distribution and/or on social stratification? By longitudinal studies involving repeated sampling of the same households, a panel data set can be constructed and used to study how remittances affect relative incomes of migrant versus other households and also how they affect social mobility within communities. For instance, do remittances allow landless farmer households to become owner-cultivators, leasehold-cultivators, or perhaps self-employed? This is an aspect of the migrant-entrepreneur question raised in the preceding paragraph.

Finally, governments of migrant receiving countries could benefit from further research on the pull factors which give rise to large clandestine inflows of immigrant workers. What are the costs and benefits of regularisation of such flows? How can shortages in domestic labour markets be most effectively addressed? To answer these questions, research is needed on the degree of complementarity/substitution between foreign and domestic workers; also, on the degree to which allowing sizeable unskilled labour imports retards the process of economic restructuring towards more skill-intensive activities.

Notes

1. During the 1980s, when foreign direct investment inflows were a mere trickle and portfolio investment had not yet taken off, India borrowed quite heavily from international banks; from 1981 to 1991 the central government's external debt rose from $14 billion to $36 billion. The structural reforms initiated in the latter year were in part a response to the macroeconomic imbalances to which the public debt contributed.
2. The government has raised the quota recently by 50 per cent, from 20 000 to 30 000 workers per year.
3. In the early 1990s, Singapore's government proposed instituting a system of competitive bidding by employers for work permits (for low skilled workers) in an effort to discourage heavy reliance on foreign workers; see United Nations 1994, p. 144.
4. There is some question about the exact size of the Mexican labour force: the 1990 Census of Population reports it as 24 million while the Ministry of Labor reports 30 million. See Martin (1993), p. 96.
5. Few of the essays in this volume explore systematically the effects on sending economies of so-called "brain drain" type migration, thought there are suggestions, notably in Knerr, that they have been significant in some cases — e.g., Bangladeshi and Pakistani doctors. Also, in the construction sector, the outmigration of skilled craftsmen appears to have reduced the quality of the remaining labour force by undermining the apprenticeship system.
6. Even if a highly skilled professional migrant were to remit only a tiny fraction of his/her foreign earnings, it could well amount to a multiple of his/her potential earnings in the home country.
7. The social cost of the withdrawal of skilled labour from the domestic economy certainly exceeds that of the withdrawal of unskilled labour. Whether the higher remittances sent by skilled migrants are sufficient to compensate for that loss is not known. The social costs may well exceed the private costs to the household of the migrant's departure if there are certain positive externalities associated with the presence of skilled and educated individuals in the country — e.g. role model or community leadership benefits.
8. Unofficial remittances or remittances in kind also have positive balance-of-payments (BOP) effects, though the former are likely to show up on the errors and omissions line in the BOP accounts while the latter represent imports financed out of foreign-earned income.

9. See the Faini paper by Martin and Taylor on this subject published in the companion workshop volume edited by Taylor, J.E. (1995) *Development Strategies, Employment and Migration: Insights from Models,* Development Centre, Paris.

10. See Faini, R. and J. de Melo paper that looks at the Morocco case in a CGE model framework, published in the companion workshop volume edited by Taylor, J. E. (ed.) (1995) *Development Strategies, Employment and International Migraton: Insights from Models*, Development Centre, Paris.

11. See for example Addleton, J. (1992) *Undermining the Centre: The Gulf Migration and Pakistan*, Oxford University Press, Oxford, or Amjad, R. (ed.) (1989) To *the Gulf and Back: Studies on the Economic Impact of Asian Labour Migration,* UNDP/ILO, New Delhi, for various articles that discuss some of these issues.

Bibliographical References

ADDLETON, J. (1992) *Undermining the Centre: The Gulf Migration and Pakistan*, Oxford University Press, Oxford.

AMJAD, R. (ed.) (1989), *To the Gulf and Back: Studies on the Economic Impact of Asian Labour Migration*, UNDP/ILO, New Delhi.

FAINI, R. and J. DE MELO (1995), "Trade Liberalisation, Employment and Migration: Some Simulations for Morocco", in J.E. Taylor (ed.), *Development Strategy, Employment and Migration: Insights from Models*, OECD Development Centre Study, Paris.

GODFREY, Martin (1991), "Wage Statistics for Employment Monitoring and Labour Market Analysis", DEPNAKAR (Ministry of Manpower)/UNDP/ILO Information System for Employment Development and Manpower Planning, INS/90/001, Report Series A, No. 9 (Technical Report), Jakarta, December.

MARTIN, Philip L. and J. Edward TAYLOR (1995), "The Anatomy of a Migration Hump", in Taylor (ed.), *op.cit.*

PANG Eng Fong (1993), *Regionalisation and Labour Flows in Pacific Asia*, OECD Development Centre Study, Paris.

RANIS, Gustav (1993), "Labor Markets, Human Capital and Development Performance in East Asia", Economic Growth Center Discussion Paper No. 697, Yale University, September.

RICHARDSON, Ray. and SOON Lee Ying (1990), "Wage Trends and Structures in Malaysia", mimeo, February.

RODRIGO, C. and R.A. JAYATISSA (1989), "Maximising Benefits from Labour Migration: Sri Lanka", in M. Amjad (ed.), *To the Gulf and Back: Studies in the Economic Impact of Asian Labour Migration*, UNDP/ILO, New Delhi.

STARK, Oded (1994), "On the Microeconomics of Return Migration", paper presented at OECD Workshop on Development Strategy, Employment and Migration, Paris, 11-13 July.

TAYLOR, J. Edward (ed.) (1995), *Development Strategy, Employment and Migration: Insights from Models*, Paris.

TAYLOR, J. Edward (1995), "International Migration and Economic Development: A Micro Economy-Wide Analysis", in Taylor (ed.), *op. cit.*

TURNHAM, David. (1993), *Employment and Development: A New Review of Evidence*, OECD Development Centre Study, Paris.

WORLD BANK (1993), *The East Asian Miracle: Economic Growth and Public Policy*, Oxford University Press for the World Bank, Washington, D.C.

PART I

GROWTH, STRUCTURAL CHANGE, AND LABOUR MARKET ADJUSTMENT

Structural Change and Labour Migration in East Asia

by Manolo Abella* and Hiromi Mori**

Summary

Rapid development sustained over several decades in Japan, Korea, and Chinese Taipei has largely exhausted domestic labour surpluses, particularly of unskilled workers, turning all three countries into magnets for labour migration from elsewhere in the region. During the early decades of high growth, the strong demand for wage labour in manufacturing and services was met largely through the transfer of workers from agriculture and self-employment and rising female labour force participation. In recent years, continued labour shortages in large firms have been met largely through transfer of workers from small-scale enterprises. The latter are faced with growing difficulties finding workers.

In all three countries, the *ageing* of the population, the slower growth of the labour force, and the decline in youth participation rates as young people extend years of schooling will make it increasingly difficult to satisfy growth in labour demand through additions to the native labour force. Moreover, with higher levels of education, young people are reluctant to accept unskilled, insecure and dangerous jobs. Such jobs are most often found in small-scale enterprises, which also face the greatest difficulty investing in automation or in offshore production in response to tight labour market conditions at home.

Governments have only begun to confront the labour scarcity problem. In Chinese Taipei, the government has chosen to legalise the employment of a limited number of immigrant workers. The Japanese and Korean governments have stopped short of legalisation, but they have permitted some companies to import short-term "trainees" as a stopgap. Nevertheless, given the potential rewards, illegal migration is becoming more widespread, forcing governments to give more attention to migration policy.

---

*   ILO, Geneva
** Faculty of Economics, Hosei University, Tokyo.

Introduction

Japan, Chinese Taipei and the Republic of Korea are today strong magnets of labour migration in East Asia. Although the three countries have been uniquely successful in reaching high levels of industrialisation without drawing on supplies of foreign labour, the current shortages of labour appear to be breaking down the barriers to the entry of foreign workers waiting at their doorsteps. The Governments of all three countries have lately been at pains to find a way of easing the shortage through the controlled entry of temporary labour from abroad without abandoning a long standing policy of avoiding the immigration of foreigners. Whether they will succeed in keeping the process under control remains to be seen but the growth of labour immigration during the past few years has been explosive. Japan today has an estimated 1.2 million foreign workers including about 400 000 illegals compared to only 700 000 in 1985. Korea had a few thousand foreign workers in the early 1980s but their numbers are now estimated at anywhere from 60 to 100 000. In Chinese Taipei the number of foreign workers has quickly climbed to 190 000 from only about 40 000 in 1990 (Tsay, 1991b, 1994).

The contemporary flows of labour migration in East Asia had their beginnings in the late 1970s but only gained momentum after the Plaza Agreement which led to the revaluation of the currencies of Japan and of the newly-industrialising Asian states. This paper analyzes this emerging phenomenon and relates it to adjustments in the labour markets of these countries during recent periods of economic expansion. Of particular interest is the growing role of foreign labour as a new source of labour supply flexibility after all other sources of national labour have dried up. We consider the evidence of "mismatches" in the labour market which has been blamed for the worsening of the labour shortage in Japan during the recent "Heisei boom", and in Korea during the current economic boom. The paper examines in some detail the characteristics of the labour shortage and considers why adjustments by industries through such measures as automation or relocation of production offshore through direct foreign investments are unlikely to solve it. We argue that while these countries have been successful in achieving high levels of industrialisation without importing foreign labour, they have now reached a stage where the import of foreign workers cannot be avoided even if economic growth considerably slows down.

Economic Growth and Emergence of Labour Shortages

These countries passed through the classic pattern of development and labour absorption. There is some disagreement among economists as to when Japan passed the phase of development with unlimited supplies of labour at the subsistence wage level (Fei and Ranis, 1964), but all three countries have passed the neoclassical phase of rising real wages and the massive transfers of labour from agriculture to industry. After the war the return of millions of former soldiers and civilians to rural areas in Japan created a temporary labour surplus in agriculture but this was soon eliminated in the early 1960s. Chinese Taipei reached the Lewisian turning point a decade or so later, and the Republic of Korea sometime in the late 1970s.

The sustained rapid growth of these economies over the last three decades led to very large intersectoral reallocation of labour. In Japan some 4.38 million workers left agriculture in the ten years between 1965 and 1975, while industry added 2.7 million to its employment. In Chinese Taipei and Korea the agricultural sector continued to absorb labour into productive employment up to about the mid-1970s but lost many workers thereafter. As many as a million additional workers were absorbed into the primary sector in Chinese Taipei between 1970 and 1975. Korea's primary sector added another half a million. There has been a steady decline however in the following period, from 1975 to 1990, with the primary sector losing 637 000 in Chinese Taipei and as many as 2.1 million in Korea.

The exhaustion of surplus labour in agriculture was followed by the increased participation of women in the labour force and by transfers of unpaid family labour to paid employment. While more young people were spending more years in school and postponing entry into the labour market, all the older age groups of females were drawn by rising wages to work outside their homes. Female participation rates in the 20-24 age group rose to 75.6 per cent in Japan, 65.4 per cent in the Republic of Korea and 62.6 per cent in Chinese Taipei. Although the withdrawal for a few years after marriage suggests the very strong values attached to rearing children, overall female participation rates had already risen by 1992 to 50.7 per cent in Japan, 47 per cent in the Republic of Korea and 45 per cent in Chinese Taipei, or rates that are almost as high as in Western Europe and North America.

In the 1970s and 1980s Chinese Taipei and the Republic of Korea were still able to draw more people into the workforce permitting the early phase of labour-intensive industrialisation to continue. A crude measure of employment elasticity shown in Table 1 indicates a pattern of "job-full" growth especially in Chinese Taipei up to the 1970s and in the Republic of Korea up to the early 1980s. In Japan the growth of employment was slower but the rising employment elasticity reflects the increasing importance of services as a source of output growth since the 1970s.

The intersectoral transfers of labour have reached the phase where additional labour supplies are coming mainly from the small-industry sector where working conditions are generally less attractive than those in services or in the large industries. In Japan and also to a large extent in the other two countries this sector has always served as a source of secondary labour for large industry during periods of expansion and as an absorber of labour during economic downturns. The unique relationship between large and small-scale enterprises has been credited for the resilience of Japanese industry and the relative stability of employment.

A striking feature of these economies is the size and durability of the small industry sector in their industrial structures. Despite the progressive shifts in manufacturing from simple-technology labour-intensive manufactures to more and more sophisticated consumer durables and capital goods, small industries continued to account for a dominant proportion of industrial employment. In Japan enterprises with fewer than 30 workers accounted for 52.6 per cent of all persons employed in industry in 1966 and for 55 per cent in 1991. Similarly, in Chinese Taipei enterprises with fewer than 50 workers slightly increased their share of employment from 70 per cent in 1980 to 72.7 per cent in 1992. In the Republic of Korea the same size industries increased their share of total industrial employment from 39 per cent in 1981 to 48 per cent in 1991.

Table 1. **Output and Employment Growth in Japan, the Republic of Korea and Chinese Taipei**
(in per cent)

	Annual GNP Growth Rate (1)	Annual Labour Force Growth Rate (2)	Annual Employment Growth Rate (3)	Employment Elasticity (3)(1)
Japan				
1970/75	4.5	1.2	0.5	0.11
1975/80	4.6	1.1	1.2	0.26
1980/85	3.8	1.0	1.0	0.26
1985/90	4.6	.9	1.5	0.33
Korea				
1970/75	8.9		4.0	0.45
1975/80	7.5	3.9	3.0	0.40
1980/85	8.4	1.5	1.7	0.20
1985/90	10.2	3.5	3.8	0.37
Chinese Taipei				
1973/75	3.0	2.5	1.9	0.63
1975/80	10.6	3.4	3.5	0.33
1980/85	6.7	2.6	2.6	0.39
1985/90	8.7	2.0	2.2	0.25

Sources: IMF International Financial Statistics; Japan: Statistics Bureau, Management and Coordination Agency; Japan Statistical Yearbook; Chinese Taipei: Budget Accounting and Statistics, Executive Yuan, Chinese Taipei: *Abstract of Employment and Earnings Statistics, 1992*, May 1993; Korea: National Statistics Office, *The Economically Active Population Surveys*, Seoul.

In the three countries the entry of foreign labour appears to be closely linked not only to the general shortage of labour but more importantly to the increasing difficulties faced by small industries to attract more native workers. The latter is well known and by now well documented. While wage levels in small firms are not always lower than those in larger firms they generally experience a higher turnover of workers and are reported to have higher vacancy rates. Scale economies operate against them in seeking a way out through automation and robotisation; hence recourse to foreign labour has become an attractive alternative. In 1990 as much as 10.7 per cent of small industries in Tokyo were reported to be employing some foreign labour (Tokyo Metropolitan Institute of Labour, 1991).

Dimensions of Recent Migration Flows

Using a residual method (disembarkation less embarkation) Mori calculated that the aggregate net inflow of foreigners into Japan over the period 1975 to 1990 reached 633 700 workers (Mori, 1992). Asian countries — notably the Philippines, the Republic of Korea, China and Chinese Taipei — account for 76 per cent of these net inflows. Up to 1983 the net inflows averaged only 3 000 a year but the flows have been explosive ever since, as shown in Figure 1. The dotted line shows the net inflows from Asian countries and the bold line for all nationalities.

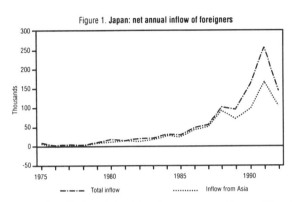

Figure 1. Japan: net annual inflow of foreigners

Three stages can be distinguished in these recent flows. The first consisted of Asian females mainly from the Philippines and Chinese Taipei who were recruited for the fast-expanding entertainment industry. The number of such workers admitted legally for short periods of stay rose from 13 132 in 1978 to 34 569 in 1985. The second stage emerged in the mid-1980s and was characterised by the entry of male foreign workers into industrial employment. Single, male Chinese, Koreans, Pakistanis, Bangladeshis and Filipinos constituted the bulk of this foreign workforce, finding employment as secondary labour in the so-called "3-D jobs" in metal casting and fabrication, plastic moulding, machine assembly, road construction and repairs, building construction and demolition. The Asians were later joined by Iranians who at the time found easy entry to Japan because of a reciprocal visa exemption agreement. The absorption of foreigners reflected the serious and persistent labour shortages in these industries and occupations which were progressively being shunned by young workers on account of poor working conditions.

There was a significant rise in the employment of foreign students in the service industries since the mid-1980s suggesting that education has become another avenue for entry into the Japanese labour market. College and pre-college students from China and later from the Republic of Korea filled vacancies in the urban labour market as store clerks, waiters, dishwashers, newspaper delivery boys, cleaners, movers and building maintenance workers. They were hired mostly by small service companies which could no longer find Japanese workers to perform these jobs.

Since their employment was not allowed by law there are no direct records of the numbers of these workers. Apprehensions of "illegals" jumped from 1 889 in 1982 to 32 900 since 1991. The sex composition reflected the progressive increase in the proportion of male workers, and in 1988 the apprehended male "illegals" actually outnumbered the females. From the residual method employed by Mori it appears that the net inflows into Japan from 1980 to 1992 had grown to over a million foreign workers. Of these some 733 600 came from Asia (mostly East Asia: 132 100 from China, 62 400 from Chinese Taipei, 121 500 from the Republic of Korea; and from Southeast Asia: 136 500 from the Philippines, 85 000 from Thailand, and 61 800 from Malaysia). Of those coming from outside the region, Brazilians numbering 135 700 and Peruvians numbering 35 000 were the most prominent.

The legalised employment of unskilled foreign workers in medium and large industries marked the onset of the third stage in the absorption of foreign labour in Japan. Large industries which developed their own large internal labour markets have found no difficulty obtaining labour and distanced themselves from the practice of hiring foreign labour. (This situation — as will be seen later — has begun to change and labour shortages have started to affect them.) The arrival on the scene of South Americans of Japanese ancestry (the so-called "South American Nikkeis") after an amendment of the Immigration Control Act which among others offered a "long-term resident" status to Nikkeis of third generation as well as to non-Nikkei spouses of second generation Japanese, opened up a new labour pool which heretofore was not available. These workers, mainly from Brazil and Peru, quickly found employment in medium to large-size automobile assembly plants, auto parts companies, and in the electrical industries. They took on the monotonous jobs in assembly line operations which were becoming less and less attractive to the native Japanese (Chiba, 1994). They constitute secondary labour filling up jobs during peak months as temporary workers, as trainees, or as "contract" workers supplied by job-contractors. The number of Nikkei people all over the world is estimated to be from 2.2 to 2.5 million (Kawakami, 1993).

Significant flows of foreign labour to Chinese Taipei started in 1987-1988 (Tsay, 1991a) following the revaluation of the Chinese Taipei dollar. Since at the time no policy had yet been adopted to admit unskilled foreign workers for employment, these migrant workers entered the country as tourists or as trainees for subsequent employment in overseas subsidiaries of national companies. The numbers are difficult to establish because they are mostly illegal but from the immigration data on arrivals and departures Tsay estimated that there were 40 000 foreign workers in Chinese Taipei by the beginning of 1990 (Tsay, 1991a). Recognising the severity of the labour shortage, the Government in Chinese Taipei gradually relaxed curbs on the employment of foreign labour. In 1989 foreign workers were allowed only in the fourteen Government-sponsored construction projects which were lagging behind schedule. In 1991 certain types of industries were given permission to hire foreign labour. These included textiles, fabricated metals, electrical and electronic products, electrical machinery and equipment, and construction. Since 1992 employment of foreign household helpers (domestic workers) was allowed for families with at least one handicapped member or working parents.

Up to the mid-1980s the Republic of Korea was a major exporter of labour through its construction projects abroad especially in the Gulf and in North Africa. Some 2 million Korean workers at one time or another found their way to work as contract labour abroad since the 1960s (Park, 1991). By 1990 Korea was still sending workers abroad (about 56 000) but it was clear that fewer and fewer Korean

Table 2. **Foreign Workers in Japan, Republic of Korea, and Chinese Taipei Legal Admissions and Estimated Stocks**

	Japan[a]	Republic of Korea	Chinese Taipei
Flows: Legal admission			
1966-1970	16 567[b]		
1971-1975	38 652[b]		
1976-1980	125 725		
1981-1985	190 880		
1986-1990	372 172	27 835[c]	42 000[d]
Stocks: Estimates			
1980	783 000[e]		
1985	850 600[e]		
1990	1 298 300[e]		40 000
1993		100 000	150 000

a. Includes all foreigners allowed to work and granted residence status in Japan for business, teaching, entertainment, skilled work, as employees of Japanese companies abroad, and as language teachers (see Mori, Hiromi, 1992).
b. Calculated as net inflows (disembarkation less embarkation of foreigners).
c. Foreigners allowed entry to Korea for employment reasons including entertainers. Those foreigners allowed entry for business (some 570 000) are not included although some of them may have the intention of finding employment (see Park, Yong-bum, 1991).
d. Total disembarkation less embarkation for period 1985 to 1988 only for Southeast Asian countries where most migrant workers come from (see Tsay, Ching-lung, 1991a).
e. Includes ethnic Korean and Chinese population of about 340 000 in 1990.

workers would be working abroad in the years to come. Instead, Korea began to attract increasing numbers of foreign workers. As Table 2 shows, the number of foreign workers in Korea in 1993 was estimated at about 100 000.

As would be expected, the mostly illegal foreign workers in the three countries take up the jobs that are shunned by nationals. These include blue collar jobs in small-scale manufacturing, hazardous work in construction, and low-productivity jobs in the services sector. According to the 1990 Population Census of Japan, 45 per cent of all foreign nationals residing and working in Japan are in manufacturing (see Table 3). This heavy concentration in manufacturing is possibly due to the large number of long-term Korean permanent residents covered. Another distribution, this time based on new entrants or foreigners who entered Japan between 1985 and 1990, shows that only a third are in manufacturing. A larger percentage of the newly admitted foreign workers are employed as menial labour in services.

In both Japan and Korea, official policy remains one of keeping the front door shut to unskilled foreign labour but allowing their entry through the side-door under so-called training schemes. In Japan the Government envisages that 100 000 overseas trainees will be accepted by the end of the century. Under such schemes, some 37 566 foreigners came to Japan in 1990, which was above the provisional limit earlier set by the Japanese Government. Meanwhile the Korean Government has set a limit of 20 000 overseas trainees but requests received in the spring of 1994 alone from some 5 400 companies already totalled 25 000. These schemes which are being carried out in the two countries through various business

Table 3. **Foreign Labour's Sectoral Distribution in Japan, Korea and Chinese Taipei**
(in per cent)

	Japan[a]	Japan[b]	Chinese Taipei	Korea
All Industries	100	100	100	100
Construction	9	7	64	39
Transport & Communications	5	3		
Manufacturing	33	45	36	45
Less than 30 workers		5c	8	
30 to 99		23c	12	
100 to 299		35c	11	
300 and over		38c	5	
Trade & Services	53	45		16

a. Distribution of foreign workers who arrived in Japan between 1985 and 1990;
b. Distribution according to 1990 Population Census;
c. Ministry of Labour material, June 1993.

Sources: Tsay, Ching-lung, "Labour Recruitment in Taiwan: A Corporate Strategy in Industrial Restructuring", in *Environment and Planning* 1994 Vol. 26; Abella M. and Y. M. Park, Foreign Workers' Issues in Korea: Report on ILO/KLI Survey 1994.

organisations appear to be aimed at responding specifically to the current labour shortages being encountered by small-scale industries.

Labour Shortage and Foreign Workers in Japan

There were two periods in Japan's recent history when the economy experienced severe shortages of labour. The first developed during the "Isanagi" boom which started in the latter half of 1965 and lasted till the mid-1970s. The second had its beginnings during the economic upswing of the "Heisei" boom which began in late 1986 and lasted till the beginning of 1991. The conditions in the labour market during these two periods were broadly similar as both displayed a marked rise in the rate of growth of employment and real wages. Some 3.48 million persons found employment during the five years from 1965 to 1970 while 4.36 million more were employed from November 1986 to December 1990. Figure 2 shows that levels of unemployment did not go beyond 1.5 per cent from the beginning of the 1960s up to the first oil crisis in the mid-1970s. From then on unemployment levels showed a rising trend until Japan's economic recovery in the late 1980s marked another turning point, bringing the level down but not quite to the depths reached in the earlier period.

What makes these two boom periods interesting is the difference in the way the labour market adjusted to the shortage. The first lasted over a longer period and the associated labour shortage was more severe than in the second, but it was only in the latter period that use of foreign labour emerged as a response to the tightening conditions in the labour market. In this section we look at how the labour market in Japan adjusted during the two periods of rapid economic expansion and look at possible explanations for the growth of employment of foreign labour in the later period.

Figure 2. **Japan: unemployment and labour shortage**

We trace the changes in the labour market that have been stimulated by these two periods of economic expansion from data available on the sources of labour force growth and some rough indicators of the intersectoral reallocation of labour. The growth of the workforce consisted of three components: new graduates entering the labour force for the first time, the increased participation of women especially from the ranks of former home-makers, and the re-activation of aged workers who had already left the workforce. The intersectoral (and geographical) reallocation of labour in turn consisted largely of transfers of workers from agriculture, and from low-productivity occupations and trades outside agriculture (mostly the self-employed and family workers). Table 4 shows the broad dimensions of the changes in the labour market during the two periods of economic expansion. There may be some overlap between "new graduates" and those coming from categories other than the aged but these are expected to be negligible.

Table 4. **Japan: Sources of Labour Supply During Two Periods of Economic Expansion**
(in 10 thousand persons)

Sources	1965-70	1986-91
Increase of Labour Force <Additions to the Workforce>	443	542
New Graduates	904	697
Additional Women Employed (outside agriculture)	149	288
Reactivated Aged Employed*	9	89
<Intersectoral Transfers>		
Employed in Agriculture and Forestry	-246	-73
Self-employed and Family Workers (outside agriculture)	57	-53

a. Aged employed of 65 years old and over.

Sources: Statistics Bureau, Management and Co-ordination Agency and Ministry of Education.

As mentioned earlier, the intersectoral transfers of labour were very significant during the Isanagi boom. In the 1960s Japan still had a large reservoir of labour in agriculture which provided much of the flexibility in the labour market. Some 4 million workers left agriculture between 1960 and 1969 and another 1.2 million between 1970 and 1973. Throughout the rest of the 1970s another 1.8 million left agriculture and by the turn of the decade it was evident that only the aged workers were left behind. During the later economic boom from 1987 to 1990 only 180 000 workers left the sector for work elsewhere.

In the Isanagi boom period the net increase of labour force was 4.43 million, while in the Heisei boom period it was 5.42 million. The data in Table 4 also reveal some differences between the two periods in the significance of each source of additional labour. During the more recent boom the number of workers coming out of agriculture was less than one-third of what it had been during the earlier period. The mining industry had stopped operation much earlier and was no longer a potential source of workers. There was an increase in the number of the self-employed and the family workers during the early period but in the 1970s and 1980s their numbers declined by a half million, suggesting transfers to large industry and wage employment. What helped during this later economic expansion were three developments. The first was the increase in the rate of participation of women in the labour force. Female participation rates grew by 4 per cent during the 1970s and by 3.2 per cent during the 1980s. There were 23.3 million women employed in non-agricultural industries in 1990 compared to 15.6 million in 1970. The second was the growth in the number of the aged workers who were re-employed, and the third was workers transferred from the self-employed sector.

For the two periods the labour market adjustments that brought about these changes were not very different from each other. Large wage differentials between large and small firms existing prior to the expansions narrowed considerably with the tightening of the labour market as shown in Figure 3. During the earlier economic upswing two trends emerged which explain the closing of the wage gap. One was the acceleration of the increase in starting wages and salaries for new entrants to the labour force. They increased annually at 3 to 6 per cent in the latter half of the 1950s but climbed steeply at 13 to 18 per cent during the upswing in the 1960s (Ujihara, 1989). With the growing labour demand, companies had to outbid each other to attract new graduates to join them. Small companies where working conditions are generally less favourable than in others had to offer higher wages to offset this disadvantage. Consequently the level of starting salaries paid by secondary-sector sub-contractors exceeded more often than not those in large, primary-sector firms (Japan Institute of Labour, 1963).

Another outcome of the tightening of the labour market was the improvement in the employment status of most temporary workers. During the early stages of the economic expansion firms tend to hire temporary workers to meet their increasing requirements for labour. Temporary workers generally received lower wages than regular workers and were not entitled to fringe benefits. With the growing scarcity of labour as rapid growth continued, more and more workers were taken into regular employment as firms sought to avoid the costly and disruptive high turnover of their workforce. This partly explains the narrowing of the wage gaps among different kinds of workers which were very large prior to the period of rapid growth.

Figure 3 shows that the wage differentials between large and small firms widened after the first oil shock which precipitated an economic recession in Japan. This trend continued till the mid-1980s and was only reversed with the recovery of the late 1980s when the renewed growth of labour demand gave rise to a similar process of narrowing of wage gaps as had occurred during the earlier economic upswing. Starting salaries in smaller companies rose faster than those in the large ones, and salary levels in smaller companies not infrequently exceeded levels paid by the latter. The period also saw a closing of the salary gap between regular and irregular workers. For example, hourly wages paid to female part-time workers in Tokyo establishments with 30 or more employees in two large sectors (manufacturing, and wholesale and retail trade including restaurants) rose by 36.6 and 40.4 per cent, respectively, from 1985 to 1992, whereas the corresponding average increases in the wages of regular employees were 31.2 and 33.4 per cent.

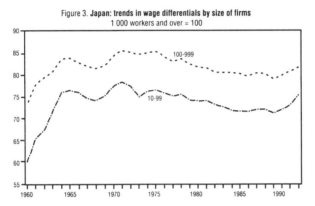

Figure 3. **Japan: trends in wage differentials by size of firms**
1 000 workers and over = 100

While the inflows of foreign workers were insignificant during the earlier Isanagi boom, their numbers grew rapidly during the later Heisei boom. Before the mid-1980s most of the foreign workers were females recruited for Japan's burgeoning entertainment industry. We earlier referred to this as the first stage of labour migration to Japan. The large inflows came with the second and third stages which are evidently closely related to the rapid rate of economic expansion. We postulate that demand for foreign labour is not only due to the general tightening of the labour market but also the consequence of growing mismatches in the labour market. One reason for the mismatches may be simply the consequence of the virtual disappearance of agricultural workers who would be willing to do unskilled blue collar work in construction or small industries. The young entrants to the workforce with much higher educational attainment than earlier cohorts of the working population are not interested in employment in small industries, especially in bottom-end jobs and in the so-called 3-K jobs.

We earlier referred to the tendency for large industry to attract workers away from small industries during periods of labour scarcity. Table 5 shows the rate at which job openings were filled in different size firms from 1983 to 1992. During the earlier years from 1983 to the end of 1986, when unemployment was rising, all the firms regardless of size experienced progressively fewer difficulties in finding workers. However 1987 was the turning point and from then on the largest firms (with 1 000 or more workers) had the opposite experience from smaller-size firms: while the labour market as a whole became tighter with the economic upswing, large firms (1000 and over) experienced a higher rate of placement; on the other hand, the smaller firms encountered more and more difficulties filling up their vacancies. Disparities in the labour sufficiency rate between large firms and others have become especially prominent since 1989. This happened in spite of the narrowing of wage gaps observed during the period of high economic growth, when it was not uncommon to find certain occupations paid better in small than in large industry.

Table 5. **Japan: Labour Sufficiency in Different Size Firms**
(in per cent)

	All firms	1000 and over	500 to 999	300 to 499	100 to 299	30 to 99	5 to 29
1983	25.5	20.3	23.1	24.7	25.9	27.1	25.0
1984	25.6	21.0	24.7	25.1	26.1	27.2	25.1
1985	26.9	28.1	24.7	26.5	27.3	28.7	26.1
1986	27.8	20.3	25.8	26.3	28.7	29.7	27.2
1987	28.4	29.6	28.2	27.5	29.5	29.8	27.6
1988	23.3	33.6	22.4	21.7	22.9	23.4	23.1
1989	19.8	39.5	17.8	18.9	19.0	19.4	19.5
1990	17.7	31.1	17.0	16.2	16.7	16.9	17.7
1991	17.5	27.4	17.2	16.2	16.7	17.0	17.8
1992	20.6	32.3	17.9	19.1	19.6	20.4	20.7

Notes: Labour sufficiency rate = number of people placed in regular and seasonal jobs/number of regular and seasonal job openings X 100. Part-time workers are not included.

Sources: Ministry of Labour.

It is not surprising that the labour shortage was more serious in the sectors usually associated with hazardous jobs such as those in construction, transport, and some manufacturing industries like metal working and woodworking, dirty jobs such as those found in dyeing factories and in restaurants, and monotonous jobs such as in textile and some large assembly plants, than in others. The Ministry of Labour reported that from 1985 to 1989 the labour shortage for all industries worsened by 12.7 per cent (as measured by a labour sufficiency index calculated as the ratio of job placements to total new openings for regular employees). The least affected sector was finance and insurance, the sector that has the highest requirement for higher educational attainment. However, in the other sectors the problem worsened. In construction there were slightly more than 2 placements for every 5 openings in 1985, but only one out of every 4 new openings by 1989. In transport there was almost one placement out of every three new openings in 1985 but this worsened to one out of every 5 by 1989 (MOL, 1990).

These developments in the labour market are of course not surprising and become even more understandable given the changes in the educational attainment of the Japanese population. In 1955 only about half of those who completed primary education proceeded to secondary schools. By 1990 over 95 per cent of primary school graduates went to secondary schools. In the 1950s only 10 per cent of those who graduated from secondary schools proceeded to university, but by the end of the 1980s the proportion had gone up to 38 per cent. New entrants to the workforce are therefore better educated than earlier cohorts and are expecting jobs offering not only better salaries but also higher status. There has in fact been an increased employment turnover for workers in the young age groups reflecting the search not merely for better wages but for jobs which carry higher social status.

Restructuring of the Japanese Economy

The Japanese economy also experienced considerable restructuring on the demand side in response to external shocks and the rising cost of labour. The oil crisis in the 1970s which raised energy prices to new heights prompted a shift away from energy-dependent heavy chemical industries which in an earlier period had led economic growth. As wages rose firms, especially the large ones, invested heavily in factory and office automation to boost productivity and competitiveness. Rationalisation of production also often took the form of "externalising" less profitable, labour-intensive operations such as transport, building maintenance, and data processing. This contributed in turn to the proliferation of various business service industries.

The appreciation of the Japanese yen *vis-à-vis* all other currencies following the Plaza Agreement gave some industries little choice but to move production offshore if they were to survive. The total stock worldwide of Japan's direct foreign investment rose by a huge $173 billion, from $78 billion to $251 billion, between 1987 and 1992 (UN, 1993). Of this, about 18 per cent went to Asian countries.

While these changes have led to reducing the demand for labour, developments elsewhere are contributing to its growth. The growth of urbanisation and the diversification of consumption in an increasingly affluent society have led to increased demand for services. Urbanised life, especially the increased involvement of housewives in the labour market, has led to another form of "externalisation", this time involving the purchase from outside the household of a large variety of personal services previously produced within it, from pre-cooked meals to care for the aged. Urbanisation may therefore be said to have given added stimulus to the expansion of the services sector through its impact on diversification of consumption.

Labour Shortage and Foreign Workers in Chinese Taipei

The profound structural transformation of Chinese Taipei over the last 30 years is reflected in the sectoral allocation of labour. Labour continued to be absorbed into high productivity agriculture until the mid-1970s but the sector has since progressively lost labour to industry and trade. The percentage of the employed workforce in agriculture steadily declined from 46.5 per cent in 1965 to only

12.3 per cent in 1992. The share of the industrial sector, on the other hand, jumped from about 20 per cent in 1965 to 41.5 per cent in 1980, after which there has been a small but noticeable decline in favour of the services sector.

The success of the export-led and labour-intensive industrialisation in Chinese Taipei is well documented and need not be elaborated on in this paper. Instead we focus on how four decades of high economic growth have affected wages and the labour market and created the labour shortages that gave rise to inflows of foreign labour. During the 1980s, the labour force in Chinese Taipei grew the fastest among the region's newly-industrialising economies and Japan, but a rapid decline of fertility has begun to have a telling effect on its rate of growth and on the age of the current labour force. Birth rates declined to half of their 1963 level within two decades and are now barely a third of it. During the decade of the 1980s the Island's labour force grew by 3.49 per cent annually but during the current decade its growth will average only 1.66 a year (Bauer, 1990).

During the past three decades unemployment rates in Chinese Taipei exceeded 2 per cent only in 1975, after the first oil price shock, and during the period from 1982 to 1986. From several years of double-digit growth, GNP growth rate in Chinese Taipei slowed down from 1979 to 1982 but quickly recovered thereafter. The period of relatively high unemployment therefore did not coincide with the slowdown of the economy but actually occurred during the earlier stage of recovery. The main reason for this is simply the large rise (27 per cent) in the number of women who entered the labour force between 1982 and 1986 but could not be absorbed into employment as in the earlier period of recovery. Overall employment actually grew by 3.2 per cent annually during the period. Drawn by the rapid growth of demand for labour in export industries, the number of employed women in Chinese Taipei rose by 2.2 million between 1965 and 1992. Their overall rate of participation in the labour force rose from 34.1 per cent in 1960 to 44.8 per cent in 1992.

In recent years, the Council of Labour Affairs under the Executive Yuan has undertaken monthly surveys of establishments excluding agriculture to assess the dimensions of the labour shortage in different sectors of the economy. The data for 1990 and 1991 indicate that the sectors hardest hit by labour shortages are construction and manufacturing. Some 172 000 vacancies were reported to be waiting to be filled at the beginning of 1990, representing 3.8 per cent of all the regular employees of the establishments surveyed. We summarise in Table 6 the reported labour shortages for the months of January and June of these two years.

While there has been a secular decline in the time that people spend at work, their real earnings have risen steadily since the beginning of the 1980s. Average monthly working hours of employees on payrolls of establishments show a decline in almost all sectors from 1978 to 1992 but earnings have risen by about two and a half times during the same period. Up to about 1980 real earnings in construction, financial services, and manufacturing were stable but from about 1980-1981 there was a very clear rising trend in all sectors. Figure 4 shows the movement of the indices of average real monthly earnings of Chinese Taipei workers in manufacturing, construction, commerce, and financial services and real estate.

Table 6. **Chinese Taipei: Labour Shortage in Selected Industries 1990-91**
(number of workers in thousands;
labour shortage rate within brackets in per cent)

	1990 January	1990 June	1991 January	1991 June
All sectors	172 (3.8)	198 (4.5)	124 (2.9)	144 (3.4)
Manufacturing	138 (5.6)	137 (5.8)	112 (4.8)	127 (5.6)
Construction	25 (5.5)	42 (8.8)	7 (1.7)	13 (3.0)
Commerce	37 (4.9)	10 (1.3)		
Transport & Communication		2 (0.6)		1 (0.3)
Financing/ins./ business services	4 (1.4)	.6 (0.2)		
Community/social/ personal services	5 (1.7)	7 (2.9)	5 (1.8)	3 (1.0)

Notes: > Labour shortage rate = number of vacancies/total number of regular employees X 100.

Sources: The Council of Labour Affairs, Executive Yuan, R.O.C.

Figure 4. **Chinese Taipei: Indices of real average monthly earnings by industry** (1978=100)

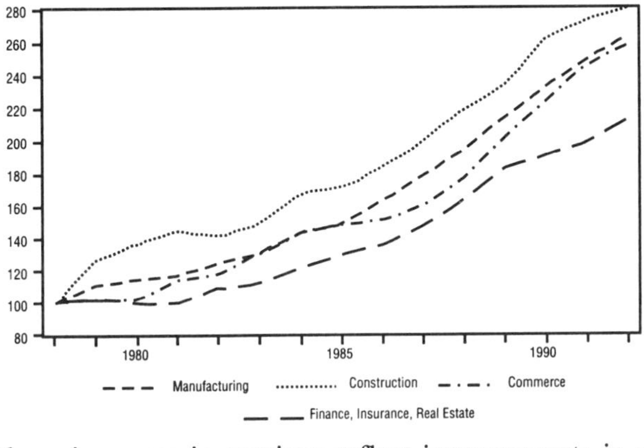

--- Manufacturing .... Construction — . — . Commerce
___ Finance, Insurance, Real Estate

Some of these increases in earnings reflect improvements in productivity, but the faster rise in wages compared to productivity undermined the Island's international competitiveness in labour-intensive industries. During the eight years from 1978 to 1986 labour productivity was estimated to have risen by 30 per cent in manufacturing, or much slower than the growth of real wages of some 62 per cent. The following six years both wages and labour productivity increased at faster rates but wages still slightly outstripped productivity. From 1986 to 1992 productivity was estimated to have increased by 59 per cent while wages rose by 62 per cent.

Adjustments to the Growing Labour Shortage

Firms in Chinese Taipei began relocating labour-intensive industries in neighbouring low wage countries at the beginning of the 1980s. Amounts of direct foreign investment however did not take on major dimensions until after the revaluation of the Chinese Taipei currency in 1987. Its foreign investments climbed to about $750 million in 1987, then jumped to over $4.1 billion the following year, and reached a peak annual outflow of $7 billion in 1989. Since then the flows have slowed down but were still running at almost $2 billion in 1991 (UN, 1993).

The recourse to foreign investment as an avenue for adjusting to the labour shortage is surprising in the light of the Island's industrialisation experience which, unlike that of Japan and the Republic of Korea, was built mainly on small industries. By international standards most of these industries were very small. In 1980 only 4 per cent of all employed were working for enterprises with 500 or more workers while 70 per cent were working for enterprises with fewer than 50 workers. Few small firms have the know-how and the capital resources to venture into investments abroad, and few have done so on their own. It is the traditional family links in China and the extensive network of Chinese business clans in Southeast Asia which have facilitated the investments of small firms from Chinese Taipei abroad.

This structure of industry in Chinese Taipei has remained virtually unchanged in spite of rapid economic growth and the considerable restructuring of exports from the earlier dominance of textiles and clothing to the current large share of technology-intensive manufactures, notably machinery, electronic office equipment and components, and chemicals. The technology upgrading of enterprises in Chinese Taipei which began in the late 1970s did, however, serve to make medium-scale producers predominant, displacing both small and large firms (Liu *et al*, 1993). Their share in value added rose but because of their relatively high capital intensity their share of total employment did not rise correspondingly.

During the earlier labour-intensive phase of export-led development, industries in Chinese Taipei drew heavily on cheap family labour. Subcontracting networks were very extensive in Chinese Taipei's export manufacturing industries (Shieh, 1990; Kuo, 1983; Lau, 1986). The use of homeworkers through subcontractors has been a pervasive practice because of the flexibility it offers to reduce labour costs. Subcontracting networks have been able to absorb fluctuations in demand for light industrial goods; such flexibility has been achieved through the employment of homeworkers largely on piece rates which were kept constant for a long time. Tsay explains that "with invariably low wages and no benefits such as sick leave, homeworkers mobilised hidden family labour and adjusted the working time to meet the deadlines of contractors" (Tsay, 1994 p. 585).

By the beginning of the 1980s most of the unpaid family workers had already found regular employment. Confronted with rapidly rising wages and the higher reservation wages of new entrants to the labour force who, as in Japan, had much higher educational attainment than earlier cohorts, enterprises in Chinese Taipei had to pursue a variety of strategies to survive. A survey by the Council of Labour finds that only 3.7 per cent of the enterprises considered moving overseas. Most firms planned on standardising operations and introducing some labour-saving machinery.

A large proportion also planned on cutting down on unprofitable operations and products. Equally common was the plan to shorten work hours, presumably to attract workers.

The use of part-time workers could be another source of additional labour but apparently part-time workers are less common in Chinese Taipei than in other industrialised countries, accounting for only about 2 per cent of the total employees in the industrial sector (Tsay, 1994). They are more frequently used in the construction industry and small manufacturing companies. Females constitute a large proportion of such workers. Tsay finds from analysing a 1992 study of the Census Bureau that the use of part-time workers is of very limited significance in meeting the labour shortage. Part-time working was found by many enterprises to be unsuited to their production systems. Other reasons cited are that part-time workers are difficult to manage; they are relatively inefficient, hard to train, and tend to have a high rate of turnover.

Foreign workers still represent a minute proportion of all workers employed in Chinese Taipei. A recent survey of establishments shows that foreigners represent only 1.87 per cent of the workforce employed by all industries (DGBAS, 1992). They were only a little more significant in the construction industry where they account for 6.5 per cent of the industry's workforce. They were unevenly distributed in manufacturing, being fairly noticeable in textiles, basic metals, and plastics. Approximately 4 per cent of all industries in Chinese Taipei have reported hiring foreign workers.

The population of Chinese Taipei is expected to continue growing, although at a declining rate, through the first half of the 21st century. Due to the shrinking proportion of the young population, the relative importance of the older age cohorts (15 years old and over) is anticipated to increase from 74.6 per cent in 1993 to 78.2 per cent in 2000 and 79.8 in 2010. If we assume that the long-term trend in labour participation rates would continue, the year 2002 will be the turning point when estimated labour demand will exceed the estimated labour supply. The shortage is expected to reach 553 000 in 2010 and up to 2 million in 2026.

The aforementioned survey however reveals that over three-quarters of the establishments faced serious difficulties finding nationals to work for them and about 17 per cent stated they were going to hire foreigners. The last four years have seen the progressive relaxation of restrictions on the legal employment of foreign workers in the country no doubt due to the pressures exerted by business on the Government. The latest move to allow domestic helpers under certain conditions is no doubt intended to draw out more women in the middle age groups to leave home and enter or re-enter the labour market. This development could easily lead to a further escalation in the inflows of foreign workers as has happened in Singapore and Hong Kong.

We should underscore the significance of the legalisation of the employment of foreign workers in Chinese Taipei, in contrast to Japan and Korea. Foreign workers in Chinese Taipei are now able to gain entry into some sectors of the primary labour market including jobs in the more modern sectors of industry. Being covered by labour laws, they can now expect to be given the same wages as national workers who do the same jobs and take part in trade union activities. They may in fact be disadvantaged by the high cost of emigrating from their countries and of getting recruited for employment in Chinese Taipei, but unlike in Japan and the Republic of Korea they are no longer confined to unprotected sectors of the labour market. We could not, however, document these changes since the only data available on their employment are those that describe the earlier situation when almost all foreign workers had irregular status.

Labour Shortage and Foreign Workers in the Republic of Korea

Like the other two countries, the Republic of Korea is facing a labour scarcity which appears to be structural in nature. The Republic of Korea was an agrarian society until very recently, but its successful industrialisation gave rise to massive migration of the rural population to the urban areas and by the mid-1970s it is said to have passed the Lewisian era of unlimited supply of labour (Uh, 1993). Real per capita GNP rose five times between 1965 and 1975 and 3.7 times between 1975 and 1985. Real wages grew on average by 4.8 per cent between 1971 and 1975, but in the following five years their growth averaged a remarkable 11.6 per cent a year.

During the 1970s, when the Republic of Korea was undergoing the labour-intensive phase of its industrialisation, the labour force grew at a rapid rate of 3.8 per cent a year. Employment in manufacturing tripled during the first ten years of rapid economic growth between 1965 and 1975. In the following decade industrial employment grew at over twice the rate of growth of overall employment. By the beginning of the 1990s there were six and a half times more people employed in manufacturing than in 1965, while the number in agriculture had actually declined by 1.6 million.

While the past three decades have been characterised by considerable flexibility of labour supply, the future growth of the labour force will be much slower on account of several developments: the slowdown in the growth of the labour force as a consequence of the early demographic transition, the exhaustion of the rural labour surplus, and the declining participation rate of the young (15 to 19 age group) due to longer schooling. For the current decade the annual labour force growth of Korea is expected to average only 1.81 per cent compared to 2.84 per cent during the previous one.

The decline of the total fertility rate from 6.0 in the 1960s to 1.6 in 1988 has already made an impact on the growth of the working age population. In 1960 slightly over half of Korea's population were young (below 20 years old). In 1990 they accounted for only 36 per cent of the population. The National Office of Statistics projects that by the turn of the century the population of ages 15 to 19 would decline to 3.4 million from about 4.6 million in 1990. The whole working age population will still grow for some time but the rate of growth has considerably slowed to 1.3 per cent during the current decade.

Intersectoral transfers of labour have taken place on a large scale in the past. Between 1957 and 1980, Bauer (1990) estimates that 11 million South Koreans moved from rural to urban areas seeking jobs in manufacturing and services. The dramatic impact of these transformations is reflected in the fact that by 1992 the agricultural workforce consisted mainly of older workers with a large proportion of elderly women. In the whole agricultural sector there were altogether only 151 000 male and female workers below 30 years of age. About 62 per cent of the male and female workers were over 50 years old. Thus agriculture has long ceased to be a source of flexible labour supplies for industry.

Dimensions of Labour Shortage

The *Monthly Labour Surveys* of the Ministry of Labour show that the labour shortage has worsened considerably since 1985. Survey findings shown in Table 7 reveal that the shortage rose from 1.8 per cent of total employed in 1985 to 5.7 per cent in 1992. They also show that the problem has become quite acute for unskilled production work where the shortage was as high as one out of every five employees in 1991. The 1993 data from the ILO/Korea Labour Institute survey indicates that the shortage has become even more serious than before for production workers, with a growing deficit for skilled workers.

Table 7. **Republic of Korea: Measures of Labour Shortage**

	Min. of Labour Survey			ILO/KLI Survey	
	1985	1990	1991	1992	1993
By type of workers					
Total employees	1.8	4.3	5.5	5.7	9.2
Office workers	0.9	1.3	1.3	1.7	2.1
Production	2.4	6.9	9.1	8.0	12.2
Skilled	2.0	5.3	7.3		9.5
Unskilled	4.9	16.2	20.1		16.8
By Size of Firm					
Less than 30				9.5	21.1
30 - 99				7.3	12.1
100 - 199				6.5[a]	7.8
200 or more				3.3[b]	4.7

Note: Labour shortage ratio = unfilled vacancies/current employees.

Sources: For 1985 to 1991 see Table 3.8 in Uh, Soo-Bong "Employment Structure" in Park, Young-bum (ed.) *Labour in Korea*, Korea Labour Institute, Seoul, 1993; the ILO/KLI Survey for 1993 data. a. for firms with 100 to 299 workers; b. for firms with 300 to 499 workers.

Table 7 gives a breakdown of the shortage by size of establishment for the more recent years. It shows that the shortage in the smallest-size establishments is four to five times more than in the largest firms. The problem also apparently worsened in 1993 for all sizes of firm but has become particularly critical for the establishments with less than 30 workers.

The problems faced by small-scale manufacturing in finding enough workers became acute during the economic upswing which started in 1986 and particularly after the political changes in 1987 when for the first time organised labour began to assert its bargaining power. That year saw the start of the escalation of real wages in the Republic of Korea, especially in the large enterprises where the unions were concentrated. Table 8 shows how nominal wages and consumer prices have risen since 1971. Nominal wages rose by double-digit figures over most of the period but inflation ate up most of these gains in the 1970s. Real wages lagged behind productivity during the first half of the 1980s but from 1987 onwards they began to outpace it by a sizeable margin, reflecting the impact of factors such as the increased influence of organised labour. Measured in US dollars (see the last column of Table 8), unit labour costs rose steeply from 1987 to 1989. According to Lee (1993), the change in the won-dollar exchange rate as well as wage increases which exceeded labour productivity caused the sharp rise in unit labour costs. Japan, Singapore and Hong Kong experienced a much slower rise in unit labour costs.

Table 8. **Republic of Korea Growth Rates of GNP, Wages and Productivity**
(in per cent)

	GNP	CPI	Nominal All Industries	Wages Manufacturing	Labour Productivity[a]	Unit Labour Cost[b] 1986=100
1971-75	8.3	15.4	20.9	22.0	21.7	
1976-80	7.1	17.2	30.8	30.7	25.4	
1981-85	8.4	7.1	13.0	12.9	12.9	
1986-90	10.8	5.4	14.6	17.0	7.8	
1986	12.9	2.8	8.2	9.2	10.4	100.0
1987	13.0	3.0	10.1	11.6	2.2	118.8
1988	12.5	7.1	15.5	19.6	12.8	145.8
1989	6.8	5.7	21.1	25.1	3.4	177.4
1990	9.3	8.6	18.8	20.2	12.0	182.5
1991	8.4	9.3	17.5	16.9	12.5	
1992	4.7	6.2	15.2	15.7	11.6	

a. Growth of labour productivity is based on rate of growth of value added in current prices/number of workers.
b. Unit labour cost = nominal wage index/exchange rate to US$/ labour productivity index.

Sources: Bank of Korea, *National Accounts*, relevant issues; Ministry of Labour, *Report on Monthly Labour Survey*, relevant issues; for unit labour cost: Korea Productivity Center.

What was the response of Korean industries to the rising cost of labour? At the macro level one notes that there may have been considerable relocation of production to low wage countries. Sizeable foreign direct investment (FDI) outflows from Korea coincided with the escalation of real wages and went largely to low wage countries in the region. From less than $66 million in 1985, FDI outflows rose to almost $321 million in 1987, $813 million in 1990 and $1 037 million in 1991 (NSO, 1993). A large proportion of these investments has evidently been stimulated by soaring labour costs at home since most of the industries involved were labour-intensive manufactures. Compared to Japan and Chinese Taipei, Korea's investments abroad are still small but the pressure to relocate production has come more recently than in the case of the other two.

Unlike in Chinese Taipei the size structure of Korean industry changed significantly after the 1960s. From 1963 to 1987 the share of large industry (more than 200 workers) in total value added in manufacturing rose from 47 to 68 per cent while that of small (less than 20 workers) firms declined to just a third of the earlier level (Rhee 1990). In terms of employment, the largest expansion was also in the large industry sector which accounted for half of all workers in manufacturing in 1987 compared to only a third in 1963. The medium size firms gained a little in their employment share (from 37 to 40 per cent) but their share in value added actually declined from 33.5 to 27.5 per cent. These shifts left only 10 per cent of the manufacturing workers in small-scale enterprises, down substantially from a 29 per cent share in 1963.

The Korean Government has played a very active role in directing structural adjustments in Korean industry to cope with the growing scarcity of labour through the use of a combination of standard macroeconomic policies, special financing schemes and subsidies, large investments in technology research, and at times unconventional methods of intervention. The results have been no less than spectacular as indicated by the swift transformation of Korean industry from the production of simple consumer manufactures to the production and export of high technology intermediate and capital goods, but apparently these efforts have not been sufficient to avert the conditions which give rise to the employment of foreign workers.

Growing Segmentation of the Labour Market

While the wage gap between industry and services was considerably narrowed between 1980 and 1992 (Park, 1993), that between the largest firms and smaller ones became wider. As suggested earlier, the latter is largely due to the liberalisation of trade union activities which had more impact on the large firms because most of them had unionised labour. Table 9 shows how the gap widened especially between firms with 500 or more workers and those employing fewer than 100 workers. Bohning (1994) argues that the intensification of the segmentation of the labour market between large and small firms reflected in this widening wage gap is partly responsible for the difficulties now faced by the latter in attracting more workers. The wage differential worsens the disadvantage seen in working for small enterprises which includes less job security, longer working hours, and a generally less attractive working environment. It compounds the problem of what Bohning calls the unfilled "undesired jobs" in Korea that seem to have increased in number as a consequence of rapid economic and employment growth, urbanisation, development of the welfare state, and higher levels of educational attainment, and political liberalisation.

During a period of rapid economic expansion, the size of the primary labour market expands giving more opportunities for workers who might otherwise be stuck in the secondary labour market. As in Japan and Chinese Taipei, this is evidently what has happened, but it is notable in the case of the Republic of Korea that there is no corresponding flexibility of the labour market during periods of slump. Large enterprises end up hoarding labour for a number of reasons but largely on account of a legal restriction on laying off workers which generally applies with greater force to the larger enterprises.

Table 9. **Republic of Korea: Wage Structure by Size of Firm (Biggest Firms = 100)**

Size of enterprise	1980	1985	1987	1990	1992
10-29	93	90	88	74	73
30-99	99	91	91	77	78
100-299	97	90	90	81	83
300-499	102	99	98	94	90
500+	100	100	100	100	100

Source: Park, 1993b, Table 4.10.

Over the long run, as Korea becomes a high-income country, the rate of economic growth will naturally slow down and so also the demand for labour. But, as Bohning points out, very sizeable unemployment would have to occur before more nationals would take on the "undesired jobs" (Bohning, 1994). In this regard, relatively high current unemployment among people with high educational attainment (Park, 1993, p. 10) is indicative. The most realistic scenario in Korea for some time to come, and one to which most Government planners in Seoul subscribe, is a continued fast pace of economic growth which would exacerbate the current labour shortage.

The possibilities for automation have been exaggerated in many of the discussions of solutions to the shortage. For the small enterprises which face the most acute shortages, automation possibilities are often limited because of the size of investment required, the risks involved, and their lack of knowledge how to apply it to their present production systems. In a survey of Korean small and medium enterprises by the Korea Labour Institute, it was found in most industries that fewer than one out of every four enterprises have considered or tried automation. Most have shied away from it because of the financial investments required, the risks involved, and because they thought automation technically ill suited for their requirements (see Annex Table 2). Enterprises risk going under if they make the mistake of investing heavily in automation where the business is characterised by significant market volatility.

The same survey revealed that only a very small percentage of firms engage irregular or part-time workers, who are usually housewives or older workers. Only a few industries have done so because of the observed high rates of absenteeism among young mothers whose family responsibilities often require them to change their schedules. Firms have found it difficult to organise production on the basis of using part-time workers since different stages of production have to be synchronised and balanced (Abella and Park, 1994).

The Government's response to pressures from business to allow the import of foreign workers was at first to close its eyes to the growing numbers of foreigners illegally working in the country. Foreign workers were on the average receiving only about 40 per cent of what the average male Korean production worker gets. The size of the foreign labour pool apparently was not large enough to moderate the growth of wage rates. Fearing the collapse of many small industries, particularly those generating export revenues, the Government yielded in 1993 to pressures to let business import unskilled foreign workers and decided to adopt a "foreign workers training scheme", as Japan had done, which would let them work legally in the country. Current limitation on the numbers of workers admitted under the scheme suggest that it would not go far towards relieving the supply constraints facing small industries and thereby extending the life of the less efficient ones. This phase of industrial restructuring is however raising many social concerns and there is an apparent acquiescence of Government to pressures to let them survive through the use of temporary labour from abroad.

Concluding Observations

The migration movements in East Asia have been stimulated largely by the dynamic developments in Japan, Chinese Taipei and the Republic of Korea which have virtually exhausted their own supplies of labour. In this paper we reviewed the dimensions of the labour market changes that have accompanied the rapid economic growth of these economies and found that the emerging labour shortage, which gave rise to the entry of foreign labour, is unlikely to be remedied by short-run measures to increase the participation of the native population in the labour force. The exhaustion of labour reserves in agriculture has brought to a trickle the supply of unskilled labour for many production jobs which an increasingly educated national workforce is reluctant to take up. Although the three countries have been reluctant to open their borders to foreign workers, the emerging labour shortages will no doubt lead to larger inflows of foreign workers in the future.

The three countries are late importers of foreign labour (Pang, 1994) and have been more successful than others in avoiding the need to import foreign labour at comparable stages of their industrialisation. They have done so through a combination of measures to promote the restructuring of industries and the relocation of labour-intensive industries abroad, and through tight immigration policies. But the persistence of labour shortages indicates that the import of foreign labour can now be avoided only at the cost of high inflation or through a considerable slowing down of the rate of economic growth and increase in the rate of unemployment. These options pose difficult policy choices for all three countries.

In Japan, the working age population will start to decline before the end of the current decade and this will further accelerate the ageing of the population. The cost of supporting its elderly population in terms of old age pensions alone is expected to rise from 6.6 per cent of national income in 1988 to 20.2 per cent in the year 2020

(Koshiro, 1991). A high level of economic growth would thus be needed to sustain the level of social support. Although the other two countries have not yet quite reached the same stage in their demographic transition, it is only a question of time before they face the same problems.

The comparison of the symptoms of labour shortages during the two boom periods in Japan reviewed in this paper illustrates the changes in the labour market which have been caused not only by the decline in the growth of the labour force but also by the dualism which characterises this market. Even during the height of excess demand for labour in the Heisei boom, the supply of labour in the primary market serving large industry was relatively abundant as workers left the small manufacturing industries to get better jobs elsewhere. Thus, while the wage gap between large and small industries considerably narrowed during both booms, labour shortages facing small industries were even more pronounced at the height of the Heisei boom, suggesting considerable segmentation of the labour market which was not observed earlier.

The causes of the labour shortage in Chinese Taipei and the Republic of Korea bear many similarities to those in Japan. The reallocation of labour to higher productivity sectors has taken place at a rapid pace during the last several years and opened the way for foreign workers to take their places in the occupations and sectors which have always depended on the migration of unskilled labour from agriculture. The social changes taking place in these countries such as the growing bargaining strength of the trade unions have added to productivity differences in widening the wage gaps between different sectors of industry. Efforts to provide remedies through the restructuring of industries and the relocation of labour-intensive industries abroad have already reduced the elasticity of employment in these countries but the persistent shortages of labour suggest that these alone would not be sufficient to reverse the trend towards greater dependence on foreign workers.

Annex Table 1. **Structural Change in Employment in Japan, Korea and Chinese Taipei**
(in thousand persons)

Sector	Primary	Secondary	Tertiary
Japan			
1965-70	-1 657	+2 432	+3 828
1970-75	-2 720	+270	+3 228
1975-80	-1 243	+640	+3 379
1980-85	-692	+468	+2 586
1985-90	-908	+1 784	+3 345
Korea			
1970-75	+509	+870	+1 576
1975-80	-767	+830	+1 812
1980-85	-936	+559	+1 607
1985-90	-430	+1 274	+2 257
Chinese Taipei			
1970-75	+1 000	+649	+296
1975-80	-404	+847	+584
1980-85	+19	+304	+557
1985-90	-233	+307	+780

Sources: Japan: Budget Accounting and Statistics, Executive Yuan; Chinese Taipei: *Abstract of Employment and Earnings Statistics, 1992*, May 1993; Korea: National Statistics Office, *The Economically Active Population Surveys*, Seoul.

Annex Table 2. **Korea: Constraints to Automation in Small Manufacturing Industry**

Industry	Number of firms*	Constraints (per cent of firms)			
		Financial	Technical	Risk	Information
Cast-iron	14	71	7	22	¾
Forging	2	100	¾	¾	¾
Heat Treatment	9	67	11	22	¾
Gold Coating	15	40	33	27	¾
Dyeing and Finishing	29	51	35	10	4
Machinery	16	50	44	¾	6
Electrical Machinery	14	50	21	14	14
Electronics	14	29	43	21	7
Footwear	16	50	25	25	¾
Leather Goods	10	50	50	¾	¾
Glass	7	43	29	28	¾
Textile	5	80	20	¾	¾
Metal Fabrication	2	¾	100	¾	¾
Coating with Paint	1	¾	100	¾	¾

Notes: Only 154 firms out of 240 responded to the question. Column shows number of firms that responded for each industry.

Bibliographical References

ABELLA, Manolo (1991), "Structural Change and Labour Migration Within the Asian Region" in *Regional Development Dialogue* Vol. 12 No. 3, Autumn.

ABELLA, M. and Y.B. PARK (1994), *Foreign Workers Issues in Korea: Report on ILO/KLI Survey of Small and Medium Scale Enterprises*, International Labour Office, Geneva.

BAUER, John (1990), "Demographic Change and Asian Labour Markets in the 1990s" in *Population and Development Review*, 16. No. 4, December.

BOHNING, W.R. (1994), *Undesired Jobs and What One Can Do to Fill Them: The Case of the Republic of Korea*, Paper presented at the Korea Small Business Institute Seminar, Seoul, April.

CHIBA, Tatsuya (1994), "Problems of Foreign Workers in Contemporary Japan" (in Japanese), *Bulletin of Japan Statistics Research Institute*, Hosei University, Tokyo.

DGBAS, *Abstract of Employment and Earnings Statistics in Taiwan Republic of China 1992*, Directorate General of Budget Accounting and Statistics, Executive Yuan, May.

FEI, John and Gustav RANIS (1964), *Development of the Labor Surplus Economy: Theory and Policy*, Homewood, Il. Richard D. Irwin.

FIELDS, Gary (1994), "The Migration Transition in Asia", in *Asia and Pacific Migration Journal*, Vol. 3 No. 1.

Japan Institute of Labour (1963), *Labour Market under Economic Growth* (keizai seicho ka no rodo shijo).

KAWAKAMI, T. (1993), *The Migration in the Asian and Pacific Regions — The Nikkei People Overseas, Past and Present.*

KOSHIRO, Kazutoshi (1991), *Labor Shortage and Employment Policies in Japan*, Paper presented at Second Japan-ASEAN Conference on International Migration, ILO-UNU, Tokyo.

KUO, S.W.Y. (1983), *Taiwan: Economy in Transition*, Westview Press, Boulder, CO.

LAU, L. (ed.) (1986), *Models of Development*, Institute of Contemporary Studies, San Francisco, CA.

LEE, Seon (1993), *Wages: The Levels, Structure and Criterion for their Determination, Labor in Korea*, ed. by Young-bum Park.

LIU, P, Ying-Chuan LIU, Hui-Lin WU (1993), *The Manufacturing Enterprise and Management in Taiwan*, DP9304, Institute of Economics, Academia Sinica, Taipei.

Ministry of Labour (MOL) (1993), *Report on Employment Security*, Yearbook of Labor Statistics.

MIZUNO, A. (1987/88), "Wage Flexibility and Employment Changes", *Japanese Economic Studies*, Vol XVI, No. 2, New York, Winter.

MORI, Hiromi (1992), "The Role of Immigrant Workers in the Adjustment Process of Labour Imbalance in Japan", *Economic Journal*, Hosei University, Tokyo, Vol. 60-1.2.

National Statistics Office (NSO) (1993), *Yearbook of Statistics 1993*, Seoul.

PANG, Eng Fong (1994), "An Eclectic Approach to Turning Points in Migration", in *Asian and Pacific Migration Journal* Vol. 3 No. 1.

PARK, Young-bum (1991), *Foreign Labor in Korea: Issues and Policy Options*, paper presented at second Japan ASEAN Forum on International Labour Migration in East Asia, Tokyo.

PARK, Young-bum (1993), *Labor in Korea*, Korea Labor Institute, Seoul.

PARK, Young-bum (1994), "The Turning Point in International Labour Migration and Economic Development in Korea", in *Asia and Pacific Migration Journal* Vol. 3 No. 1.

RHEE, Sungsup (1990), *Promoting International Competitiveness and Efficient Resources Utilization in Manufacturing: Case of the Republic of Korea* ESCAP, Bangkok, December.

SHIEH, G.S. (1990), *Manufacturing 'Bosses' Subcontracting Network under Dependent Capitalism in Taiwan*, PHD Dissertation in Sociology, University of California, Berkeley, CA.

Tokyo Metropolitan Institute of Labour (1991), *Employment and Working Conditions for Foreign Workers in Tokyo: Final Report* (Japanese), Tokyo.

TSAY, Ching-lung (1991a), *Clandestine Worker Migration to Taiwan*, paper presented at conference on International Manpower Flows and Foreign Investments in Asia, Sept. 9-12, Tokyo.

TSAY, Ching-lung (1991b), *Labour Flows from Southeast Asia to Taiwan*, paper presented at second Japan ASEAN Forum on International Labour Migration in East Asia, Tokyo.

TSAY, Ching-lung (1993), "Industrial Restructuring and International Competition in Taiwan", in *Environment and Planning* Vol. 25.

TSAY, Ching-lung (1994), "Labor Recruitment in Taiwan: A Corporate Strategy in Industrial Restructuring", in *Environment and Planning* Vol. 26.

UH, Soo-Bong (1993), "Employment Structure", in *Labor in Korea,* ed. by Young-bum Park, Korea Labor Institute, Seoul.

UJIHARA, Hojiro (1989), *Japanese Economy and Employment Structure* (nihon keizai to koyo kozo), Tokyo University Press, Tokyo.

UN (1991), *Industrial Restructuring in Asia and the Pacific*, ESCAP, Bangkok, March.

UN (1993), World Investment Report 1993, *Transnational Corporations and Integrated International Production*, New York.

Malaysia and Chinese Taipei: Labour Market Experiences Compared

by Pang Eng Fong *

Starting from very different initial conditions, Chinese Taipei and Malaysia have pursued similar industrial development strategies and witnessed similar changes in their labour markets, including growing shortages of unskilled workers which have forced them to rely more heavily on immigrant labour.

Chinese Taipei was already a full-employment economy by the early 1980s, while Malaysia has approached full employment only in the early 1990s — though labour shortages in the plantation and construction sectors were already evident earlier. With a slight lag, Malaysia has experienced the same structural changes in its labour market as Chinese Taipei: rising female participation rates, sustained declines in the share of agricultural employment, and an expansion of wage employment. Malaysia's industrial development is still at a relatively early stage, where the employment elasticity of manufacturing output remains high and the proportion of production workers in the labour force is still rising. In Chinese Taipei, the fast-growing service sector absorbs an increasing proportion of the labour force while both the agricultural and manufacturing shares decline. In both countries, workers have enjoyed significant improvements in real earnings and, while the rate of increase has been much higher in Chinese Taipei than in Malaysia, wages in the latter have tended to rise even during periods of high unemployment, possibly indicating less flexible labour markets.

In contrast to Chinese Taipei, Malaysia began receiving a sizeable inflow of foreign workers — mostly from poorer ASEAN neighbours — well before its domestic labour force had approached full employment. In Chinese Taipei, as labour shortages became more acute in the mid-1980s, many companies responded by investing overseas, but this option is not always available, especially in the non-tradeables sector. Thus, since the late 1980s, Chinese Taipei has also witnessed a sizeable influx of foreign workers. As the two economies have come to depend more heavily on immigrant labour, both governments are searching for policies that would balance the short-term demands for such labour with the need to maintain political and social cohesion. In the longer term, they are seeking to promote economic restructuring to reduce the demand for unskilled labour.

* National University of Singapore

Introduction

Malaysia and Chinese Taipei stand out among countries in the fast-growing East Asian region[1]. Malaysia is the first country in the region (and the world) with a Muslim majority population to transform itself from a commodity exporter into a newly-industrialising economy. A multiethnic society and a stable parliamentary democracy since independence in 1957, it is also the only middle-income, highly-urbanised country in the region that is both a significant importer and exporter of unskilled labour. Chinese Taipei, in contrast, is an ethnically homogeneous society[2] that started on the road to industrialisation under military rule and introduced democratic reforms only from the late 1980s, a quarter century after it began promoting exports. In the past thirty years, economic progress in Chinese Taipei has been extraordinary, not only in terms of GDP growth rates and sustained improvements in living standards, but in the way rapid growth was combined with equity[3].

This paper examines one aspect of the rapid export-oriented industrialisation of Malaysia and Chinese Taipei, namely, their labour market experiences, especially since 1980. It analyses how public policies have affected the labour market, with particular attention to policies on unskilled foreign labour, the volume of which has expanded rapidly in both economies since the late 1980s. The central thesis of the paper is that even though the two economies are at different stages of development, the fundamental forces shaping significant labour market changes in these economies are similar. In the labour market area, as in many other policy areas, their policy responses to emerging problems are increasingly similar.

Initial Conditions and Development Strategies[4]

Despite their common experience as colonies, initial conditions in Malaysia and Chinese Taipei could not have been more different. At independence in 1957, Malaysia was a resource-rich, outward-looking economy, highly dependent on commodity exports, and prosperous in comparison with its Southeast Asian neighbours. In contrast, Chinese Taipei was a backward, natural resource-poor, agricultural island province of China when the Kuomintang (Nationalist Party) took over in 1949.

Independent Malaysia continued the *laisser-faire* policy of the colonial period, encouraging foreign investments in export-oriented agriculture and import-substituting manufacturing while promoting rural development and investing in physical and human capital. The economy remained open and vulnerable to external market forces, particularly fluctuations in the prices of rubber and tin, the two main exports. The *laisser-faire* policy produced economic prosperity but its fruits were unequally divided. Growth was concentrated in the modern sector where immigrant Chinese and Indians dominated, and western enterprises flourished. The Malays who lived mostly in the traditional rural sector fell further behind economically. Malaysian politics became increasingly polarised along ethnic lines, and racial riots broke out after the 1969 general elections.

In response, the Malay-dominated government launched a New Economic Policy (NEP) in 1971 to address the problems of persistent poverty and racial imbalances in income and employment opportunities. The NEP's operational targets were (a) to make the ethnic composition of the workforce in each sector similar to that in the population as a whole; and (b) to raise the Malay share of corporate sector ownership from 2.4 per cent in 1970 to 30 per cent in 1990. These targets were to be achieved by a redistribution-through-growth strategy rather than by redistributing wealth and employment opportunities from economically advantaged to economically disadvantaged groups.

Some progress was made in achieving the NEP targets in the 1970s. Economic growth exceeded Plan targets in both the Second (1971-75) and Third (1976-80) Malaysia Plan periods, reaching 7.4 per cent and 8.7 per cent respectively. Strong external demand for commodities and light manufactures contributed to this good performance, as did rapid increases in public investment and consumption. Malay educational enrolments and wage employment expanded much faster than for Chinese and Indians. Increases in Malay corporate shareholdings were held mainly by state enterprises since Malay individuals and firms did not have the resources to buy over equity from Chinese or foreign firms. This development, together with a greatly increased number of public sector jobs which went disproportionately to Malays, resulted in a much enlarged role for the public sector.

Besides rapidly expanding public sector employment, the government extended controls over the private sector in the 1970s. The Industrial Coordination Act passed in 1975 required firms beyond a certain size to comply with NEP goals on the ethnic distribution of employment and shareholding, while the Petroleum Development (Amendment) Act which was passed in the same year allowed the government to control companies in the petroleum and petrochemical sectors through management shares. In consequence, state controls over the private sector expanded significantly, with adverse effects on private sector investment and efficiency.

Unlike Malaysia, the Chinese Taipei government did not inherit a free trade colonial policy when it came to power in 1949. It pursued instead a mercantilist policy, a policy which was relaxed only in the late 1980s when, partly under pressure from its major trading partners, it embarked on an active programme of import liberalisation. Unlike Malaysia, ethnically homogeneous Chinese Taipei did not face the problem of ethnic imbalances. From the early to the late 1950s, its development strategy promoted agricultural growth and import-substituting industries, whose success was facilitated by infrastructure laid down during the Japanese colonial period, by well-executed land reform programmes (which helped narrow rural-urban income inequalities), and by US military aid. When the limitations of an import-substituting strategy in a small domestic market became clear in the late 1950s, Chinese Taipei began promoting exports through policies such as a unified exchange rate, low-interest loans and preferential treatment for export firms, reduced tariffs for the import of raw materials and inputs, and the establishment of export processing zones where free trade is permitted with the rest of the world. This export drive — the most important shift in the development strategy of Chinese Taipei — was hugely successful because many local entrepreneurs seized the opportunities created by an expanding world economy and turned the island into a major exporter of light industrial and consumer goods by the early 1970s.

In both Malaysia and Chinese Taipei, the export push did not lead to a complete withdrawal of support for import-substituting industries. Malaysia continued until the mid-1980s the modest import-substitution regime inherited from the 1960s, while expanding incentives and facilities for natural resource exports as well as light manufactured exports, particularly textiles, footwear and garments. It embarked in the early 1980s on a programme of heavy industrialisation financed largely by external debt, moving away from this strategy only after the economy had suffered several external shocks including falling commodity prices, and fiscal and current account deficits had risen sharply[5]. In Chinese Taipei, import restrictions continued even as the export push gathered momentum in the 1970s. In Chinese Taipei, as in Malaysia, there was a secondary import substitution phase in the late 1970s when capital-intensive, heavy, and petrochemical industries were promoted to produce raw materials and intermediate goods for export industries.

Both Malaysia and Chinese Taipei have followed since the mid-1980s market-friendly policies, adjusting them in response to new or adverse circumstances. Economic difficulties in the mid-1980s prompted Malaysia to de-emphasize heavy industrialisation and to initiate a wide-ranging reform programme involving privatisation, import liberalisation and deregulation. Foreign investment rules were liberalised, new export incentives were introduced, and the Industrial Coordination Act was suspended to stimulate both domestic and foreign private investment. These changes, together with favourable external factors including currency realignments which improved Malaysia's international competitiveness, resulted in a huge influx of new foreign investment, much of it from Japan and Chinese Taipei. Manufactured exports have expanded by more than 20 per cent a year since 1987, and account for more than half of export earnings. Their rapid expansion has helped boost Malaysia's GDP growth rate to over 8 per cent every year since 1988.

Unlike Malaysia, the pressing problem in the mid-1980s in Chinese Taipei was not growing trade or fiscal deficits, but a huge current account surplus and foreign reserves of over $80 billion. Its successful export drive accounted for only part of this surplus. Extensive import, currency and financial market controls which restricted domestic purchasing power and consumption also contributed to it. As a result of this surplus, Chinese Taipei came under protectionist pressures in its export markets, especially the United States, its leading trade partner. These pressures, together with the recognition that it was losing competitiveness in many labour-intensive industries due to rising costs, prompted the government in Chinese Taipei to pursue a strategy of economic liberalisation and internationalisation from the mid-1980s. Restrictions on imports were relaxed, exchange controls lifted, and state enterprises privatised. High-technology industries including computers and biotechnology were given priority attention, and manufacturers encouraged with tax incentives to diversify and upgrade their operations and to invest in research and development. In 1985 the government launched fourteen major public sector projects costing $300 billion to remedy deficiencies in infrastructure and improve the business and living environments. It also expanded support for science and engineering education and provided incentives for skilled nationals living abroad to return to the island. These policy changes eased protectionist pressures on Chinese Taipei, quickened the adjustment of the Island's firms to rising costs, and triggered a huge surge of outward investments to Southeast Asia in the late 1980s, and to China since the early 1990s with the warming of Chinese Taipei-China relations and the growth of investment opportunities in China.

Though Malaysia and Chinese Taipei began industrialising with different resource bases and trade orientations and are at different stages of their export-driven industrialisation, their development policies have converged since the late 1980s. Internal and external pressures have pushed the two economies to pursue similar policies of economic liberalisation, financial deregulation, and industrial upgrading. A similar convergence is appearing in the labour market as both economies look for ways to improve wage and labour flexibility and to manage a growing influx of unskilled foreign labour.

Economic Growth and Labour Market Changes

Labour Demand and Supply Changes

As in the other fast-growing countries in the Asia-Pacific region, economic growth has resulted in significant labour market changes in Malaysia and Chinese Taipei. Malaysia entered the 1970s with a growing unemployment and underemployment problem because the labour supply was growing faster than demand, especially in the rural areas and among high school leavers[6]. The urban unemployment rate was 11.4 per cent. In the rural areas, though the open unemployment rate was not high, a large proportion of the workforce was underemployed and earning low incomes. By the end of the 1970s, the unemployment problem had improved greatly because sustained economic growth averaging 7 per cent a year created jobs at a faster pace (3.7 per cent a year) than the increase (3.4 per cent a year) in the labour force[7]. In 1980, open unemployment stood at 5.6 per cent. Labour shortages appeared in some sectors, e.g., rubber and oil palm plantations and construction, and for a variety of skills in the manufacturing sector. By 1980, Malaysia had made some substantial progress in achieving its goal of restructuring ethnic employment patterns. There was a relative decline in the proportion of Malays employed in the agricultural sector, and an increase in their involvement in the modern sectors of the economy, especially the public sector.

Unlike Malaysia which was moving towards but not at full employment in 1980, Chinese Taipei at the beginning of the 1980s was already a fully-employed economy, thanks to more than a decade of rapid export-led growth which created more jobs than could be filled by new labour force entrants, including many women drawn into the labour force for the first time who entered the expanding manufacturing and services sectors. But many of the structural labour market changes that appeared in Chinese Taipei in the 1970s have also occurred in Malaysia (and also other newly-industrialising economies[8]). These include a slowdown in the growth of the labour force, rising female participation rates, sustained declines in the proportion of the workforce engaged in agriculture, increases in the employment shares of manufacturing and services, and an expansion of wage employment[9].

Table 1. **Population, Labour Force and Unemployment, Malaysia and Chinese Taipei**

		1980	1985	1990	1992	Average Annual Growth Rate (%)		
						1980-85	1985-90	1990-92
Population ('000)	MAL	13 879	15 791	17 877	18 600[a]	2.6	2.5	2.0
	TAI	17 641	19 132	20 235	20 652	1.6	1.1	1.0
Labour Force ('000)	MAL	5 122	6 039	7 047	7 461	3.3	3.1	2.9
	TAI	6 629	7 651	8 423	8 765	2.9	1.9	2.0
Labour Force	MAL	65.4	65.8	66.5	66.9			
Participation Rate (%)	TAI	58.3	59.5	59.2	59.3			
Male	MAL	82.9	87.4	85.7	85.7			
	TAI	77.1	75.5	74.0	73.8			
Female	MAL	40.6	44.3	47.3	47.8			
	TAI	39.3	43.5	44.5	44.8			
		1980	1985	1990	1992	1993		
Unemployment Rate (%)	MAL	5.6	6.9	6.0	5.4	3.0[b]		
	TAI	1.2	2.9	1.7	1.5	1.5[c]		

Notes:
MAL   Malaysia
TAI   Chinese Taipei.
a.   Rounded.
b.   Estimate by Manpower Department.
c.   Jan-Oct average.
Unemployed persons are those aged 15 years and over who are without work, currently available for work, and seeking work.
Unemployment rate is the ratio of unemployed persons to the total labour force aged 15 and over (15-64 for Malaysia) during the reference period.
Source: Malaysia, *Economic Report 1993/94*, Pillai (1992), Lim (1988). Chinese Taipei, *Statistical Yearbook* (Taipei, 1993); *Monthly Bulletin of Statistics of the Republic of China* (1993).

As Table 1 shows, the general employment picture in Malaysia and Chinese Taipei changed greatly in the mid-1980s. In the first half of the 1980s, economic growth rates decelerated in both Malaysia and Chinese Taipei because the recession in industrial countries reduced demand for manufactured goods from developing countries. In Malaysia, weak export growth together with falling commodity prices and a slower rate of expansion of public sector employment resulted in employment growth not being able to keep pace with labour force growth. Unemployment climbed to 6.9 per cent in 1985. In Chinese Taipei, the labour market became less tight, as unemployment rose to 2.9 per cent in 1985. A recovery in economic growth after 1985 combined with declining labour force growth triggered a rapid decline in unemployment in both Malaysia and Chinese Taipei. In Malaysia, the unemployment rate fell steadily from nearly 7 per cent in 1985 to an estimated 3 per cent in 1993. Together with other indicators — widespread labour and skill shortages, a rising inflow of (mostly illegal) foreign workers, rapidly increasing wages in most sectors — this unemployment level suggests that the Malaysian economy was approaching or at full employment in 1993. As for Chinese Taipei, a situation of over-full employment has prevailed since the late 1980s, a situation alleviated only partly by the influx of unskilled foreign workers from Southeast Asia and by the movement of the Island's labour-seeking firms to Southeast Asia and China.

Table 1 also shows that in both Malaysia and Chinese Taipei, the overall labour force participation rates have levelled off since the mid-1980s. Female participation rates have continued to rise in both countries in the 1980s, in large part because of expanding employment opportunities for women in the manufacturing and service sectors. But they are still low compared to developed economies like the United States or Japan where about 60 per cent of working-age women are in the workforce. Higher female participation rates would reduce labour market pressures in both economies, as would better use of underemployed workers and a reduction in the economically inactive population.

Chinese Taipei has lower male and female labour force participation rates than Malaysia. The higher participation rates in Malaysia arise in part because Malaysia has relatively more workers in the agricultural sector which has high participation rates. In Chinese Taipei, the male rates are low because of the much higher enrolment of men in tertiary educational institutions[10].

Industrial and Occupational Shifts

In both Malaysia and Chinese Taipei, export-led industrialisation has greatly changed the sectoral and occupational patterns of employment. As Table 2 shows, the main difference between the sectoral employment pattern of Malaysia and Chinese Taipei lies in the employment share of agriculture, a share that is recognised to be a good indicator of a country's stage of industrialisation[11]. In Malaysia, the agricultural sector is still the largest employer, but its employment share has fallen steadily from 50.5 per cent in 1970 to 37.2 per cent in 1980 and 25.6 per cent in 1992 (Table 2). Manufacturing is the second largest employer, its share nearly doubling between 1970 and 1992. The expansion of manufacturing employment has been especially strong since 1985 as a result of a surge of investments into the

Table 2. **Employed Persons by Industry (%), Malaysia and Chinese Taipei, 1970-92**

Year		1970	1980	1985	1990	1992	Average Annual Employment Growth Rate (%) 1985-92
Agriculture	MAL	50.5	37.2	31.3	27.8	25.6	0.6
	TAI	36.7	19.5	17.5	12.8	12.3	-2.8
Mining	MAL	2.6	1.3	0.8	0.6	0.6	-1.4
	TAI	1.6	0.9	0.5	0.2	0.2	-9.1
Manufacturing	MAL	11.4	15.5	15.2	19.5	20.5	7.8
	TAI	20.9	32.7	33.5	32.0	30.1	0.6
Construction	MAL	4.0	5.6	7.6	6.5	6.8	1.6
	TAI	5.1	8.4	7.0	8.2	9.1	6.0
Electricity	MAL	0.8	0.7	0.8	0.7	0.7	1.0
	TAI	0.4	0.4	0.5	0.4	0.4	1.2
Transport	MAL	3.4	3.9	4.3	4.3	4.4	3.4
	TAI	5.4	5.9	5.2	5.5	5.3	2.4
Trade	MAL	10.9	14.9	16.3	18.7	19.6	6.0
	TAI	13.6	16.0	18.0	19.7	20.7	4.2
Finance	MAL	0.9	2.9	3.5	3.5	3.5	3.2
	TAI	1.4	2.1	2.6	4.3	4.7	11.4
Govt/Other services	MAL	15.5	18.0	20.1	18.5	18.0	1.7
	TAI	14.9	14.1	15.4	16.8	17.2	4.2
Total ('000)	MAL	3 340	4 835	5 625	6 621	7 060	**3.3**
	TAI	4 576	6 547	7 428	8 283	8 632	2.2

Source: Malaysia, *Economic Report 1977/78, Yearbook of Statistics,* 1988, 1992 (estimates for 1992), Onozawa, (1991) Chinese Taipei, *Statistical Yearbook* (Taipei, 1993).

manufacturing sector. If its recent rate of employment creation is maintained, it will likely overtake agriculture as the largest employer in Malaysia before the year 2000.

In Chinese Taipei, agriculture employed over a third of the workforce in 1970. By 1980, manufacturing had displaced it as the largest employer and it has maintained its position as the largest absorber of labour. However, since 1985, its employment share has declined as Chinese Taipei firms relocated production to other countries in response to the rise in labour costs, the relaxation of rules on outward investments, and the appreciation of the Chinese Taipei dollar.

In both Malaysia and Chinese Taipei, trade and government and other services are the third and fourth largest employers respectively. In both economies the employment share of the trade sector has risen steadily, an increase that reflects a number of factors including rising incomes and tourism growth. Government and other services absorbed a growing proportion of the workforce in Malaysia until the mid-1980s. Since then its share has fallen, mainly because of slower growth of public sector employment and the privatisation of government-owned firms. In Chinese Taipei, the employment share of the government and other services sector remained largely the same in the 1970s. But since around 1980, it has increased rapidly, reaching 17.2 per cent in 1992 due in part to the huge infrastructure-building programme which added many workers to the public payroll.

Table 3. **Employed Persons by Occupation, Malaysia and Chinese Taipei**
(Percentage shares)

Year		1980	1985	1990	1992
Professional/	MAL	6.7	7.5	7.8	7.9
Technical	TAI	5.5	6.1	7.8	8.2
Administrative/	MAL	1.9	2.3	2.2	1.8
Managerial	TAI	0.9	0.8	1.0	1.1
Clerical	MAL	8.3	9.8	9.8	9.9
	TAI	13.0	13.6	16.1	16.7
Sales	MAL	9.8	11.1	11.3	11.4
	TAI	12.4	13.7	14.8	15.2
Service	MAL	9.0	11.4	11.4	11.5
	TAI	7.1	8.4	9.4	9.9
Agricultural	MAL	35.8	30.4	26.2	25.9
	TAI	19.3	17.3	12.8	12.3
Production/	MAL	28.5	27.5	31.3	31.6
Labourers	TAI	41.9	40.1	38.1	36.8

Source: Malaysia, *Yearbook of Statistics*, 1988, 1992.
Chinese Taipei, *Statistical Yearbook*, 1993.

The occupational employment patterns in Malaysia and Chinese Taipei reflect their stage of industrialisation. As Table 3 reveals, Malaysia has relatively more agricultural workers and fewer production, professional and technical workers than Chinese Taipei — a consequence of its later start and success in export-oriented industrialisation. In Malaysia, the proportion of production workers in the labour force has risen rapidly since 1985 in line with the growth of the manufacturing sector. In contrast, Chinese Taipei has experienced a relative decline in the number of production workers, a decline due in part to the shift of workers to the faster-growing services sectors and in part to a shift of manufacturing production by labour-seeking Chinese Taipei firms to overseas locations. There are relatively more administrative and managerial workers in Malaysia than in Chinese Taipei, a difference attributable to the larger size of Malaysia's public sector.

Employment and Output Growth

Table 4 shows employment-output elasticities which measure how employment has changed in relation to output changes[12]. For Malaysia, the employment intensity of output growth (Gn/Gy) has increased from 0.42 in the period, 1970-1985, to 0.46 in the period, 1985-1992. In contrast, Chinese Taipei experienced the opposite trend, its Gn/Gy ratio falling steeply from 0.39 to 0.26 in the comparable two periods. Whereas Malaysia's economic growth has been associated with more employment expansion, in Chinese Taipei it has turned less employment-intensive since 1980.

Both economies reveal wide sectoral variations in the Gn/Gy ratio. For Malaysia, the large labour-absorbing modern sectors like manufacturing and commerce have higher-than-average ratios in both periods. In a few sectors for example, finance and construction the Gn/Gy ratio has fallen, indicating a lower level of employment creation with output growth. In Chinese Taipei, the fall in the Gn/Gy ratio between the two periods is sharp in the two largest sectors, namely, manufacturing (from 0.64 in 1970-85 to 0.10 in 1985-92) and commerce (from 0.65 to 0.39). One explanation for this decline is higher productivity gains due to greater investments in machinery and human resources and the shift to higher value-added activities within the sector[13].

Wage Changes and Economic Growth

In both Malaysia and Chinese Taipei, rapid employment growth in the 1980s has not been at the expense of falling real wages. Sustained economic growth in a stable macroeconomic environment that produced low inflation has led to rising real wages. Between 1980 and 1991, the average rate of annual inflation was 1.7 per cent in Malaysia and 3.2 per cent in Chinese Taipei[14]. These rates are lower than the nominal wage increases for Malaysia and Chinese Taipei in roughly the same period shown in Tables 5 and 6. Between 1981 and 1990, the average nominal monthly wage in Malaysian manufacturing — the fastest-growing sector — rose by 5.2 per cent a year, three percentage points faster than the inflation rate. In Chinese Taipei, the index of the average earnings of employees in most sectors has doubled since 1986[15]. The index for manufacturing employees, for example, rose 94 points between 1986 and 1992, a period when the inflation rate averaged less than 4 per cent a year.

In Malaysia, real earnings of manufacturing workers rose even between 1980 and 1985 when unemployment was rising and manufacturing employment was stagnant. The pattern was somewhat different in Chinese Taipei where manufacturing employment expanded by 12 per cent between 1981 and 1984 before dipping

Table 4. **Employment and Output Changes, Malaysia and Chinese Taipei, 1985-92**
(Percentages)

	Malaysia						Chinese Taipei					
	Growth Rate of Employment (Gn)		Growth Rate of GDP (Gy)		Gn/Gy		Growth Rate of Employment (Gn)		Growth Rate of GDP (Gy)		Gn/Gy	
	70-85	85-92	70-85	85-92	70-85	85-92	70-85	85-92	70-85	85-92	70-85	85-92
Agriculture and fishing	-0.1	0.6	5.3	3.5	-0.02	0.16	-1.7	-2.7	1.5	0.9	-1.15	-2.95
Manufacturing	7.5	7.8	11.9	13.2	0.63	0.59	6.6	0.6	10.2	6.2	0.64	0.10
Utilities	n.a.	1.0	6.1	10.7	n.a.	0.10	4.7	1.2	12.0	3.1	0.39	0.39
Construction	10.9	1.6	8.8	4.4	1.24	0.37	5.6	6.0	8.8	11.7	0.63	0.51
Transport and communication	4.1	3.4	9.2	9.0	0.45	0.38	3.0	2.4	8.8	8.2	0.34	0.29
Commerce	5.6	6.0	7.7	7.2	0.73	0.84	5.2	4.2	8.0	10.8	0.65	0.39
Financial and business services	n.a.	3.2	9.3	9.8	n.a.	0.33	7.4	11.4	10.9	13.7	0.68	0.83
Other services	5.0	1.7	7.8	4.8	0.64	0.35	3.3	4.2	7.6	9.8	0.44	0.43
Total	3.5	3.3	8.4	7.2	0.42	0.46	3.3	2.2	8.4	8.3	0.39	0.26

Sources: Malaysia, *Economic Report 1977/78*, *Yearbook of Statistics*, 1988, 1992 (estimates for 1992).
Chinese Taipei, *Statistical Yearbook* (Taipei, 1993).

slightly in 1985 because of a recession, and nominal earnings rose by more than 20 per cent. Institutional factors account for the relative inflexibility of real wages in the first half of the 1980s in Malaysia, factors that make the Malaysian labour market different from that of Chinese Taipei. In Malaysia, even though only a quarter of the workforce was unionised in 1985 and there are restrictions on union organisation in export-oriented manufacturing firms, wage setting practices found in collective agreements are widely followed by large non-unionised firms including multinationals. These practices include multi-year contracts which result in wages not adjusting quickly to changing labour demand, and long salary scales which provide for automatic annual wage increments based on seniority regardless of market conditions[16]. The combined effect of these practices is reduced wage flexibility and a longer adjustment period to a decline in employment[17]. These practices are not widespread in Chinese Taipei where the industrial sector is dominated by unorganised highly-competitive small and medium-sized enterprises. Even in Malaysia, they appear not to have adversely affected growth.

Table 5. **Indices of Average Earnings of Employees by Industry in Chinese Taipei, 1980-x92**

1986=100	1980	1985	1990	1992
Mining	67.22	95.00	151.35	182.90
Manufacturing	57.48	90.83	158.54	194.03
Electricity	51.09	98.18	175.60	222.60
Construction	55.43	97.46	164.70	205.17
Trade	60.89	91.82	157.57	182.11
Transport	58.62	93.99	155.90	194.73
Finance	60.69	95.19	156.68	189.00
Other services	68.09	91.71	161.51	198.63

Source: Chinese Taipei, *Statistical Data Book* (1993).

Table 6. **Average Monthly Wage by Sector in Malaysia**
(ringgit)

	1981	1983	1985	1987	1990	Average Annual Growth (%) 1981-1990
Manufacturing	438	541	639	637	691	5.2
Construction	471	569	609	590	634*	3.8*
Mining	766	986	1 395	1 915	1 731*	10.7*
Rubber Estates	273	309	303	334	356	3.0
Banking	1 249	1 483	1 678	1 679	1 878	4.6

* Figures are for year 1989.

Source: Malaysia, *Economic Report 1992/93*.

Institutional Interventions and Labour Market Flexibility

The efficiency and flexibility of labour markets have a strong influence on economic growth. Efficient labour markets encourage workers to invest in skills and move to better-paid jobs in higher value-added industries, thus enhancing productivity growth. If their functioning is distorted by institutional interventions, their contribution to economic growth would be reduced. In both Malaysia and Chinese Taipei, institutional factors — government legislation, public sector wage leadership, and trade unions — have not distorted greatly labour market outcomes in the 1980s. In Malaysia, rapid employment growth moderated the efficiency-reducing labour market impact of the NEP which imposed racially-based hiring quotas on employers. With the suspension of the Industrial Coordination Act in 1985, employer hiring flexibility has expanded. Unions have not had a powerful influence on wages as they are restricted or not allowed in export-oriented manufacturing firms where employment demand is strong and where concerted union action could raise wages above levels in non-unionised sectors. In the public sector, union scope for industrial action is restricted by government legislation which prohibits strikes in a wide range of industries deemed to be essential or important to national security. Minimum wage legislation exists in Malaysia but, as it covers less than 5 per cent of the workforce, its impact on employment and wages has been minimal, especially as the minimum wages set are low in comparison to wages for unskilled workers[18]. In Malaysia, statutory job security provisions are reported to have no discernible impact on employment[19]. Malaysia also has statutory minimum fringe benefits which add 10-15 per cent to the wage costs of employers. There is, however, no evidence that these benefits have had a strong negative effect on employment growth in the private sector.

In Chinese Taipei, as in Malaysia, the government did not repress wages, which increased because output and exports expanded rapidly. But in Chinese Taipei, unlike Malaysia, there was labour repression. Until the mid-1980s, Chinese Taipei discouraged the growth of independent unions, unlike Malaysia which allowed independent unions but restricted their activities. After the lifting of martial law in 1986, unions were allowed to take industrial action and opposition parties were recognised, changes which politicised unions and made them more militant. Although labour was no longer repressed, the unionisation rate remains low — about 25 per cent of the workers were union members in the late 1980s, the same proportion as in Malaysia — because of three factors: the dominance of small and medium-sized enterprises which increases the difficulty of organising large unions with market power; high labour turnover rates which reduce the benefits of union membership to workers; and intense wage competition among labour-short employers which means that workers could improve their wages by changing jobs rather than by joining unions. Thus, although unions became more active after 1986, they did not become powerful enough to cause distortions in the labour market. As in the pre-martial law period, labour supply and demand factors, rather than institutional interventions, have been the main determinants of wage changes in Chinese Taipei's labour market since the late 1980s.

The Chinese Taipei government passed the Labour Standards Act in July 1984. Setting standards higher than those in many developed countries, the Act was not well received by employers who came under pressure from workers and unions to implement its provisions. Labour disputes increased sharply, especially after 1987. Far from promoting peaceful industrial relations, the Act has increased conflicts between employers and workers (Gee, 1991, pp. 46-47). As many of its provisions including the minimum-wage provision are not enforced, the Act has had no significant adverse impact on labour market efficiency or flexibility.

Fields (1992, p. 415) has concluded that:

"the Taiwanese [Chinese Taipei] labour market is better characterised as integrated and well-functioning rather than segmented and pathological. The major institutional interventions that segment labour markets in other countries — minimum wages, unions, public sector pay policies, multinational corporations, and labour codes — have little distortionary effect in Chinese Taipei. The labour market in [Chinese Taipei] is almost a textbook case of a smoothly-operating labour market in which employment and earnings reflect the scarcity value of labour".

This conclusion also applies to Malaysia, especially after 1985 when the implementation of the NEP's employment restructuring goals was relaxed, and steps were taken to reduce the expansion of the public sector[20].

Economic Growth, Unskilled Foreign Labour and Policy Responses

Recent Trends in Labour Inflows

The structural labour market changes that occurred in Malaysia and Chinese Taipei in the 1970s and early 1980s have continued in the late 1980s and early 1990s. One labour market development of particular concern in both countries is the growing shortage of unskilled labour, a shortage that has led to a large inflow of unskilled foreign labour, legal as well as illegal. In both economies, the general causes of the growing unskilled labour shortage are similar. Employment opportunities, especially in the export-oriented urban manufacturing sector, have expanded faster than the local supply of workers which, despite being boosted by internal migration and the influx of women workers, has been insufficient to meet rising demand. The plentiful supply of jobs created by export-led industrialisation has also widened the range of jobs available to citizen workers, more and more of whom are shunning physically demanding work in such sectors as agriculture and construction. The volume and timing of the unskilled foreign labour inflow in the two economies are, however, strikingly different because of their different geography and historical development.

Like Singapore but unlike Chinese Taipei, Malaysia is a racially diverse country with a long history of receiving migrant workers. Indeed, its current ethnic make-up is the consequence of British colonial policy which brought workers from China and India to work in the tin mines and on rubber plantations in Peninsular Malaysia. As the only Asian country which shares common borders with all the other Asian countries (Brunei, Indonesia, Philippines, Singapore and Thailand), Malaysia has strong cultural, economic and religious ties with its Asian neighbours. With a higher level of economic development than its neighbours (except Singapore), it has long attracted immigrants from neighbouring countries fleeing from unstable conditions at home or simply seeking a better life. Since labour shortages first appeared in the plantation and construction sectors in the early 1970s, Malaysia has tolerated an inflow of illegal unskilled foreign workers from neighbouring countries including Indonesia, Thailand, and the Philippines[21]. Successful industrialisation since the late 1980s has increased Malaysia's attraction to unskilled foreign workers[22].

Estimates of the number of foreign workers in Malaysia vary. Pillai (1992, p. 33) calculates that 1.2 million workers or 17 per cent of Malaysia's labour force of 7.0 million in 1990 are foreigners. The proportion of foreigners in the workforce ranges from 70 per cent in construction to 30 per cent in agriculture and 3 per cent in manufacturing. Most foreigners are employed illegally because Malaysia issued only 67 000 work permits to unskilled foreigners in Peninsular Malaysia between 1985 and 1991.

Concerned about their fast-growing number and its economic, health and security implications, Malaysia started a drive to register foreign workers in 1992. By early 1994, some 430 000 foreign workers had registered, though many have yet to be issued work permits (*Straits Times*, 27 April 1994). Another 200 000 are believed to be still unregistered. In addition, an estimated 800 000 unskilled workers, mostly from the Philippines, are reported to be working or living in Sabah and Sarawak, the two states that comprise East Malaysia. In all, there may be as many as 1.4 million foreigners in Malaysia's current labour force of about 7.8 million persons. Assuming they are as productive as the average Malaysian worker, foreigners account for nearly a fifth of Malaysia's GDP, a proportion that is significantly higher than that in many labour-receiving countries[23].

Apart from an influx of people from the Chinese mainland in the late 1940s, Chinese Taipei did not receive any significant inflow of foreigners until the late 1980s, more than a decade after its economy had reached full employment. Its experience contrasts strikingly with that of Malaysia, which began receiving a large inflow of foreign workers long before it approached full employment. In Malaysia's case, its common borders with several poorer ASEAN countries, structural labour shortages in plantation agriculture and construction, and a history as an immigrant country combine to induce several streams of unskilled labour inflow. These facilitating factors are absent in Chinese Taipei. The later arrival of a significant number of unskilled foreign workers into the Island compared with Malaysia is not due to the emergence of large wage differences between Chinese Taipei and the labour-sending countries in the late 1980s. These differences existed in the early 1980s, but they induced no inflow from poorer countries. Lee (1992, pp. 345-347) attributes the sudden influx of mostly male foreign workers into Chinese Taipei to the surge of outward investments in Southeast Asia. These investments expanded trade ties between Chinese Taipei and Southeast Asian countries, increasing knowledge about Chinese Taipei in these countries and diffusing information (partly through workers trained in Chinese Taipei) about employment opportunities in the Island[24]. This would explain why most illegal workers in Chinese Taipei are from Southeast Asian countries, in particular, Malaysia, Thailand, and the Philippines, rather than South Asian countries. Cultural and social links between Southeast Asian countries and Chinese Taipei also reduce information and transaction costs for job-seekers from Southeast Asia. One factor not mentioned by Lee is the development of a resourceful international labour recruitment industry which began channelling foreign workers to the booming economies of Asia from the mid-1980s after the demand for contract workers in the Middle East had begun to wane in the early 1980s.

In Chinese Taipei, as in Malaysia, estimates of the foreign worker population vary widely[25]. Using immigration data, Tsay (1992) calculates that Chinese Taipei had in 1990 41 000 over-stayers from five countries — Indonesia, Malaysia, the Philippines, Sri Lanka and Thailand. Most of these over-stayers are working illegally[26]. Tsay's estimate excludes overseas Chinese who came in under the category of nationals or persons who entered the country illegally. It also excludes large numbers of mainland Chinese who have entered Chinese Taipei illegally in fishing boats or who are employed on board ships owned by local inhabitants. The Council of Labour Affairs estimates that as many as 36 000 Chinese from the mainland are working illegally in Chinese Taipei[27]. In all, the population of illegally employed foreign workers in 1993 was probably greater than 100 000, a number which represents just over 1 per cent of the Island's labour force of 9 million.

Policy Responses and Effects of Labour Inflows

Malaysia and Chinese Taipei share similar concerns about their growing dependence on unskilled foreign labour, even though they have significantly different levels of dependence on foreign labour. Like other labour-receiving countries, they are concerned about the economic, social, political, and security implications of hosting a large and growing number of migrant workers. They fear that an excessive reliance on unskilled foreign workers may slow industrial upgrading, even though these workers help to relieve labour shortages and boost production[28]. They also worry that foreign labour may threaten social stability by increasing tensions among locals who are differentially affected by an influx of foreign workers, and between locals and foreigners. In Malaysia, there is also increasing concern that a large flow of immigrants from neighbouring countries, particularly Indonesia, could change the ethnic mix of the country in favour of the *bumiputera* (sons of the soil). For a multiracial society like Malaysia where politics and political parties are organised along communal lines, this shift could expand the support base of Malay-based political parties at the expense of others. It could also strain relations with sending countries, especially Indonesia. In both Malaysia and Chinese Taipei, opponents of foreign labour have argued that illegal immigrants, many of whom live in squalid conditions and are often poorly nourished, may raise the crime rate and spread diseases including tuberculosis and AIDS[29]. In short, foreign labour is a divisive and controversial issue in Malaysia and Chinese Taipei, as it is also in other labour-receiving countries.

Since the beginning of the 1990s, the need in Malaysia and Chinese Taipei for coherent policies to manage their rising dependence on unskilled foreign workers has become an urgent issue. The challenge facing policy makers in both countries is two-fold: how to restructure the economy to reduce its long-term need for unskilled workers; and how to maximise the benefits while minimising the costs of a growing pool of foreign workers. Despite major differences in their historical and economic circumstances, Malaysia and Chinese Taipei have evolved an approach to the management of foreign labour that is similar in important aspects. Essentially, this approach emphasizes policies that hasten industrial restructuring while allowing the legal entry of unskilled foreign workers into a few selective sectors. At the same time, the approach imposes sanctions on errant employers and illegal workers. The difference between them lies in the way they carry out this approach, the success of which depends on striking a proper balance between allowing foreign workers into labour-starved sectors in the short term and encouraging employers to upgrade and reduce their dependence on foreign workers in the long term. Because of its porous borders and much greater dependence on foreign workers, Malaysia faces much more severe management problems than Chinese Taipei does.

Although Malaysia has been receiving large inflows of unskilled foreign workers since the early 1970s, it did not formulate a comprehensive policy to address the problems of foreign labour until 1991[30]. In October 1991, the Malaysian government announced a programme to protect the rights of citizens to employment and to register illegal workers. Under the programme, foreign workers would be allowed into selected sectors including construction and manufacturing. They would be entitled to the same wage and statutory benefits as local workers. But they may not change employers. Employers must pay a levy varying between M$360 and M$2 400 a year for each worker they import[31]. Before they can import workers, employers must provide documentary evidence that locals cannot be found to fill the vacancies. In addition, they must sign employment contracts with foreign workers and submit proposals to solve their labour shortages. The new policy thus seeks to balance the national stake in political stability and economic upgrading with the interests of disparate groups, some of whom like labour-short employers and recruiting agencies have much to gain from an increasing reliance on foreign labour while others like unskilled local workers and trade unions may suffer a decline in their bargaining power.

Included among the more than 430 000 illegal workers who were reported to have registered with Malaysian authorities by the end of 1993 were nationals of not only neighbouring Asian countries but also nationals from Bangladesh, Myanmar, India, Sri Lanka, Pakistan, and a few African countries including Botswana and Tanzania, many entering Malaysia as tourists, others smuggled into the country by well-organised labour syndicates. In January 1994 the government imposed a temporary ban on the recruitment of unskilled foreign workers so that the authorities could find and deport the 200 000 illegal immigrants who had not registered and were believed to be working in the country[32]. In April 1994, this ban was extended by two months to allow the government to review a report being prepared on the "security, social ills and health implications" of foreign workers (*Business Times*, 28 April 1994). A month earlier, the Manpower Department had released a report that foreign labour, by easing labour shortages and moderating wage increases, has helped improve Malaysia's investment climate (*New Straits Times*, 31 March 1994). One outcome of Malaysia's ambivalent, stop-and-go management of foreign workers is great confusion about the country's foreign worker policies and programmes not only in the private sector but also in the public sector. Until Malaysia develops a coherent policy toward foreign workers and implements it effectively, this confusion seems likely to continue.

With little experience in managing unskilled foreign workers, Chinese Taipei did not evolve a policy allowing the legal importation of foreign workers until 1990 when the problem of illegal foreign workers became a major public issue. In that year, after offering an amnesty to illegal foreign workers, it introduced new rules allowing the recruitment of unskilled foreign workers in 15 different occupations. Six industries — textiles, basic metals, metal manufacturing, machinery, electronics and construction — were given access to unskilled foreign labour. The new rules increased the number of workers that contractors undertaking government infrastructure projects could import and imposed penalties on employment brokers and companies hiring workers without government approval. In August 1992, the government allowed labour-short manufacturing and construction firms to bring in 40 000 foreign workers and maids[33]. As in Malaysia, foreign workers can be employed only for two years, and employers hiring them must have plans to upgrade their production technology and facilities[34].

In April 1992, the government in Chinese Taipei passed the Employment Service Law which imposed a fee on employers who import foreign workers (Lee, 1992, p. 117). The fee will be used to train and upgrade the skills of local workers. In addition, the law also provides for severe penalties (including jail sentences) for employers found guilty of employing illegal workers.

In July 1992, Parliament in Chinese Taipei approved the "Statute for Relations Across the Taiwan Strait" after nearly two years of debate on its 96 articles. The statute lifts the ban on a wide range of contacts with China. One of its articles empowers the Cabinet to import thousands of Chinese workers. A large flow of Chinese labour would have far-reaching effects on the Island's labour market as it would not only alleviate current labour shortages but also strengthen the growing trade and investment ties between Chinese Taipei and China, especially the Fujian province which has received a large proportion of investments of Chinese Taipei on the mainland. It could also reduce the Island's growing dependence on unskilled Southeast Asian labour.

In Chinese Taipei, as in Malaysia, the effects of unskilled foreign workers are the subject of much debate[35]. In both countries, there is clear evidence of its positive effects: unskilled foreign labour has alleviated labour shortages, dampened wage pressures, and increased production capacity in many sectors, particularly manufacturing and construction. Allowing families access to foreign maids has enabled many women to enter or remain in the labour force, boosting the pool of educated workers. Evidence on the negative economic impact of unskilled foreign labour on industrial upgrading, domestic wage rates and employment of local workers, and public services, is, however, more controversial and less clear. Lee and Wu (1991, pp. 114-116), citing studies of other countries, reached the following conclusions regarding these negative effects as far as Chinese Taipei is concerned. One, no close correlation exists between labour shortages and economic upgrading because firms in Chinese Taipei have adjusted to labour shortages by relocating production to other countries. Barring employers in Chinese Taipei from importing unskilled workers will not necessarily impel them to innovate or upgrade. On the other hand, allowing unskilled foreign workers into the modern sectors, including construction, may quicken economic restructuring. Two, more unskilled foreign workers do not necessarily depress the wages of local workers or reduce their employment prospects; much depends on whether they complement or displace local workers. In Chinese Taipei, as also in Malaysia, foreign workers are not in direct competition with local workers as most of them are employed in sectors or activities shunned by locals. Three, international evidence on the effects of unskilled foreign workers on public services is mixed. In Chinese Taipei, the influx of foreign workers has apparently not resulted in an unacceptably high level of demand for public services or caused severe congestion costs. In short, the available evidence indicates that Chinese Taipei has so far enjoyed positive net benefits from importing unskilled foreign workers.

As for Malaysia, the economic benefits of unskilled foreign labour have been substantial. Foreign labour has expanded output in important sectors of the Malaysian economy and helped make the labour market more flexible and efficient. The economic and social and political costs, however, are much harder to evaluate, in part because they cannot be easily quantified. One study (Nagayam, 1992) suggests that the employment of foreign labour in Malaysia has prolonged the country's comparative advantage in plantation agriculture but at the cost of deterring investments in new labour-saving technologies. On balance, it seems likely that Malaysia, like Chinese Taipei, has derived net benefits so far from unskilled foreign labour. But the balance between costs and benefits could alter quickly if the influx of foreign labour were to continue unchecked, taking on a momentum of its own and creating security and public health problems for Malaysia while hampering its transition to an industrialised economy by the year 2020.

While both countries realise the need for better management of foreign labour, they are also implementing broadly similar restructuring policies to slow the demand for unskilled labour and to expand the supply of skilled labour. They have provided incentives for firms to shift to higher value-added and knowledge-intensive activities that use less unskilled labour. They have also increased greatly investments in skills and in research and development.

Chinese Taipei has attracted home many of its engineers and scientists who have been trained and working abroad in developed countries. These returnees have played an important part in the Island's move into higher technology areas. This move is taking place at the same time that firms in Chinese Taipei are shifting production of labour-intensive activities abroad to escape rising costs and labour shortages at home. This largely labour-seeking internationalisation process, which accelerated in the late 1980s, has shrunk manufacturing employment and alleviated labour shortages. But it has engendered serious concern about the hollowing out of manufacturing sector, especially as a large number of relocating firms are small and have weak linkages to the Island's domestic economy after they go overseas.

Compared to Chinese Taipei, Malaysia has yet to launch a programme to lure home its citizens who are working abroad, although many of its nationals have returned to fill openings for skilled professionals created by rapid industrialisation. Being a later industrialiser than Chinese Taipei, it has also yet to experience a large volume of outward investments, although some Malaysian companies have ventured overseas and established new regional and international linkages. For Malaysia, the "hollowing out" of the industrial sector is not yet a major policy issue.

Conclusions

In both Malaysia and Chinese Taipei, rapid economic growth has come about principally because of policies that promoted international trade and investments while ensuring macroeconomic stability. In both economies, a successful export push has led to similar and major labour market changes including a steady shift of the workforce from agriculture to manufacturing and modern services, increases in real wages, and the greater participation of women in the workforce. Institutional interventions have been modest, especially in Chinese Taipei. As a result, the labour market has been efficient and flexible, moving workers into sectors of growing demand and providing signals to workers to invest in training.

In both economies, economic success has created shortages of unskilled labour which have led to an influx of unskilled foreign workers. The problems caused by this influx are therefore the problems of managing economic success. Both Malaysia and Chinese Taipei are using similar short- and long-term strategies — industrial restructuring, internationalisation, privatisation, legalisation of unskilled labour inflows along with employer sanctions and levies, etc. — to deal with these problems. If they remain pragmatic and flexible — qualities that have served them well so far — there is every reason to believe that they can meet the inescapable challenge of industrial restructuring while extracting the greatest benefit from their growing dependence on unskilled foreign labour.

Notes

1. For an analysis which emphasises the role of both well-functioning markets and institutions in the region's superior economic performance, see World Bank, 1993a, pp. 8-12.
2. The Chinese population in Chinese Taipei comprises two main groups: the native inhabitants of the island who are active in commerce and industry, and the mainlanders who came to the island in 1949 and are disproportionately represented in the government and state enterprises. The differences between these two groups, once sharp, have become much less distinctive over the years, in part as a result of social and political changes brought about by rapid economic growth.
3. For analyses of Taiwan's exceptional economic performance and transformation, see Fei, Ranis, and Kuo, 1979; Kuo, 1983; Ranis, 1992; and Fields, 1992.
4. This section uses materials from Lim and Pang, 1991, pp. 21-30, and World Bank, 1993a, pp. 131-135.
5. The current account deficit as a percentage of GDP rose rapidly from 1.1 per cent in 1980 — the year the heavy industrialisation programme began — to 13.4 per cent in 1982, while the budget deficit stood at about 15 per cent of GDP in the period 1980-83, twice the level in the 1970s.
6. For a detailed analysis of Malaysia's labour market changes in the 1970s, see Onozawa, 1991.
7. In the 1970s, the largest employment-creating sectors were, in order of importance, manufacturing (which accounted for a quarter of the total employment growth), commerce, government services, and agriculture.
8. For an analysis of labour market changes in dynamic Asian economies, see OECD, 1991, pp. 63-83.
9. In Malaysia, the rise of wage employment among Malays in the 1970s was dramatic as Malays moved in large numbers from the rural to the urban areas. In 1980, 55 per cent of Malays were employees compared to 36 per cent in 1970 (Onozawa, p. 326).
10. Hsu and Hwang (1992) estimate that a labour reserve of 800 000 workers comprising mostly underemployed and women workers existed in Chinese Taipei in 1989. Contrary to Fields (1992) and World Bank (1993a), they argue that the existence of this reserve "along with shortages of certain types of labour faced by industries in Chinese Taipei reflect the malfunctioning of the labour market" (p. 526). But their argument is not persuasive as the simultaneous appearance of shortages and under-utilised labour does not necessarily imply the absence of a well-functioning labour market. In the short term, market disequilibria can and do occur because of time lags and imperfect information. A malfunctioning labour market occurs only when the labour market is

segmented and workers of similar skills are paid vastly different wages because of institutional interventions like government legislation or union pressure.

11. In Malaysia, expanding manufacturing and service employment opportunities together with the government's NEP restructuring programme have led to significant changes in industrial and employment patterns by race and location, changes which have transformed Malaysian society and politics. There has been a massive migration of rural Malays or *bumiputeras* to the urban areas in search of wage employment. In 1990, Malays employed in the manufacturing sector outnumbered the mostly urban Chinese (Onozawa, 1993, p. 327). In 1990, Malays were under-represented only in two job categories: managers and administrators, and sales workers — a sea-change from 1970 when they were vastly over-represented in traditional agriculture and under-represented (in relation to their population share) in modern sector jobs. Employment restructuring under NEP and rapid economic growth have created a new and growing Malay middle class.

12. The choice of base and end years affects these elasticity calculations. The year 1985 was one of slow output and employment growth in Malaysia and Chinese Taipei.

13. For an analysis of the contribution of human capital formation to increased productivity in Chinese Taipei, see Liu, 1992, pp. 373-376, and Pack, 1992, pp. 88-89.

14. These figures are from World Bank, 1993b.

15. The narrow spread in wage increases across sectors whose output grew at vastly different rates suggests a well-functioning and integrated labour market. If the market was segmented because of union power or government legislation, wage changes across sectors would strongly reflect sectoral output or demand growth.

16. For a more detailed analysis of the effects of these practices, see Mazumdar, 1993, pp. 372-373. These wage practices are not unique to Malaysia but are found in most former British colonies including Singapore. Since the mid-1980s, Singapore has introduced wage reforms, shortening the period of collective agreements and salary scales, and increasing the variable component in wages and tying it more closely to productivity and economic performance (Pang, 1991, pp. 87-90). Malaysia has yet to move strongly in the same direction.

17. Real earnings in Malaysia fell in 1986 and 1987 when employment was rising. The fall reflects the delayed wage adjustment of firms to weak labour demand in the early 1980s.

18. Freeman (1993, p. 128) has argued that minimum wages which can be expected in theory to have a distortionary effect on the labour market are in practice often more benign in their impact. Countries are sensitive to the costs and benefits of minimum wages, rarely setting them at levels that seriously reduce employment. And if the minimum wage is set too high, it will not be observed by employers who have reason to collude with workers to avoid the law.

19. Standing (1989, pp. 46-48) reports most firms in an ILO survey said that government job security provisions have had no influence on their employment levels.

20. In Malaysia, the government expanded public sector employment to provide job opportunities for Malays in the 1970s and first half of the 1980s. Had it not cut back on public sector employment growth after 1985 because of budget deficits, the affirmative action programme it instituted would have reduced the efficiency and flexibility of the Malaysian labour market.

21. Indonesians, for example, entered Malaysia, most of them surreptitiously with assistance from illegal syndicates or social networks; a small number were brought in to meet the labour needs of private estates and government agricultural schemes. Their growing inflow strained relations between Malaysia and Indonesia. In 1984, the two

22. countries signed in Medan, Sumatra an agreement that required Malaysian employers to import Indonesians only through official channels. But the agreement failed to stem the flood of illegal immigrants as there was little incentive for employers to go through the costly and time-consuming procedures required to import workers.

22. Even as it attracts more unskilled foreign workers, Malaysia continues to send unskilled workers abroad, mostly to Singapore which is estimated to have about 100 000 workers from Malaysia, the majority of them employed in unskilled or semi-skilled jobs in the manufacturing and construction sectors. There are also large numbers of Malaysian workers in Chinese Taipei and Japan. One estimate suggests there were over 30 000 illegal Malaysian workers in Chinese Taipei, and about 18 000 in Japan in 1991 (Pillai, 1992, p. 42).

23. Even if one assumes that the number of registered and illegal foreign workers totals only one million, foreign workers would still comprise 13 per cent of Malaysia's labour force, which is much higher than in the northeast Asian countries, namely Japan, South Korea and Chinese Taipei, where unskilled foreign workers, most of them employed illegally, form less than 2 per cent of the labour force.

24. While foreign direct investment in Southeast Asia may explain partly the country origin of foreign workers in Chinese Taipei, its explanatory power appears limited when applied to Japan or South Korea which have attracted large numbers of illegal workers from the Indian sub-continent even though their direct investments in South Asia are small, especially in relation to their investments in Southeast Asia.

25. Local papers give estimates ranging 12 000 to 200 000 in the late 1980s (Selya, 1992, p. 793).

26. In 1991, 25 000 illegal workers in Chinese Taipei agreed to leave in return for a tax amnesty and a right to return legally.

27. Cited in the *Far Eastern Economic Review*, 5 August 1993.

28. Mehmet (1988) argues that foreign workers have slowed wage increases in the agricultural sector and delayed restructuring in the manufacturing sector.

29. Twelve of 5 000 immigrant workers randomly tested in Malaysia in August 1992 were found to be infected with the AIDS virus. In April 1994, it was reported that nearly 30 per cent of foreign workers who were given medical tests in Malaysia had contagious diseases (*Business Times*, 28 April 1994).

30. Before 1991, the government made a number of efforts to control illegal immigration, entering into agreements with several governments for the supply of labour into selected sectors (Nayagam, 1992, pp. 479-480).

31. Originally, the levy was set higher for skilled and professional workers than for unskilled workers, which contradicts the policy of encouraging skill development and discouraging unskilled foreign labour inflow. The levy rates have since been revised to be consistent with the objectives of the foreign worker policy.

32. Employers who were given approval before January 1994 were allowed to bring in foreign workers after that date.

33. The government also eased restrictions on the import of white-collar workers as part of its effort to boost foreign investment.

34. There are other restrictions on the hiring of foreign workers. Employers can only hire them through agencies approved by the Office of Labour Affairs. They must pay each new foreign worker NT$ 11 040 (US$ 420) a month as well as post a cash bond of five months' pay for each worker. A legally recruited foreign worker can be expelled if he arrives with dependents, gets married in Chinese Taipei, fails to pass a physical examination (workers are tested for HIV antibodies, syphilis, and hepatitis), becomes ill

or injured, workers for someone other than his official employer, or violates "social order and good customs".

35. See Bohning (1984, pp 86-122) and Greenwood and McDowell (1986) for reviews of the mixed evidence on the short and long-term impact of unskilled immigration in North America and Europe.

Bibliographical References

BOHNING, W. R. (1984), *Studies in International Labour Migration*, Macmillan.

BUSINESS TIMES, (1994), "Asia extends freeze on hiring of unskilled foreign labour", 28 April.

FAR EASTERN ECONOMIC REVIEW (1993), "Human Wave", 5 August.

FEI, John C.H., Gustav RANIS, and Shirley W.Y. KUO (1979), *Growth with Equity: The Taiwan Case*, London, Oxford University Press.

FIELDS, Gary (1992), "Living Standards, Labour Markets and Human Resources in Taiwan", in Ranis, pp. 395-433.

FREEMAN, Richard B. (1992), "Labour Market Institutions and Policies: Help or Hindrance to Economic Development", *Proceedings of the World Bank Annual Conference on Development Economics*, pp. 117-144.

GEE, San (1991), "Emerging Issues of Industrial Relations and Labour Markets in Taiwan", in Lee and Park, pp. 35-55.

GREENWOOD, Michael and John McDOWELL (1986), "The Factor Market Consequence of US Immigration", *Journal of Economic Literature*, Vol. XXIV, No. 4 (December), pp. 1738-72.

HSU, David Y.C. and Jen Te HWANG (1992), "Labour Shortage and Unutilized Labour Reserve in Taiwan", *Journal of Contemporary Asia*, Vol. 22, No. 4, pp. 514-528.

KUO, Shirley W.Y. (1983), *The Taiwan Economy in Transition*, Boulder, Colorado, Westview Press.

LEE, Chung-hoon and Fun-koo PARK (1991), *Emerging Labour Issues in Developing Asia*, Korea Development Institute and East-West Centre.

LEE, Joseph S. (1992), "Capital and Labour Mobility in Taiwan", in Ranis, pp. 305-355.

LEE, Joseph S. and Hui-lin WU (1991), "Unskilled Foreign Workers in Taiwan: Causes and Consequences", *Asia Club Papers*, No. 3, pp. 107-121.

LIM, Linda Y.C. and PANG ENG FONG (1991), *Foreign Direct Investment and Industrialisation in Malaysia, Singapore, Taiwan and Thailand*, Paris, OECD Development Centre.

LIU, Paul K.C. (1992), "Science, Technology and Human Capital Formation", in Ranis, pp. 357-394.

MALAYSIA, *Economic Report*, various years.

MALAYSIA, *Yearbook of Statistics*, various years.

MAZUMDAR, Dipak (1993), "Labour Markets and Adjustment in Open Asian Economies: The Republic of Korea and Malaysia", *The World Bank Economic Review*, Vol. 7, No. 3 (September), pp. 349-380.

MEHMET, Ozay (1988), *Development in Malaysia: Poverty, Wealth and Trusteeship*, Insan, Kuala Lumpur.

MINISTRY OF FINANCE, Malaysia (1993), *Economic Report 1992/93*.

NAYAGAM, James (1992), "Migrant Labour Absorption in Malaysia", *Asian and Pacific Migration Journal*, Vol. 1, No. 3-4, pp. 477-494.

NEW STRAITS TIMES (1994), "Help from foreign workers", 31 March.

ONOZAWA, Jun (1991), "Restructuring of Employment Patterns Under the New Economic Policy", *The Developing Economies*, Vol. 29, No. 4, pp. 314-329.

ORGANISATION FOR ECONOMIC CO-OPERATION AND DEVELOPMENT (OECD) (1991), *Employment Outlook*, Paris, OECD, July.

PACK, Howard (1992), "New Perspectives on Industrial Growth in Taiwan", in Ranis, 1992, pp. 73-120.

PANG Eng Fong (1991), "Emerging Issues of Labour Markets and Industrial Relations in Singapore", in Chung-hoon Lee and Fun-koo Park, pp. 79-97.

PANG Eng Fong (1993), *Regionalisation and Labour Flows in Pacific Asia*, Paris, OECD Development Centre.

PILLAI, Philip (1992), "Malaysia: Nature, Contributory Factors and Consequences of Cross-Country Labour Mobility", *Asia Club Papers* No. 3.

RANIS, Gustav (ed.) (1992), *Taiwan: From Developing to Mature Economy*, Boulder, Westview Press.

REPUBLIC OF CHINA (1993a), *Statistical Yearbook*, Taipei.

REPUBLIC OF CHINA (1993b), *Statistical Data Book*, Taipei.

REPUBLIC OF CHINA, (1993c), *Monthly Bulletin of Statistics of the Republic of China*.

SELYA, Roger Mark (1992), "Illegal Migration in Taiwan: A Preliminary Overview", *International Migration Review*, Vol. XXVI, No. 3 (Fall), pp. 787-805.

STANDING, Guy (1989), "The Growth of External Labour Flexibility in a Nascent NIC: A Malaysian Labour Flexibility Survey", *ILO World Employment Programme Working Paper 35*, Geneva.

STRAITS TIMES (1994), "Ban on hiring unskilled workers extended", 27 April.

TSAY, Ching-Lung (1992), "Clandestine Labor Migration to Taiwan", *Asian and Pacific Migration Journal*, Vol. 1, Nos. 3-4, 1992, pp. 637-655.

WORLD BANK, (1993a) *The East Asian Miracle: Economic Growth and Public Policy*, Washington, D.C.

WORLD BANK, (1993b) *World Development Report 1993*, Washington, D.C.

PART II

LABOUR MARKET AND MIGRATION TRANSITIONS

Thailand: Development Strategies and Their Impacts on Labour Markets and Migration

by Chalongphob Sussangkarn*
and Yongyuth Chalamwong**

Summary

   With a combination of abundant natural and human resource endowments, a stable macroeconomic environment and a market-oriented development strategy, Thailand has enjoyed an annual growth rate of 5 per cent in per capita income over the past three decades. The consequences of sustained high growth for Thailand's labour market have been significant. While agriculture continues to be the major source of employment, absorbing 60 per cent of the labour force, there has been a dramatic shift within agriculture from own account and unpaid family labour to wage employment. Not only have open unemployment rates been consistently low, but under-employment is also low even in rural areas, suggesting a well functioning labour market. Real wage trends show an improvement since 1984, with urban wages growing much faster than those in rural areas. Furthermore, the wages of skilled workers have outpaced those of unskilled workers. If, as would appear to be the case, the demand in the manufacturing sector for workers with a secondary education grows faster than the supply, the wage gap between the educated and uneducated should continue to widen for some time.

   Internal migration has long been a significant feature of Thailand's labour markets. Wide inter-regional income differentials have stimulated sizeable internal movement, both temporary and permanent. Overseas migration has been occurring since the mid-1970s, peaking in the early 1980s before beginning to decline as demand slackened in the Middle East and employment opportunities improved at home. While Thailand continues to export some unskilled and semi-skilled workers,

---

*   Director, Human Resources and Social Development Program, Thailand Development Research Institute
**   Researcher, Human Resources and Social Development Program, Thailand Development Research Institute

it has become a sizeable importer of labour — at both the upper and the lower ends of the skill distribution. Shortages of skilled labour and a fairly liberal immigration policy have attracted highly educated migrants, while high rates of growth of urban unskilled employment have drawn large numbers of young people out of agriculture, leaving vacancies which are increasingly filled by immigrants from neighbouring countries. The fact that a sizeable portion of the native workforce continues to work in agriculture has caused some concern that the influx of migrant workers may be depressing rural unskilled wages — though further research in this area is needed.

Introduction

This paper reviews Thailand's past development pattern and its impacts on the labour market and migration. The paper is divided into four sections. The first section discusses the past development success in Thailand and highlights some key underlying factors. The second section examines the labour market adjustments that have take place. General labour market operations and the sectoral and regional imbalance in Thailand are discussed, and wage trends over the past two decades are analysed. The third section discusses migration patterns. This section looks at inter-regional migration patterns, the flow of Thai workers abroad, and foreign workers in Thailand. Finally, the last section discusses some policy directions.

Thailand's Past Development Success and Key Underlying Factors[1]

Good Economic Growth and Reduction in Poverty Incidence

Over the past 30 years or so, the Thai economy had performed fairly well. Table 1 shows that, between 1960 and 1990, the average rate of real GDP growth was about 7.4 per cent per annum, a rate which can be regarded as quite satisfactory. The growth rates achieved in the immediate aftermath of the two oil shocks were lowest: 1970-75 and 1980-85. However, the 5.6 per cent average growth achieved during these periods was very high when compared to the experiences of other countries. After 1986, the economy began a period of unprecedented rapid growth. Driven on by fast growth of manufactured exports, as well as tourism, in 1987 growth reached 9.5 per cent, and between 1988 and 1990, the rate of growth was above 10 per cent per annum, resulting in an average growth rate of 9.9 per cent per annum between 1985 and 1990.

Table 1. **Growth of GDP, Population, and GDP Per Capita**
(Annual percentage change)

	1960-65	1965-70	1970-75	1975-80	1980-85	1985-90	1960-90
Real GDP at 1972 Prices	7.2	8.6	5.6	7.9	5.6	9.9	7.4
Population	3.0	3.0	2.6	2.4	2.0	1.7	2.4
Real GDP Per Capita at 1972 Prices	4.2	5.6	3.0	5.5	3.6	8.2	5.0

Source: NESDB, National Income of Thailand, various issues.

With the introduction of the very successful National Family Planning Program in the early 1970s, the rate of population growth also declined rapidly. From a rate of about 3 per cent per annum in the 1960s, the rate fell to about 1.7 per cent per annum between 1985 and 1990. This contributed to high growth of real GDP per capita, which averaged about 5 per cent per annum between 1960 and 1990, reaching about $1 434 in 1990 (current prices).

A result of the relatively high rate of per capita GDP growth was that the incidence of poverty also declined substantially from the level of the 1960s. According to the 1962/63 Socioeconomic Survey, 57 per cent of Thailand's population had income below the poverty line (Table 2). Since then, the incidence of poverty has shown a clear downward trend with some fluctuations, and in 1988/89 it was reduced by more than half from the 1962/63 level, reaching 23.7 per cent. The decline was particularly rapid for urban areas, but even for the rural areas, poverty incidence declined by more than half between 1962/63 and 1988/89. Poverty fluctuated somewhat, in particular showing a sharp increase in 1985/86. This was because of changes in various economic conditions affecting incomes of the population. The increase in poverty between 1980/81 and 1985/86 was due to the downward trend of the world and domestic prices of all the major crops, which had a severe adverse effect on the income of Thai farmers. In addition, in the aftermath of the second oil shock, the Thai economy was in a period of relatively slow growth, so that opportunities to supplement farm income through work in industry and services were limited.

Table 2. **Poverty Trends in Thailand**

	1962/63	1968/89	1975/76	1980/81	1985/86	1988/89
Per cent of Population Under Poverty Line						
Whole Kingdom	57.0	39.0	30.0	23.0	29.5	23.7
Rural Areas	61.0	43.0	32.9	25.8	33.9	28.5
Villages	n.a.	n.a.	36.2	27.3	35.8	29.4
Sanitary Districts	n.a.	n.a.	14.8	13.5	18.6	13.2
Urban (Municipal) Areas	38.0	16.0	12.5	7.5	5.9	6.7
Population in Poverty (millions)	16.464	13.679	12.753	10.994	15.491	13.069

Sources: NSO, Socioeconomic Surveys, various years, as analysed in Meesook (1979), Jitsuchon (1989) and Hutaserani and Tapwong (1990).

The absolute number of people under the poverty line has shown a slight decline, from 16.5 million in 1962/63 to 13.1 million in 1988/89. While this decline was not dramatic, it has to be remembered that between 1962/63 and 1988/89 the population of Thailand increased by about 26 million persons. Thus, to have been able to reduce the absolute number of people living under the poverty line during this period, when the size of population nearly doubled, was certainly some achievement.

The progress on the economic front also went along with good progress on the social front. As already mentioned, the rate of population growth declined rapidly from the early 1970s. Life expectancy at birth increased from 58 to 66 for females, and from 54 to 62 for males, between 1965 and 1986. Infant mortality rates declined from 88 per 1 000 live births in 1965 to 28 in 1989. Over the last decade or so, much progress has also been made in tackling the problem of child malnutrition. In 1982, about 15 per cent of children less than five years old suffered from severe malnutrition (2° and 3°). By 1990, the incidence of 2° and 3° malnutrition had dropped to less than 1 per cent[2].

The provision of basic education to the population is another area in which Thailand had also made substantial progress over the last three decades. Expansion of primary enrolment has been sizeable, and currently there is almost universal enrolment. This was a rather impressive feat considering the high rate of population growth during the 1960s and early 1970s. A rough indicator of the improvement in basic education of the population is the adult literacy rate[3]. Table 3 shows that the adult literacy rate in Thailand increased from 67.7 per cent in 1960 to 93.0 per cent in 1990. Compared to other Asian countries, the current adult literacy level is one of the best in the region.

Table 3. **Adult Literacy Rates for Selected Asian Countries**
(Per Cent)

	1960	1970	1980	1985	1990
Thailand	**67.7**	**78.6**	**86.0**	**91.0**	**93.0**
Hong Kong	70.4	77.3[a]	90.0[b]	88.0	n.a.
India	27.8[c]	34.1[a]	36.0[d]	43.0	48.0
Indonesia	39.0[c]	56.6[a]	62.0[e]	74.0	77.0
Malaysia	52.8[f]	58.5	60.0	73.0	78.0
Philippines	71.9	82.6	75.0[b]	86.0	90.0
Singapore	n.a.	68.9	83.0	86.0	n.a.
South Korea	70.6	87.6	93.0	n.a.	96.0
Sri Lanka	75.0[f]	77.6[a]	85.0[b]	87.0	88.0

Notes: a=1971, b=1979, c=1961, d=1981, e=1978, f=1962.

Sources: World Bank, World Tables 1983, and World Development Report 1991, 1994.

Some Key Factors Underlying Successes

Obviously, many factors contributed to the past development successes, but if some factors are to be singled out, then these include the economic and political stability during the last several decades, and the quality of the natural and human resources base.

Macroeconomic stability has certainly been the hallmark of Thailand's past development history. When comparing the past macroeconomic data of Thailand with many other countries, two aspects of Thai macroeconomic development stand out very prominently. First is the minimal movement in the exchange rate between the baht and the US dollar over the past 30 to 40 years, and second is the relatively low inflation rate, which has been very close to the US inflation rate over many decades (see Table 4).

Table 4. **Relative Thai/US Inflation Index and Baht/$ Exchange Rate**

Year	Relative Thai/US Inflation Index	Exchange Rate Baht/US$
1960	1.00	21.18
1965	1.04	20.83
1970	0.95	20.93
1975	1.10	20.38
1980	1.15	20.51
1985	1.12	27.19
1990	1.11	25.64

Note: Relative Inflation Index indicates the ratio between Thai CPI and US CPI (Base Year 1960).

Sources: International Monetary Fund, Year Book of International Financial Statistics, 1986, and Bank of Thailand, Monthly Bulletin and Key Economic Indicators, various issues.

Being able to maintain almost a fixed exchange rate with the US dollar over the last 30 to 40 years and attain low inflation rates, implied a great deal of monetary and fiscal discipline. It was not the case that Thailand had abundant domestic resources that could be used to invest in the country's development without adversely affecting the domestic saving-investment gap, or equivalently the current account deficit. Rather, there had always been sufficient monetary and fiscal discipline to keep the problem of the saving-investment gap from cumulating out of control. When problems became severe, as in the aftermath of the second oil shock, then it became just about the main policy priority to try to maintain macroeconomic stability.

With the importance attached to the maintenance of macroeconomic stability, it is not surprising that Thailand managed to emerge from the post second oil shock period without any serious macroeconomic overhang. The recovery in the world economy in mid-1980s, and particularly the exchange rate realignment between the Japanese yen and the dollar and major European currencies in 1986, benefited the Thai economy enormously. This, in effect, led to a substantial depreciation of the baht against the average currency of Thailand's trading partners, as the baht was tied mostly to the dollar. It also led to changes in comparative advantage between Japan and the Asian NIEs (South Korea, Chinese Taipei, Hong Kong and Singapore), whose currencies at the time were also very much tied to the dollar, and allowed the latter countries to push more strongly into the export market for technologically advanced and skill-intensive manufactured products, such as cars and sophisticated electronic consumer products. In fact, by the mid-1980s, the Asian NIEs were probably already near to losing their comparative advantage in domestic production of labour-intensive semi-skilled manufactured products (such as basic garment products) to other economies with plentiful supplies of low wage semi-skilled workers. The changes in the international economic environment in the mid-1980s simply accelerated the transition of the Asian NIEs. Comparative advantage in semi-skilled labour-intensive manufactured commodities now lies with countries at a lower level of development compared to the Asian NIEs, in particular Thailand and some of the other East Asian economies, such as Malaysia, Indonesia and China. Without a serious overhang from the post second oil shock period, Thailand was in a position to benefit fully from the changes in comparative advantage.

Apart from macroeconomic stability, Thailand also benefited from long periods of relative political stability. Of course, over the past three decades there were military coups, and changes in governments and Prime Ministers. However, apart from some tragic episodes, the latest of which occurred in May 1992, the changes in regimes or Prime Ministers took place relatively painlessly. There was little overhang from political changes, in the sense that a situation of continual conflict between different factions struggling for power and for revenge was generally avoided. Also, changes in government hardly affected the basic development philosophy or development strategy of the country. There were no distinct differences in development philosophy (for example, socialist versus conservative) between different political factions, be they factions within the military or the various political parties. The political game was not to change the direction of the ship, but rather to become captain while the ship continues to sail on in the same general course. Continuity in development direction was provided through bureaucrats and technocrats, who have generally stayed through several changes in governments.

What also contributed to the stability in development direction was that Thai governments were relatively weak. They have had to balance the interests of, and generally share benefits with, many different pressure groups, such as different industrial and trading interests, bureaucrats, technocrats, labour groups etc. After balancing all these interests, what emerged at the end was basically a continuation of the status quo, even if at the beginning new governments may have wanted to do things in substantially different ways from past governments.

In addition to macroeconomic and relative political stability, Thailand is relatively well endowed with agrarian natural resources. The natural resource base and the agriculture it supports has in the past been a mainstay of the Thai economy. Between 1960 and 1980, Thailand managed to achieve a very respectable average real GDP growth rate of over 7 per cent per annum which was driven in large part by extensive agricultural expansion. Cultivated area in agriculture increased rapidly. In the 1970s, up to 1978, cultivated area expanded by over 3 per cent per annum, faster than the rate of increase of the agricultural population, so that the land/man ratio in agriculture was actually rising[4].

The abundance and quality of Thailand's natural resource base is attested to by the country's position in world agricultural trade, being the largest exporter of rice and cassava, and ranking high in the export of rubber, sugar cane, and aquaculture products. Even though agriculture's contribution to GDP is now very small, this sector is still very important to the livelihood of the majority of the population in Thailand (see below).

The quality of the human resource base has also played a crucial role in Thailand's development success. The following can be highlighted.

1. Good Basic Education of the Population: A strong point of Thai development policy has been the provision of basic primary education to the population. Even in 1965, the primary enrolment ratio was 78 per cent (82 per cent for males and 74 per cent for females). By 1980, almost universal primary enrolment had been achieved. As already indicated Thailand has one of the highest literacy rates among countries of the region. The good basic education of the population has been an important factor behind Thailand's past development success. Jamison and Lau (1982) found that farmers with completed primary education were significantly more productive than those with less education in traditional agriculture, which covers the bulk of Thai agriculture. In the mid-1980s, having a large pool of relatively low income workers with good basic education to draw into the expanding industrial and service sectors meant that Thailand could take full advantage of changes in international comparative advantage that occurred at the time. In fact, apart from the formal educational qualifications, Thai workers appears to be highly adaptable and trainable, as many foreign companies investing in Thailand have found.

2. Highly Educated Elites: At the top of the educational hierarchy, Thailand has many well-educated people. This is due partly to the relatively good quality of the Thai universities (particularly the closed public universities). Of equal importance has been the traditional desire by the Thai elites to send their children to get the best education possible abroad, which was substantially supplemented by the availability of various scholarships. Also, the Thais who go to study abroad mostly come back to Thailand. They form an important core of bureaucrats, technocrats, and entrepreneurs, who have had important roles in guiding the direction of the country's development. The actual formal education received abroad was probably not as important as the exposure to different societies, different ways of thinking, and different economic structures and opportunities.

3. Skill Acquisition through On-the-Job Training: Another factor which contributes to the quality of the Thai workers is the extensive nature of on-the-job training in the economy. This is one area where the private sector plays a major role in human capital formation in Thailand. Based on a recent study[5], it was found that science and technology (S&T) related workers made up about 10 per cent of the labour force. However, fully 75 per cent of these workers only had primary education or less. The skills needed for the occupations in which they were employed (mostly as technicians) are learnt on the job. This shows the importance of on-the-job training as a mode of human resource formation in Thailand. It is one reason why the economy has performed well over the last three decades, in spite of past findings that Thailand has a lower stock of S&T manpower (through the formal education system) per capita compared to many other countries in the region. The experiences of countries such as Japan, Korea and Chinese Taipei have also shown that on-the-job training can make substantial contributions to rapid economic growth.

4. Capability of Thai Female Labour Force: Thailand has a very high female labour force participation rate. In 1987, of females aged 11 and above who were not attending school, 80 per cent participated in the labour force. The female labour force also had good basic education along with the men. The active participation of women in the labour market has been particularly important during the recent period, as one finds that most of the labour-intensive semi-skilled industries which are the dynamic exporting industries are big employers of female labour. Such industries as canned food, textiles and apparel, footwear, and electronics employ more women than men. Thus, female workers make a crucial contribution to exports and to growth. In addition, female labour also predominates in the service sector, and this sector is also of key importance for foreign exchange earnings, mainly through tourism.

5. Quality and Diversity of Thai Entrepreneurs: A key strength of the Thai economy is the diversity and quality of Thai entrepreneurs. First and foremost among the entrepreneurs who have been the backbone of past Thai development is the group of *Thai farmers*. That Thai farmers should be regarded as entrepreneurs stems from the fact that about 80 per cent of them are "owner cultivators" [6], not necessarily in the sense that they have formal titles to their land (because there are still millions of farmers in so-called national forests without formal legal title) but that they are own-account workers who have to decide on what and how to produce, and generally operate their own farm enterprise. The fact that they also have good basic education has contributed to their productivity as earlier indicated. The base of entrepreneurs in industry and services is also very broad. Basically, Thai society has been able to harness the available entrepreneurial talents, whatever their racial, religious, or socioeconomic background. The tolerant, compromising, practical, or "middle path" nature of Thai society is well known. This enables Thai society to avoid long-lasting and damaging social conflicts. It avoids the negative impact of social conflicts on the harnessing of available talents, whatever the racial, religious or social background. The diversity of informal sector activities in Thailand is also of importance in developing entrepreneurial skills. This sector should really be regarded as a "school for entrepreneurs". Entrepreneurial skills are certainly not something that can be easily taught formally through educational institutions. It is the past learning-by-doing that has occurred in vast amounts in the informal sector that has shaped many of the top entrepreneurs or entrepreneurial families in the Thailand of today. The quality and diversity of Thai entrepreneurs explains why the Thai economy is so diverse. The country has strength in agriculture, industry, and services.

Labour Market Adjustments

General Labour Market Operation

Aggregate indicators suggest that the labour market in Thailand operates fairly well. The rates of open unemployment[7] are very low. Table 5 gives open unemployment rates by level of education for 1980, 1986 and 1992. In aggregate, the rate of open unemployment ranges from 0.5-1.3 per cent. Between 1980 and 1986, when the economy was generally in recession in line with the recession in the world economy, the open unemployment rate rose slightly. The main problem at the time was one of educated open unemployment, especially for those with vocational education. Between 1986 and 1992, when the Thai economy grew much more quickly, the open unemployment rates became much lower. It should be noted that these open unemployment rates refer to situations during the peak agricultural season. The rates are higher during the dry season months, but the unemployment problem during the

Table 5. **Open Unemployment Rates of Those Looking for Work in Survey Week**
1980-92 Labour Force Survey: July-September
(Per cent)

Year	<=Prim	Secondary	Vocational	Teacher	University	Total
1980	0.43	3.57	8.74	3.43	2.65	0.77
1986	0.57	3.53	10.84	3.94	4.55	1.29
1992	0.20	1.22	2.50	1.45	1.65	0.46

Source: NSO, Labour Force Surveys (July-September).

dry season is somewhat different from the overall unemployment situation, as it relates to the seasonal nature of agriculture.

The fact that open unemployment rates are generally low in Thailand should not be too surprising. Most people in Thailand work as either own-account or unpaid family workers, mainly in agriculture (Table 6). Thus, it is easy for most people to work in the family enterprise. Also, as with many other developing countries, there are many informal sector employment opportunities available, where barriers to entry are low, so that most who really want to work can find something to do.

Table 6. **Structure of Employment by Sector and Work Status: 1992**

	Agriculture	Non-Agriculture	Total
Structure of Employment by Sector (Thousands)			
Own Account Workers	6 391	2 690	9 082
Unpaid Family Workers	11 024	1 402	12 426
Employer	369	394	763
Government Employee	40	2 019	2 059
Private Employee	1 880	6 174	8 055
Total	19 705	12 680	32 385
Share in Total Employment by Work Status (Per cent)			
Own Account Workers	32.43	21.22	28.04
Unpaid Family Workers	55.95	11.06	38.37
Employer	1.87	3.10	2.35
Government Employee	0.20	15.92	6.36
Private Employee	9.54	48.69	24.87
Total	100.00	100.00	100.00
Share in Total Employment by Sector (Per cent)			
Own Account Workers	70.37	29.63	100.00
Unpaid Family Workers	88.72	11.28	100.00
Employer	48.39	51.61	100.00
Government Employee	1.95	98.05	100.00
Private Employee	23.35	76.65	100.00
Total	60.85	39.15	100.00

Source: NSO, Labour Force Survey, July-September 1992.

The rates of under-employment also reinforce the efficiency of labour market operations as indicated by the open unemployment rates. The rates of under-employment are low in Thailand. Table 7 shows the proportion of those employed working less than 20 hours a week (or less than about 5 half-days a week) for 1984 and 1992. It can be seen that the rates of underemployment are only about 1.5 per cent. There are some regional variations, but in 1992 even the part of the country with the highest rate of under-employment (the rural South) had a rate of only about 4.3 per cent[8].

Table 7. **Per cent of Employed Working Less Than 20 Hours Per Week**
(July-September)

	1984	1992
North		
Urban	0.65	1.16
Rural	1.55	1.01
Northeast		
Urban	1.57	1.68
Rural	0.65	1.90
South		
Urban	0.94	2.11
Rural	3.49	4.29
Central		
Urban	0.96	0.74
Rural	1.22	1.14
Bangkok	0.76	0.62
Whole Kingdom	1.27	1.63

Source: NSO, Labour Force Surveys, 1984 and 1992 (July-September).

The own-account and unpaid family workers accounted for most of the under-employed. These workers may combine work with other activities that they do in the home, so that the under-employment rate will overstate the real problem of low-working hours while desiring more work. In fact, in 1984, only about one-third of those under-employed expressed the desire for more work (Sussangkarn, 1990). Thus, it appears that under-employment is also not a very serious problem for Thailand and that the labour market in Thailand is generally able to absorb efficiently the labour supply.

Sectoral and Regional Imbalances

Satisfactory economic growth over the past three decades has obviously led to substantial changes in the structure of production. The previous discussion showed that the labour market has been able to absorb most of the available labour supply. However, in spite of seemingly efficient labour market operation, major imbalances exist between the structure of production and the structure of employment. The most glaring imbalance is between agricultural production and employment.

Table 8 shows the shares of agriculture in GDP and in employment. The importance of agricultural production in Thailand has gradually declined over the last several decades. By 1990, the share of agriculture in GDP was only 12.4 per cent. The share of employment in agriculture has also declined. However, available employment figures indicate that the decline in the share of employment in agriculture has been at a much slower pace than that for the share of agriculture in value added. In 1990, over 60 per cent of the workforce was still employed in agriculture while the sector produces only 12 per cent of the GDP. The ratio of the share of agriculture in GDP to the share of agriculture in employment has declined from about 0.35-0.43 in the 1970s to about 0.2 in 1990. Even if the employment shares are adjusted to take into account the fact that those with main occupation in agriculture do not spend all their work time on agricultural work, it is still found that about 45 per cent of total labour time in Thailand is spent on agricultural activities (see Sussangkarn, 1992).

Table 8. **Share of Agricultural GDP (at Current Prices) and Agricultural Employment**

	1971	1975	1980	1985	1990*
Share of GDP (at Current Prices) (Per cent)	28.20	31.48	25.38	16.75	12.41
Share of Employment (Per cent)	78.90	72.99	70.95	68.40	63.50
Ratio of Share of GDP to Share of Employment	0.357	0.431	0.358	0.245	0.195

* From 1989, the Labour Force Survey (LFS) changed the definition of the active workforce to include only those 13 years or older (as opposed to 11 years or older in earlier surveys). Thus, direct comparisons of the absolute employment figures from the LFS since 1989 with earlier years are not possible without adjustments. Broad employment shares are, however, probably less affected by the change. The shares in the table are for the wet season. Dry season shares are slightly lower.

Source: NESDB, National Income of Thailand, and NSO, Labour Force Surveys (July-September).

This imbalance between agricultural production and employment is obviously a key factor in creating widening income disparities between agricultural and non-agricultural households and between rural and urban areas. In 1975/76 the mean per capita income of non-agricultural households was 2.08 times that of agricultural households[9]. In 1988/89, the ratio rose to 2.55 times[10]. Thus, between 1975/76 and 1988/89 the trend of a worsening income disparity between agricultural and non-agricultural households is clear. Against this, of course, it has to be remembered that poverty incidence declined from 30 per cent in 1975/76 to 23.7 per cent in 1988/89, so that agricultural households generally became better off during this period, but the pace of improvement was slower than that for non-agricultural households.

The slow shift of labour out of agriculture is obviously reflected in the disparity between urban and rural areas. Over the course of development, economic activities have concentrated in core urban areas[11]. However, in the case of Thailand, the extreme concentration of urban activities around Bangkok, has led to big differences between the economic conditions in the Bangkok Metropolitan Region (BMR) and the rest of the country[12]. Whereas the BMR contains 16.1 per cent of the total population in 1991, it accounted for 51.8 per cent of total GDP (Table 9). In 1991, the per capita GDP in the BMR was 142 084 Baht (about $5 600), which was 5.6 times higher than that for the rest of the country. The gap between the BMR and the rest has also widened over the last decade or so.

Table 9. **GDP and Population**

	1981	1991
Shares of GDP (%)		
BMR	45.56	51.84
Rest of the Country	54.44	48.16
Whole Kingdom	100.00	100.00
Shares of Population (%)		
BMR	14.89	16.08
Rest of the Country	85.11	83.92
Whole Kingdom	100.00	100.00
Per Capita GDP		
BMR	48 764	142 084
Rest of the Country	10 192	25 303
Whole Kingdom	15 934	44 085
Ratio BMR/Rest	4.8	5.6

Note: BMR includes Bangkok and the five surrounding provinces.

Source: NESDB Gross Provincial Product.

Wage Trends

The trend in wages can give more insight into how the labour market has adjusted in response to the development trend. First, Table 10 gives the real monthly wage rates for private employees in urban and rural areas. The pattern is consistent with the previous discussions of the development pattern. Between 1978 and 1984, when the economy grew fairly well, but before the accelerated industrialisation phase which started after 1986, real (private) wage rates increased by about 2 per cent per annum. Further, while urban wages increased faster then rural wages, the difference was not that pronounced. Between 1984 and 1992 the economy grew much faster, and the increase in real wages was much faster, averaging about 4.4 per cent per annum. With more concentration of industrialisation around the urban areas, urban wages increased much more rapidly than rural wages (4.8 per cent to 1.1 per cent), and the ratio between urban and rural wage increased from 1.59 in 1984 to 2.12 in 1992. For rural real wages, the increase was in fact slower between 1984-92 than between 1978-84. This suggests that most of the jobs created during the accelerated industrialisation phase after the mid-1980s were concentrated in the urban areas. The patterns for males and females are similar. However, it should be noticed that between 1984-92 the female real wage increased significantly faster than the male real wage, although there is still a differential in favour of males. This presumably reflects the pattern of industrial and service sector growth, where the industrial export sectors demand mainly female workers, and this is also true of many of the modern service sectors.

Table 10. **Real Monthly Wage for Private Employees by Area (1978 Prices)**

Both Sexes	Urban	Rural	Total	Ratio U/R
1978	1 267	839	990	1.51
1984	1 508	948	1 116	1.59
1992	2 192	1 036	1 578	2.12
Average Growth (%)				
1978-84	2.94	2.06	2.02	
1984-92	4.79	1.11	4.42	
Male				
1978	1 450	955	1 133	1.52
1984	1 738	1 085	1 281	1.60
1992	2 486	1 156	1 768	2.15
Average Growth (%)				
1978-84	3.07	2.15	2.07	
1984-92	4.58	0.80	4.11	
Female				
1978	975	669	774	1.46
1984	1 182	752	882	1.57
1992	1 810	866	1 322	2.09
Average Growth (%)				
1978-84	3.26	1.97	2.20	
1984-92	5.47	1.77	5.18	

Source: Nominal wages are tabulated from Labour Force Survey Data Tapes (July-September), CPI series from the Bank of Thailand Monthly Bulletins.

Table 11 looks at real wages for those private employees with just primary education or less as indicators of unskilled private real wages (henceforth referred to as unskilled real wages). The picture here is very different from that in Table 10. Between 1984 and 1992, unskilled real wages increased more slowly than between 1978 and 1984, and in rural areas unskilled real wages actually fell. For men, unskilled real wages increased more slowly between 1984-92 compared to 1978-84 in urban areas, and unskilled real wages fell between 1984-92 in rural areas. For women, unskilled real wages increased faster between 1984-92 in urban areas, but increased slower in rural areas compared to 1978-84, though at least female unskilled real wages in rural areas did not decline as for males.

Table 11. **Real Monthly Wage for Private Employees by Area: Primary Educated and Below (1978 Prices)**

Both Sexes	Urban	Rural	Total	Ratio U/R
1978	972	798	850	1.22
1984	1 129	899	953	1.26
1992	1 315	891	1 049	1.48
Average growth (%)				
1978-84	2.53	2.01	1.92	
1984-92	1.93	-0.11	1.21	
Male				
1978	1 161	905	983	1.28
1984	1 374	1 029	1 108	1.34
1992	1 518	1 011	1 192	1.50
Average Growth (%)				
1978-84	2.85	2.16	2.02	
1984-92	1.26	-0.22	0.92	
Female				
1978	678	648	656	1.05
1984	798	716	736	1.11
1992	1 069	725	860	1.48
Average Growth (%)				
1978-84	2.75	1.68	1.94	
1984-92	3.72	0.14	1.97	

Source: Nominal wages are tabulated from Labour Force Survey Data Tapes (July-September), CPI series from the Bank of Thailand Monthly Bulletins.

The differences between the two wage trend tables suggests that the benefits of the more rapid growth achieved since the mid-1980s went predominantly to the better educated employees in the country, although female unskilled employees also benefited slightly. However, it should be noted that while the real unskilled employee wage fell in the rural areas between 1984-92, this did not necessarily mean that the rural poor became worse off. The poverty trend in Table 2 above (and more detailed analyses, such as Hutaserani and Tapwong, 1989) certainly suggest that the poor benefited from the recent growth. The reason for this is that most of the poor are own-account and unpaid family workers in agriculture, who earn less than the rural average monthly wage for private employees[13]. Over time there has been a shift from own-account and unpaid family workers to wage workers (private employees) as wage employment opportunities expand (see Table 12). Thus, even though real rural wages fell, the rural poor could earn more than they previously did by shifting into wage employment where opportunities allowed. In fact, the available supply of poor own-account and unpaid family workers that can shift into wage employment is one important factor why unskilled real wages increased slowly or declined. Additional supply of (illegal) migrants from Thailand's neighbouring countries may also be another important factor (see below).

Table 12. **Employment by Work Status: 1978-92**
(Thousands)

	Government Employee	Private Employee	Own Account and Unpaid	Total
1978	1 020.5	3 573.4	17 213.9	21 807.8
1984	1 676.6	5 036.5	19 285.8	25 998.9
1992	2 059.3	8 817.4	21 508.1	32 384.8
Row Shares (%)				
1978	4.68	16.39	78.93	100.00
1984	6.45	19.37	74.18	100.00
1992	6.36	27.23	66.41	100.00

Note: Employers are included in Private Employees.

Source: NSO, Labour Force Surveys, July-September.

While the poor may have benefited from the recent growth, it is clear that the better educated and the better off benefited much more. A prior study of socio-economic mobility by one of the authors (Sussangkarn, 1992) found that the better educated took full advantage of the economic opportunities opened up by the dynamic growth in the late 1980s, while those with primary education or less benefited to a much lesser extent. Data on income distribution (Table 13) also clearly indicates the worsening trend of income inequality in Thailand. In 1975/76 the poorest 60 per cent of the population had an income share of 29.78 per cent. By 1990/91 this share has declined to 23.41 per cent.

Table 13. **Income Shares of Population by Quintiles**

	1975/76	1980/81	1985/86	1988/89	1990/91
Richest 20%	49.26	51.47	55.63	55.01	56.48
Next Richest 20%	20.96	20.64	19.86	20.30	20.11
Middle 20%	14.00	13.38	12.09	12.20	11.92
Next Poorest 20%	9.73	9.10	7.87	7.98	7.44
Poorest 20%	6.05	5.41	4.55	4.51	4.05
Richest 40%	70.22	72.11	75.49	75.31	76.59
Poorest 60%	29.78	27.89	24.51	24.69	23.41

Source: From analyses of NSO, Socioeconomic Surveys.

A fundamental reason that can explain why the less educated (equivalently the poorer segment of the population) did not benefit as much from the recent economic boom is the fact that the structure of the Thai labour force is highly skewed toward those with primary education or below. As earlier indicated, Thailand was successful in expanding basic education to benefit most of the population. However, over the last two to three decades, Thailand under-invested in the middle level of education[14]. Thailand lags far behind other countries at a comparable level of development in secondary enrolment. For example, in 1990 the gross secondary enrolment ratio for Thailand was only about 30 per cent, compared to 87 per cent for South Korea, 71 per cent for the Philippines, 57 per cent for Malaysia and 48 per cent in Indonesia[15]. While the past enrolment pattern can be fairly well understood if analysed in conjunction with the employment and production structure (see Sussangkarn, 1988), it has meant that the share of the Thai labour force with just primary education or less is extremely high. In 1990, about 83 per cent of the Thai labour force had only primary education or less.

While the recent economic boom created demand for factory workers with just basic primary education for the labour-intensive manufactured export sector, the available supply is very large. As can be seen from Table 12, while the share of private employees in total employment increased from 19.4 per cent in 1984 to 27.2 per cent in 1992, two-thirds of those employed are still own-account or unpaid family workers in 1992 (mostly in agriculture). The large available supply in addition to the still relatively small base of wage employment explains why unskilled real wages did not go up much.

The employment situation continues to change rapidly. While it may be sufficient in the early stage of labour-intensive export-led growth that workers have only primary education so long as they are trainable, currently most medium to large-scale enterprises require workers to have at least lower secondary education. This is inevitable as production processes become more complex and Thai industry is becoming more technology-intensive, so that firms perceive that the basic knowledge workers should have to be fully trainable and effective is more than that provided from primary education. Thus, for those with just primary education, who still comprise over 80 per cent of Thailand's workforce, the door to modern sector jobs is quickly closing.

Over the last few years, the authorities have made a conscious effort to increase secondary enrolment. Parents are also responding by sending more and more of their children to secondary school, as they can see that good jobs now require more than primary education. This has led to a rapid increase in the transition rate from primary to secondary school; the rate increased from less than 50 per cent five years ago to about 80 per cent currently. However, as the increase in secondary enrolment will only affect new entrants to the labour force, the Thai labour force will continue to be dominated by those with primary education or less for many years to come. Simulations have shown that by the year 2000, more than 70 per cent of the Thai labour force will have only primary education or less irrespective of how quickly the transition rate from primary to secondary school can be increased[16]. Analyses have shown that this will probably not affect Thailand's ability to grow at around 7 to 8 per cent per annum to the year 2000, as there will still be sufficient numbers of workers available with middle level of education or more who could be drawn into the modern production sectors[17]. However, the fact that the majority of Thai workers with only primary education will have less and less access to the better paying jobs will mean that income distribution will get increasingly more unequal throughout the next decade.

Migration Patterns

Internal Inter-Regional Migration Patterns[18]

From the above discussion of the past development pattern and sectoral and regional imbalances, it should not be surprising to find that the net inter-regional migration movements are mainly toward Bangkok and the surrounding areas. Table 14 gives the regional population and net migration gains for 1975-80 and 1985-90. It can be seen that in 1975-80, only Bangkok had a net migration gain. This represented 4.36 per cent of Bangkok's 1980 population. All other regions were net losers, with the Northeast (the poorest region) losing the most both in terms of absolute number and as a proportion of the 1980 population.

Table 14. **Regional Population and Net Migration Gain**
(Thousands)

	Bangkok	Central	North	Northeast	South
Net Gain: 1975-80	212	-6	-24	-181	-1
Population 1980	4 870	10 113	9 427	16 434	5 874
Rate of Net Gain (%)	4.36	-0.06	-0.25	-1.10	-0.02
Net Gain: 1985-90	366	293	-89	-554	-16
Population 1990	6 198	12 340	10 777	19 209	7 315
Rate of Net Gain (%)	5.90	2.38	-0.83	-2.88	-0.22

Note: Migration refers to inter-regional 5-year migrants aged 5 years and over.

Source: NSO, 1980 and 1990 Censuses.

Between 1985-90 the rate of net migration increased. This is to be expected given the economic boom in the second part of the 1980s and the widening sectoral and regional imbalances. Bangkok was still the largest gainer, gaining 366 000 people or about 5.9 per cent of the 1990 population. However, by the late 1980s, the economic boom and increasing congestion in Bangkok led to rapid development of the provinces surrounding Bangkok. Many factories were set up in these surrounding provinces. Thus, one finds that the Central Region (which includes the booming Eastern Seaboard area) also became a net gainer. The Central region gained 293 000 people, representing about 2.4 per cent of the region's 1990 population. The largest loser was still the Northeast, and the loss amounted to over half a million people, or about 2.9 per cent of the region's 1990 population.

While the above migration patterns are consistent with the development pattern and the sectoral and regional imbalances, a puzzle is the fact that the migration movements were not larger. Given the sectoral and regional imbalances and the urban-rural wage gap, one might expect larger migration streams to reduce the imbalances. Previous analysis of this issue suggests two main reasons why this was not the case[19]. The first is the past ready availability of forest areas which could be converted to arable land. This was the main destination for migrants from the rural areas in response to the population pressure up until about 1980. Instead of migrating to the urban areas, rural migrants would go to the forest areas (often illegally), and settle down to cultivate the land, in effect taking ownership. As indicated earlier in the 1970s the cultivated area expanded more rapidly than the rural population.

The second reason is the very high proportion of farm households who are owner cultivators in Thailand (83.3 per cent in 1981). This is likely to be a factor working against large-scale migration into the urban areas. It is likely that the market for land in the rural areas is thin, and thus owner cultivators who wish to sell their land and migrate to the urban areas may only get rather low prices. This would increase the opportunity cost of migration. Migration from self-cultivating households would therefore be limited to a few family members such as sons or daughters, and may be circulatory in nature, rather than a wholesale movement of all the family members. A factor which would reinforce the above reason is that many of the so-called "owner cultivators" in fact do not have full land titles. The migrants who went into the forest areas to open up new land were actually taking possession of the land illegally. They went into the reserved forest areas, while the authorities did not really try to enforce the law. The result is that about 30 per cent of private land in Thailand has no formal legal documents. This makes it even more costly for a farmer to abandon the land and migrate out of the rural areas.

Up until about the end of the 1970s, it was logical that many farmers migrated to open up new agricultural land. Plenty of land was still available in the forest areas[20]. Further, crop prices were high and rising. The rural-rural migration path was probably the best choice for the rural population. First, once they migrated, they ended up doing what they knew how to do well, i.e. agricultural cultivation. Second, the move also appeared to increase their assets, because they acquired *de facto* possession of the land. The problem is that once crop prices started to decline in the first half of the 1980s, it was difficult for the farmers to move out of agriculture. Those who legally own their land may face large opportunity costs in selling their land and moving to the urban areas, due to the thin land market. Those who have no legal title will get even lower prices for their land, and hence face a very high opportunity cost.

The high opportunity cost faced by the farmers were they to migrate into the urban areas leads to long lags in the migration adjustment process. However, Table 14 showed that the pace of inter-regional migration has picked up considerably in the latter part of the 1980s. Given the persistent sectoral and regional imbalances, rapid inter-regional migration flows can be expected well into the future (see Chalamwong, 1991).

Outflow of Thai Workers

Profile

The voluntary flow of labour across national boundaries is an age-old phenomenon and one which generally has made a major contribution to rising incomes, economic development, as well as personal well-being. Today, the international movement of labour between countries has become commonplace and has accelerated in the past two decades in response to internal labour-market imbalances and foreign employment opportunities/ possibilities. These flows vary in size and composition, and are subject to various legal and institutional settings, often with significant economic and political repercussions. Over the years, many Thai workers have gone to work in other countries, with the persistent income inequality in Thailand acting as a continual push factor.

Changes in the Middle Eastern countries that were brought about by the increase in oil prices since the early 1970s led to a strong demand for Asian workers. The first batch of short-term overseas contract labourers from Thailand was sent to the Middle East by foreign firms, mostly European and American, that ran construction businesses in Thailand during the Vietnam War. When these companies began to operate in the Middle East, they hired large numbers of workers from Thailand. These companies were, therefore, the main conduit for Thai workers to find employment overseas, mainly in unskilled jobs. It was not until 1977 that labour export from Thailand was conducted by private Thai recruitment agencies.

It has been widely accepted that the official international figures for contract-labour migrants from Thailand compiled by the Department of Labour are considerably underestimated. This is due to the fact that large numbers of workers are sent illegally by unregistered employment agencies. Nevertheless, the official statistics do offer an indication of the increased magnitude of overseas contract labour. These contract workers numbered fewer than 1 000 in 1975, and increased very rapidly thereafter to 117 341 in 1982 and 123 054 in 1989 before declining again to 71 710 in 1992 (Table 15). The fluctuation in numbers has corresponded mainly to a fluctuation in labour demand from the Middle Eastern oil exporting countries.

From Table 15, one can see that the major geographical destinations of Thai workers are the Middle East, Africa (Libya), ASEAN and other Asian countries (mainly Japan and Chinese Taipei). Statistics indicate that, up to the late 1980s, the great majority of this international labour flow was channelled to the Middle East countries, particularly Saudi Arabia. In 1989, some 73 422 workers, or 59.7 per cent of the total number of overseas Thai contract workers, went to the Middle East. Second to the Middle East was Asia (ASEAN and other Asia) which accounted for 25.4 per cent. The share of the Middle East (or Middle East plus Libya) has been continually declining, however, and by 1992 ASEAN and other Asian countries had overtaken the Middle Eastern oil exporting countries as the main destination of Thai contract workers. This shift can be attributed to the weakening oil price which substantially affected the earnings of the Middle Eastern countries, and also diplomatic difficulties between Thailand and Saudi Arabia over the handling of a jewellery theft episode. On the other hand, the demand for Thai workers in Asia has been steadily increasing. Singapore, Brunei and Malaysia are the most popular destinations in ASEAN. Recently, due to the attraction of very high Japanese wage levels, and easier access to the Japanese labour market, Japan has become another popular destination.

Table 15. **Thai Workers Going Abroad, by Country of Destination**
(Number of Workers)

	1977	1982	1989	1992
Middle East	3 831	104 951	73 422	17 432
Saudi Arabia	2 855	38 271	61 442	8 707
Iraq	0	3 140	2 829	¾
Qatar	0	2 825	2 328	944
Bahrain	976	10	1 773	841
Kuwait	0	611	3 473	3 313
Africa	0	9 184	13 339	5 595
Libya	0	9 034	13 215	5 407
USA & Europe	0	0	4 990	2 031
ASEAN	0	3 134	20 580	21 505
Singapore	0	1 975	11 056	6 510
Brunei	0	960	8 630	12 729
Malaysia	0	199	611	2 151
Other Asia	0	72	10 723	25 147
Japan	0	41	3 825	6 748
Total	3 831	117 341	123 054	71 710
Percentage Shares by Region				
Middle East	100.00	89.44	59.67	24.31
Africa	0.00	7.83	10.84	7.80
USA & Europe	0.00	0.00	4.06	2.83
ASEAN	0.00	2.67	16.72	29.99
Other Asia	0.00	0.06	8.71	35.07

Source: Department of Labour.

If the estimated number of illegal migrants is taken into consideration, the proportion of Thai contract workers in ASEAN would be considerably higher than it appears in Table 15. Evidence of its magnitude appeared, for example, when the Singaporean government announced tough measures to curb the illegal immigration problem in January 1989 and more than 10 000 illegal Thai workers surfaced. A large number of migrants are unrecorded because of the relative ease of travelling to these three ASEAN countries.

As for the characteristics of the international contract workers, although there is no comprehensive survey of Thai workers, available evidence from various studies (Thosanguan 1982, and Pitayanon 1986) suggests that, prior to migration, a high percentage share of the workers were farmers and unskilled workers. This share increased from 63 per cent in 1982 to 85 per cent in 1986. Due to the nature of the work, which is heavily concentrated in the construction sector, and the necessity of living in labour camps at construction sites, these contract jobs attract mainly young adults. The recruiting agents generally select only those who are likely to withstand the strains of physical and mental hardship. Data from the Department of Labour indicate that about 80 per cent of these workers are between the ages of 25 and 40. In the case of female workers, who are mainly employed in labour-intensive manufacturing types of production, a high percentage of people recruited are in the 17-30 age group. The distribution of migrants by area of residence, as compiled by the Department of Labour, indicates that in 1983 the majority (50 per cent) of the migrants were from Northeastern (the poorest region) Thailand, with 31 per cent from the North, 11.9 per cent from the Central region, and the remaining 9 per cent from the South. These patterns of labour outflow are consistent with the sectoral and regional income imbalances and the poorer prospects for those with low education in the Thai labour market.

Legal Framework and Policy

As an exporter of labour, one of Thailand's main concerns is protecting Thai workers from harsh conditions overseas, breach of contract between employer and employee, as well as fraud from labour-recruiting agencies.

The Thai Labour Law clearly encourages private sector participation in the form of employment placement agencies. Therefore, from the earliest period, the exportation of Thai workers was purely in the hands of private employment agencies. Motivated by self-interest and profit, private agencies played a significant role in matching the supply of labour and the demand for labour from abroad. High profits from overseas placement services attracted many new agencies into the market. However, the Department of Labour had strict controls on the number of local job agencies in an effort to keep the number of agencies to a manageable level and to avert cut-throat competition. Consequently, a large number of illegal agencies as well as an increasing number of unscrupulous recruitment agencies emerged. There were several problems of abuse in recruiting, with many horror stories of exploitation of workers, mainly poorly-educated with no experience in overseas travel. As a result, a new Employment Placement Act was legislated and passed in 1985. This new legislation recognises the role of the private recruitment agencies, but attempts to ensure that workers are neither exploited nor abused. Accordingly, one of provisions of this Act made the agencies responsible for all the expenses incurred by a worker, and required refund of the commission fee to the worker if the job stipulated in the agreed contract was not found.

With this new law, the number of agencies increased from 134 firms in 1982 to 324 firms in 1989, and the number of workers filing complaints against overseas placement agencies declined. The figures show that there were 3 629 cases in 1988, compared with 4 235 and 8 904 complaints in 1987 and 1986 respectively. Job agencies had to pay 18.7 million baht as compensation to 3 111 of the 3 629 workers who filed complaints in 1988, a sharp drop from the 26.4 million in 1987 and 34.5 million in 1986.

As far as an overall policy toward international labour migration is concerned, it was not until the Fifth 5-Year National Economic and Social Development Plan of 1982-1986 that specific policies on labour migration were established. Government policy with respect to Thai overseas employment is positively stated as follows:

a) To promote the export of excess Thai labour to work in foreign countries. However, care will concurrently be taken to prevent possible domestic shortages of skilled workers, particularly when they appear to affect the country's economic development.

b) To promote private, licensed recruitment agencies to carry out the business of exporting labour more effectively.

c) To assure a fairer distribution of the benefits from labour export among all parties concerned.

d) To provide more and better services to assure that the labourers are not cheated by unscrupulous recruitment agencies or employers while seeking work and while working abroad.

e) To promote and facilitate remittances via the banking system.

Impact of International Contract Labour

Remittances

Like other labour-exporting countries, Thailand has gained a considerable amount of foreign exchange from the export of labour. As a result of the rapid increase in the number of international migrants, the remittance flow has also risen dramatically between 1980 and 1985 (Table 16). Since 1985 the remittances have stabilized at around $1 billion per year, with a slight upward trend. The great bulk of the remittances was contributed by Thai workers from the Middle East. Remittances from ASEAN are rather small in relation to overall remittances. However, had the number of illegal migrants been included, this figure could have doubled or even tripled. As a share of merchandise exports, however, the ratio increased from 5.83 per cent in 1980 to 13.41 per cent in 1983, and has been declining since, reaching 3.47 per cent in 1992. Currently, with exports still increasing at around 15 per cent per annum, the contribution of remittances to total foreign exchange earnings is becoming smaller and smaller.

Remittances Through the Banking System

As for the impact of the remittances, they obviously contribute to improving the current account and the balance of payments. Prior to the boom in exports in the second part of the 1980s, remittances from overseas workers ranked among the top foreign exchange earners. Even now with remittances being a much smaller share of exports, they are still significant when compared to the size of Thailand's current account deficit; for example, in 1992 Thailand's current account deficit was 161 278

Table 16. **Remittances Through the Banking System**
(Millions of Baht)

	Remittances from			Merchandise Exports	Ratio Rem/Exp
	Middle East	ASEAN	All Countries		%
1980	4 234.0	n.a.	7 703	132 041	5.83
1981	6 753.5	111.7	10 428	150 218	6.94
1982	10 326.8	221.6	14 222	157 203	9.05
1983	15 667.6	405.5	19 457	145 076	13.41
1984	16 473.4	556.6	21 118	173 520	12.17
1985	12 931.6	790.8	23 796	191 703	12.41
1986	10 521.0	523.9	20 900	231 481	9.02
1987	9 627.8	561.1	21 596	298 099	7.24
1988	9 124.7	n.a.	23 413	405 000	5.78
1989	n.a.	n.a.	24 240	516 315	4.69
1990	n.a.	n.a.	24 907	589 813	4.22
1991	n.a.	n.a.	26 018	725 630	3.59
1992	n.a.	n.a.	28 620	824 644	3.47

Source: Bank of Thailand.

million baht, so that remittances amounted to about 17.7 per cent of the current account deficit.

The inflow of remittances benefited the poorer groups in the population, although middle-men also certainly benefited. Results from a survey of Northeastern villages (Poapongsakorn, 1989) give a micro-level view of the use of remittances. Since most of the migrants had to borrow money to finance their overseas employment and some migrants were victims of fraud, the survey indicated that 45.2 per cent of total remittances were spent on the repayment of loans (principal plus interest) and payment of loss of the commission fees. Consumption and investments constituted only 17.9 per cent and 12.6 per cent of total remittance income respectively, while saving accounted for 14.6 per cent. A considerable proportion of remittance-induced expenditures are on non tradeable goods such as land, housing, and education. In addition, most of the migrants brought home some luxury durable goods such as televisions, radios, and electrical appliances.

Skill Development

The impact of international migration on skill development is ambiguous. It is not clear whether international migration serves as a positive or negative factor in the augmentation of skilled labour supplies. So far there have been no systematic surveys or a longitudinal follow-up of the return migrants to determine the degree of skill acquisition. However, some inferences can be made from information collected from the sample of overseas workers' registration forms lodged with the Labour Department which indicate that, among those who experienced changes in occupational status, the extent of skill formation was insignificant. Figures show that 241 workers out of a total sample of 424 workers took up the same type of job as they pursued at home. Another 156 workers took up jobs that could be regarded as an improvement over their occupational status at home and hence allowed them to acquire new skills. In some 19 cases, it can be inferred that they lost skills, because they left skilled jobs in Thailand to take up unskilled jobs for better earnings, while only 8 others moved clearly into new occupations that would have imparted new skills to them.

In the case of female workers in Singapore, a small sample survey of 100 workers from Thosanguan (1985) concluded that the overseas experience does not appear to expose the workers to new technology or modes of production that could be construed as skill acquisition. Even if these female workers do acquire some new skills, the evidence from the survey indicated that most of them did not plan to work in their previous occupation upon return, and did not intend to apply new skills acquired overseas. Many of them intended to go into self-employed businesses. However, there is some evidence that they do gain confidence and worldly experience which could have some impact on their lives and future careers.

In the case of workers in rubber and palm oil plantations (mainly in Malaysia), it is also probable that there is practically no substantial net acquisition of skills. This is due to the fact that a large proportion of Thai workers in these plantations are experienced farmers and agricultural workers and already possess the skills required for plantation work.

What should be clear from this discussion is that the issue of skill formation is complex. For individual skill acquisition, a definitive answer would require that the productivity of the workers before and after their overseas work trips be measured, and that productivity gains be compared with those of a non-emigrating control group. An attempt should also be made to assess the consequences, in terms of skills, of returning workers moving out of the labour market and into self-employment.

International Co-operation

In view of the potential for mutual benefits that can be shared by the host country and the labour exporting one, mutual co-operation would be the most logical path to pursue. The three major issues that can be identified are: (i) the appropriateness of current barriers to the free flow of labour, (ii) the social problems created by migrant workers, and (iii) the protection of labour from exploitation and a "fair" distribution of mutual benefits.

The unexpectedly high turn-out of illegal Thai workers reporting for repatriation assistance at the Thai Embassy in Singapore in March of 1989 revealed a deplorable situation of exploitation and neglect. Evidence revealed that many of these Thai workers were victims of indifference and exploitation by Singaporean employers and unscrupulous Thai and Singaporean job agents. It may be argued that, in voluntary agreements that do not involve coercion, no intervention is needed because of the apparent willingness of both parties to enter into contract despite the risks. However, the present asymmetry of information allows exploitation to occur.

Given the mutual benefits to the participating countries, policy coordination is urgently needed to reduce the incidence of cheating in placement service activity. As for Thailand, efforts have to be made to punish job agents who abuse their privileges, and to educate the Thai workers about the proper procedures for seeking employment overseas. The Local Labour Offices outside Bangkok should disseminate information concerning dishonest job-placement representatives and employment agencies. Recruiting agencies will have to be made responsible for the damage that is created by themselves or their representatives. Prompt and well-prepared assistance to workers facing penalties and allegations of criminal conduct has to be provided. A simplified procedure should also be devised for workers appealing for justice. As for the host countries, the conditions for legal entry need to be re-examined to determine whether they impose excessive costs on prospective employers, so that they have to resort to illegal means of recruiting. To act as effective deterrents, legal penalties should be structured so as to offset the potential gains from illegal recruitment.

Apart from the illegal migration aspects, problems pertaining to the living conditions of Thai workers overseas need to be investigated also. The social problems that the migrants cause should be recognised as partly a consequence of the Spartan conditions under which the workers are forced to live. Although the welfare services provided by the foreign employers are generally satisfactory, there are nevertheless some problems related to daily living conditions, especially for female workers.

As for the job-seekers, the scope of public information should be expanded to provide more extensive information in the areas of laws and regulations of host countries, their religion, culture, tradition and ritual practices. For the host countries, there is a need for more public information relating to the substantial contributions that foreign workers make to the host economy by accepting menial jobs turned down by the locals, thereby effectively relieving labour shortages in the host country. Public information programmes should be designed to foster a more open and receptive attitude toward foreign workers in the local communities.

Foreign Workers in Thailand

Foreign workers in Thailand can be divided into two distinct categories: the highly-skilled, professional group, and the newly-emerging group of semi-skilled and often illegal "guest" workers from neighbouring countries.

Professional and Skilled Migrants

For the first category of workers, the issue of foreign workers has emerged as a "concern" rather than as a "problem" in Thailand. In fact, it has become a concern only from 1986 onwards when the Thai economy began to exhibit signs of imminent shortages of both professional and skilled workers in its period of economic boom. The rapid expansion of the industrial and service sectors led to a rising demand for highly-skilled and experienced manpower, leading to a tightening in the skilled labour market. In fact, prior to the boom in the latter part of the 1980s, the labour market was characterised by an excess supply of the better educated workers (Table 5). In the early 1980s, the public sector was the main absorber of the educated workers. In 1984, the public sector employed 41.4 per cent and 56.3 per cent of all workers with vocational and university education respectively (Table 17). Since the economic boom starting in the mid-1980s the picture has changed rapidly. Major demand for educated workers is coming from the private sector. The share of public sector employment of workers with vocational and university education has declined rapidly, to 29.3 per cent and 45.3 per cent respectively in 1992.

Table 17. **Share of Public Sector Employment by Levels of Education: 1984, 1992**

	1984			1992		
	Public	Total	Pub. Share (%)	Public	Total	Pub. Share (%)
Elementary and Below	441.1	23 036.4	1.91	408.0	26 561.2	1.54
Secondary	320.9	1 448.8	22.15	426.5	3 030.1	14.08
Vocational	229.3	554.6	41.35	390.4	1 332.4	29.30
Teacher Training	440.6	524.8	83.97	462.1	640.2	72.18
University	244.7	434.4	56.32	372.2	821.0	45.33
Total	1 676.6	25 998.9	6.45	2 059.2	32 384.9	6.36

Source: NSO Labour Force Survey, July-September 1984, 1992.

Obviously the fields of study that are demanded by the public sector are different from those required by the private sector. The public sector demands mainly social sciences and humanities, while the private sector needs S&T manpower and those with commercial disciplines. Shortages of S&T and highly skilled labour have become very evident, with the wages for these types of workers rising rapidly since the mid-1980s in the private sector. Brain drain from the public sector to the private sector, and from the smaller to the larger firms, has become commonplace.

To address this problem, Thailand has in its Seventh Economic and Social Development Plan (1991-1996) made important adjustments to increase the supply of skilled individuals and improve the skills and quality of manpower supply through educational and training programmes. Such a strategy, however, will require a certain amount of time to manifest results and to satisfy long-term trends in the labour market, and shortages are still expected well into the future[21]. In the meantime, contingency measures to cope with the present shortage of skilled and highly-skilled manpower will have to be adopted and pursued. One such measure concerns filling the gap with foreign professionals and technicians.

To facilitate the inflow of specific manpower to meet the requirement of the country's industrialisation, Thailand has established procedures to consider requests for entry from expatriates to work in promoted firms. The investment promotion law administered by the Board of Investment (BOI) gives foreign investors the same rights and privileges as Thai investors. Foreign companies promoted by the BOI are also entitled to various incentives, including permission to bring in foreign nationals to undertake investment feasibility studies and foreign technicians and experts to work in promoted firms, as clearly stipulated in sections 24, 25 and 26 of the Investment Promotion Act B.E. 2520 (1977). Generally, aliens in Thailand also have the same legal rights as Thais, unless a right is particularly reserved for nationals, or is denied to aliens under specific laws, such as the Nationality Act, the Land Code and the Alien Employment Act. As a developing country, Thailand has specific policies and legislation concerning immigration of human resources so as to protect the interests of its own citizens. In any case, there are very few occupations and provisions prohibited to aliens under the Alien Business Law, as shown in Appendix 1 thereto. This list of restricted occupations is mainly confined to Thai handicrafts and some traditional professions related to the arts and culture. In addition, exception is granted to aliens who have promotional privileges granted by the BOI to enable them to engage in business for a fixed period of time, subject to certain conditions.

Table 18 shows data on aliens who received work permits in the whole country, classified by occupation, which reflects the need for skilled and professional manpower in various sectors.

Table 18. **Aliens Who Received Work Permit in Whole Kingdom by Occupation**

Occupation	1985	1991
Physical Scientists & Related Technicians	85	153
Engineers and Technical Specialists	630	1 703
Machinery Fitters, Installers & Mechanics, Repairmen	62	504
Electrical Fitter & Related Electrical & Electronics	86	150
Aircraft and Ships' Officer	136	99
Medical Doctor, Professional Nurse & Related Workers	13	16
Economists and Auditors	48	43
Teachers	228	508
Workers in Religion	172	190
Authors Journalists & Related Writers	50	108
Photographers Etchers and Designers	¾	27
Musicians, Singers, Actors, Producers and Directors	602	607
Translators and Interpreters	10	39
Administrative and Managerial Workers	1 357	3 237
Specialists	476	459
Receptionist and Travel Agency Clerks		160
Managers Working Proprietors (Wholesale & Retail)	244	921
Managers and Supervisors, Catering & Lodging Service	45	166
Cooks and Related Workers	108	107
Watchmen	13	14
Farm Managers and Supervisors	5	38
Production Supervisors and General Foremen	172	1 034
Food and Beverage Processors		38
Others	591	361
Total	5 133	10 682

Source: Yearbook of Labor Statistics (various issues). Aliens Occupation Control Division, Department of Labour.

Illegal "Guest" Workers

With rapid economic development in Thailand in conjunction with long land borders with poorer neighbouring countries, it is inevitable that many illegal immigrants come to Thailand from these countries. While hard data on the extent of these illegal migrants are difficult to come by, latest estimates from the Ministry of Interior suggest that the number of illegal migrants is very large. Table 19 shows an estimate of the number of illegal migrants in various provinces. The total comes to between 200 000-300 000 people. This would just about make Thailand a net importer of labour overall, assuming that the actual Thai outflow of labour is about 2-3 times the size of the official figure when illegal emigrants are included.

Table 19. **Estimated Number of Illegal Migrants by Provinces**

Provinces	Number '000	Sectors
Chiang Mai(N), Chiang Rai(N), Mae Hong Son(N),	30	Construction
Tak(N)	20	Agriculture, Services (restaurant and food shop) Prostitution, etc.
Ranong(S)	34	Marine Fishery Factory
Ratchaburi(C) and Kanchanaburi(C)	16	Palm Oil and Coffee
Chumporn(S)	3	Plantations, Shrimp
Surat Thani(S)	3	Farms, Prostitution, etc.
Other Border Provinces	100-200	Agriculture, Services and Others
Total	206-300	

Note: N=North, C=Central, S=South.

Source: Ministry of Interior, Practical Guidelines for Solving Problems of Illegal Migrants from Myanmar to Tak and Mae Hong Son Provinces, February 14, 1994.

The extent of the problem is now of major concern to the authorities, but the issue is very controversial, with vastly different views concerning the problem even among various government agencies. On the one hand, it is suggested that it is now very difficult to find Thai workers for certain types of jobs or in certain locations. Thus, foreign unskilled workers are needed and the policy should be to ease the legal restrictions on such workers. On the other hand, it can be argued that with about 1 in 5 of the Thai population still living under the poverty line, and with widening income disparities, the presence of these illegal migrants is further harming the economic prospects of the poorer and less educated Thai workers. Therefore, no easing of restrictions should be carried out, and effective measures should be pursued to deport these illegal workers. Adverse social and security consequences of these illegal migrants are highlighted in support of this recommendation.

A fairly neutral stand at this point would be to say that both lines of argument probably contain elements of the truth. The real wage data in Table 11 is consistent with the view that these illegal migrants are depressing rural unskilled wages. On the other hand, some evidence exists of real labour shortage in some parts of the country for some types of jobs. More detailed research will be needed to guide concrete policy formulation. However, the important point is that, whatever the policy on illegal migrants might be, it is very difficult to stop movements of labour across Thailand's land borders. At present, there is an "underground" market for these illegal workers, which is clearly not desirable. Thus, in the end some effective "management" solution to this problem will need to be devised.

Some Policy Directions

The Thai economy has developed satisfactorily over the past three decades or so. Economic growth has been good and there have been substantial declines in poverty. Since the mid-1980s the pace of growth has accelerated, with rapid development of the modern sectors, both industry and services. Underlying the recent rapid growth has been the ability of Thailand to compete successfully in the world market in products previously dominated by countries which had higher per capita incomes than Thailand. As the Asian NIEs began to lose comparative advantage in semi-skilled labour-intensive manufactured exports and moved up to more technology-intensive products in the mid-1980s, countries such as Thailand penetrated the former markets. The resulting boom in manufactured exports led to rapid investment and increases in jobs and incomes (although income disparities widened). In a simple sense, the ability to compete successfully with richer countries had the effect of pulling up Thai income levels.

Yet, competition in the world market is now fiercer than ever. Countries which are at a lower per capita income level than Thailand, such as Indonesia and China, are very prominent in the labour-intensive manufactured export market, and newcomers such as Vietnam will intensify the competition. The potential for Thai manufactured exports is still abundant, but in more skill-intensive and technology-based products rather than simple labour-intensive products. The ability to upgrade the technological base of Thai industries and move up the product ladder to continue to penetrate markets dominated by countries who are richer than Thailand will hold to key to future Thai economic prospects. In fact, the Thai export structure has already changed. Table 20 gives some major manufactured export sectors. Group 1 consists of the traditional semi-skilled labour-intensive exports, and group 2 consists of the more technology-intensive products. In 1988 Thai manufactured exports were dominated by the labour-intensive group. By 1993, however, the technology-intensive products in group 2 had overtaken the group 1 products in export value. The group 1 products grew on average 16.7 per cent per annum between 1988 and 1993. On the other hand, the group 2 products grew on average 35.4 per cent per annum over the same period. Currently, the growth of the group 1 products has slowed down significantly to a range of 5-10 per cent per annum. However, group 2 products are still expanding at around 20-40 per cent per annum. Thus, in a few

Table 20. **Manufactured Exports by Some Major Sectors**
(Million Baht)

	1988	1993
Group1		
Textiles	64 053	129 347
Footwear	9 658	27 892
Furnitures and Parts	6 635	16 735
Rubber Products	4 413	11 353
Travel Goods	3 540	8 967
Sports Equipment and Related	426	6 795
Leather Products	1 783	4 244
Artificial Flowers and Related	2 038	2 594
Precious Stones and Jewelry	23 683	40 931
Toys and Games	2 429	7 924
Total Group 1	118 658	256 782
Average Growth Group 1 (1988-93)	16.7%	
Group2		
Machineries and Mechanical Appliances (Mainly Computers and Parts)	16 494	90 795
Electrical Appliances	6 274	62 624
Electrical Circuits Apparatus	29 888	75 617
Electric Cable	1 899	10 363
Transformers, Generators and Motors	1 175	10 382
Clocks, Watches and Parts	1 364	7 265
Optical Appliances	848	7 838
Vehicles, Parts and Accessories	3 770	16 531
Total Group 2	61 712	281 415
Average Growth Group 2 (1988-93)	35.4%	

years, Thai manufactured exports will be dominated by technology-intensive products.

The rapid change in export pattern shows that Thailand has the ability to exploit the opportunities in the world market, utilising new technology as necessary to produce more technology-based products. There is no doubt that the 25 per cent or so of the Thai workforce who have good education can adapt to new production technologies and form the backbone of modern industry and services in the years ahead. The real problem is the prospect for the roughly three-quarters of the Thai workforce who have only primary education, and who find it more and more difficult to find jobs in the modern sector. Most medium to large modern sector firms no longer hire those with just primary education. With technological upgrading of the production processes even in traditional labour-intensive industries, such as in the weaving sector, even those less educated workers already employed in manufacturing establishments may be asked to leave.

Without opportunities in the modern sector, the less educated will remain in traditional agriculture and low-skilled labour-intensive industries and services. Yet, low-skill-based products are facing stiff competition from countries which are poorer than Thailand, as seen from the recent slowing of export growth. If the mass of the workers are tied to low-skilled products (whether agriculture or industry) for which comparative advantage is rapidly shifting to poorer countries, it will be virtually impossible for them to increase significantly their incomes and to reduce the widening income inequality. The ability to migrate and work overseas may help a little. However, as seen earlier, the demand for Thai workers has not been growing since the late 1980s. On the other hand, the presence of illegal migrants in Thailand from neighbouring countries is likely to dampen the prospects of the unskilled Thai workers even more.

Recently, substantial progress has been made in increasing the transition from primary to secondary schools. However, as earlier indicated, this will be not be sufficient to change the educational composition of the labour force significantly in the medium term. Massive programmes to upgrade the skills and knowledge of the less educated who are already in the labour market are urgently needed. The good news is that now there appears to be close to a consensus on this need. The Ministry of Education is currently submitting a project to the Cabinet to upgrade the basic education of those working in factories to at least the lower secondary educational level. About 2 millions factory workers form the target group till the end of the decade[22]. If successful, this will serve to enhance significantly the future economic opportunities of the mass of the Thai population.

In addition to human resources development, effective programmes to deconcentrate development away from the Bangkok region are sorely needed. The traffic congestion and environmental degradation of Bangkok are well known. With public infrastructural development in Bangkok under long delays, the efficient future functioning of the country's main economic centre is in question.

Policies to achieve better spatial balance in development should focus on a three-pronged approach.

1) Agricultural Diversification and Promotion of Agro-Industries. Given the importance of agriculture to the Thai labour force, this sector cannot be ignored. However, Thailand needs to diversify its agricultural base. The past pattern of agricultural growth, which relied mainly on expansion of the cultivated area can no longer be sustained. It has led to deforestation, forest encroachment, cultivation of marginal and fragile lands, soil erosion, flooding and water shortages and other natural-resource-related problems. At the same time, it is unclear how long Thailand can remain competitive in some of the traditional agricultural crops, particularly rice. Some of Thailand's neighbours have equally fertile soil, and when their political conditions become more stable, it is likely that one will begin to see large quantities of paddy and other traditional agricultural products exported from these countries at prices which will make Thailand less competitive. Vietnam is already a major player in the rice export market (although mainly for low quality rice so far). Thus, there is a need to diversify Thai agriculture into products with higher value-added, such as fruits, vegetable, and aquaculture. At the same time, agro-processing industries should be encouraged, as these can help to increase industries in rural areas, and ultimately wages and incomes.

2) More Decentralised Planning for Effective Regional Development Strategies. To promote more regional development outside of the capital region, more effective account needs to be taken of the diversity of the various areas of the country and their development potentials. Some parts of the country have potential in agriculture and agro-related industries; some as tourist centres; some may be more suited for handicraft industries. The key to fully exploiting the potential of the various areas is to increase the participation of the local communities in development planning and management. This will ensure that local knowledge of comparative advantages and needs will be fully integrated into regional development packages. Concrete steps are needed to give the local authorities more fiscal autonomy, rather than having to rely mainly on hand-outs from the central government. Only then can local needs be effectively translated into appropriate development projects which ensure that public funds are used more efficiently than in the past and that investments more closely reflect local needs and concerns.

3) Alternative Growth Pole to the BMR. While attempts should still continue to encourage industries to move to regional cities and rural areas, it has to be recognised that the success may be rather limited. The overwhelming advantage of the capital region both in terms of physical and social infrastructures is great. If industries are to be diverted from the BMR in large enough numbers to have significant impact in diverting migrants away from the BMR, then the alternative area has to have sufficient physical and social infrastructure to be an attractive locational site. The only area of the country which could conceivably play this role is the Eastern Seaboard Region (ESB). This region has grown in importance over the past 5 years or so.

While the ESB is not that far away from Bangkok (about 150-200 km.), it is still far enough away so that substantial growth of the area will ease some of the congestion from the BMR. It already is a well-developed tourist area, and many of the elements of infrastructure required for its development into a major industrial area are already in place. In addition, new deep seaports in the ESB can divert the congestion that is very much apparent now at the Bangkok Port, particularly since the manufacturing export boom. More infrastructural development is needed over the next 5-10 years, particularly of social infrastructure like schools, hospitals and other amenities and utilities to serve the ever growing population in the area.

There is also a need to develop the transportation and communication linkages between Bangkok and the ESB. In fact, at the moment, the whole stretch linking Bangkok and the ESB is like an urban conurbation, and for effective management of the area's development, the BMR and the ESB should be viewed as an integrated whole. Between 1985-90, the surrounding provinces of Bangkok and the Eastern Seaboard region were regional net migration gainers. In terms of absolute number, the net migration gain for these regions was already approaching that for Bangkok. In the future, it is likely that these regions will be the major destinations for migrants.

Notes

1. This section draws mostly from Sussangkarn (1992).
2. From Nutritional Division, Department of Health, Ministry of Public Health.
3. Although there are many difficulties in getting an accurate measure for this.
4. This has, however, gradually led to increasingly severe problems of deforestation, soil erosion and other rural environmental problems, see e.g. Panayotou, Behrman and Sussangkarn (1991).
5. TDRI/NESDB (1989).
6. Data from the 1980/81 Socioeconomic Survey show that 83.3 per cent of farmers tend their own land.
7. The openly unemployed are those without work, but who looked for work in the survey week. If one includes those who looked for work at some time during the one month prior to the survey, the number of openly unemployed, or the rate of open unemployment, does not change very much.
8. The fact that the main rubber season in the South is not during the wet season months but during the dry season months explains why the rate in the South during July-September is the highest.
9. Households are classified according to the primary occupation of the head of the household.
10. Figures are from the Socio-Economic Surveys for 1975/76 and 1988/89.
11. See Chalamwong and Douglas (1991).
12. Bangkok is over ten times larger than the next largest city.
13. See eg. Chutikul (1989).
14. See Behrman and Schneider (1991).
15. Data for other countries refer to 1988, and are from the *World Development Report* of the World Bank.
16. See Sussangkarn (1991).
17. In 1990, only 31.8 per cent of the labour force with lower secondary education were employed in the formal sectors (basically public sector and medium-large private firms), and 34.0 per cent of those with upper secondary education were in the formal sectors. Thus, taking into account new output from the education system, there will be sufficient supply of secondary-school-educated workers to draw into the expanding modern sectors. See Sussangkarn (1991).
18. As agriculture still employs the majority of the labour force in Thailand, the seasonal nature of agricultural operations leads to sizeable seasonal variation in employment and

seasonal migration movements. For brevity, seasonal migration will not be discussed in this paper. For an analysis of seasonal migration see Sussangkarn (1987).
19. Sussangkarn (1990).
20. Subject to non-enforcement by the authorities.
21. See TDRI/NESDB (1989).
22. The aim is to transform primary educated workers into lower secondary educated workers through non-formal education along the lines suggested in Sussangkarn (1991).

Bibliographical References

ARNOLD, Fred and Nasra M. SHAH, eds., (1986), *Asian Labour Migration: Pipeline to the Middle East*, Westview Press, Boulder, Colorado.

BEHRMAN, Jere R. and Ryan SCHNEIDER (1991), "Thai Schooling Investment in an International Perspective", Research Report No. 1-4, Chai Pattana-TDRI Year-End Conference on "Educational Options for the Future of Thailand", Chon Buri, December.

CHALAMWONG, Y (1991), "A Preliminary Integration of Migration and Economic Demographic Sub-Models", Human Resources and Social Development Program, TDRI, August.

CHALAMWONG, Y. and C. M. DOUGLAS (1991), "Regional Economic Performance and Outcomes", Final Report of the National Urban Development Policy Framework Project, NESDB/TDRI.

CHUTIKUL, Sirilaksana (1989), "Equity Concerns in the Development of Human Resources in Thailand, with Particular Reference to Education", Paper presented at the Workshop on Human Resource Problems and Policies, Organised by TDRI/USAID, Hua Hin, February 24-25.

HUTASERANI, Suganya and Pornchai TAPWONG (1990), "Urban Poor Upgrading: Analyses of Poverty Trend and Profile of the Urban Poor in Thailand", Background Report No. 6-2, National Urban Development Policy Framework Project, Thailand Development Research Institute, October.

JAMISON, D.T. and L.J. LAU (1982), *Farmer Education and Farm Efficiency*, Baltimore: Johns Hopkins University Press.

JITSUCHON, Somchai (1989), "Alleviation of Rural Poverty in Thailand," Paper prepared for ILO-ARTEP, Thailand Development Research Institute, Bangkok, December.

MEESOOK, Oey Astra (1979), "Income, Consumption, and Poverty in Thailand, 1962/63 to 1975/76," World Bank Staff Working Paper No. 364, The World Bank, Washington D.C., November.

PANAYOTOU, Theodore, Jere R. BEHRMAN and Chalongphob SUSSANGKARN (1991), "Population, Environment and Development in Thailand: Concepts, Issues and Problems," Paper prepared as background for the UNFPA Programme Review and Strategy Development, March.

POAPONGSAKORN, Nipon (1989), "Consequences of Overseas Contract Labour Migration on the Rural Economy: The Case of Two Northeastern Villages", Research report submitted to the Asian Regional Programme on International Labour Migration, ILO Regional Office for Asia and the Pacific, Bangkok.

ROONGSHIVIN, Peerathep (1986), "The Socioeconomic Consequences of Labour Migration from Thailand to the Middle East," in Arnold and Shah, eds., *Asian Labour Migration: Pipeline to the Middle East*, Westview Press, Boulder, Colorado.

SUSSANGKARN, Chalongphob (1987), "The Thai Labour Market: A Study of Seasonality and Segmentation", Paper presented at the International Conference on Thai Studies, The Australian National University, Canberra, Australia, July.

SUSSANGKARN, Chalongphob (1988), "Production Structures, Labour Markets, and Human Capital Investments: Issues of Balance for Thailand," NUPRI Research Paper Series No. 46, Nihon University, Population Research Institute, Tokyo, Japan.

SUSSANGKARN, Chalongphob (1990), "Thailand," in *Human Resource Policy and Economic Development: Selected Country Studies*, Asian Development Bank, Manila, Philippines.

SUSSANGKARN, Chalongphob (1991), "Education, Labor Markets, and Economic Development: Policy Simulations," Research Report No. 1-2, Chai Pattana-TDRI Year-End Conference on "Educational Options for the Future of Thailand," Chon Buri, December.

SUSSANGKARN, Chalongphob (1992), "Toward Balanced Development: Sectoral, Spatial and Other Dimensions," Chai Pattana-TDRI Year-End Conference on "Thailand's Economic Structure: Towards Balanced Development?" Chon Buri, December.

TDRI/NESDB (1989), "S&T Manpower Situation: An Update," Human Resources and Social Development Program, TDRI, and Human Resources Planning Division, NESDB, June.

THOSANGUAN, Vatchareeya (1985), "A Study of International Migration: Case Study of Thai Female Workers to Singapore", Research Report, Faculty of Economics, Thammasat University (in Thai).

Indonesia: Notes on Employment, Earnings and International Migration

by Martin Godfrey

Summary

Indonesia's economy has shown strong performance over the last decade, with rapid diversification of the export structure away from primary commodities towards labour-intensive manufactures. In consequence, wage employment grew faster than population from the mid-1980s, though the large pool of agricultural labour kept real wages virtually flat until very recently. Since 1991, however, real wages in agriculture and construction have turned up sharply. While it is possible that this represents the onset of a period of sustained real wage growth, such an interpretation may be premature. Interpretation of recent wage trends will have to await more up-to-date productivity figures.

The number of unskilled Indonesians working in neighbouring countries particularly Malaysia is sizeable (perhaps a half million people), though most are illegal migrants so data are unreliable. Still, in comparison with the labour force their numbers are tiny. One noteworthy feature of Indonesian migration is the virtual absence of "brain drain" type migration. The high local returns to schooling may explain in part the small numbers of educated migrants, along with the opportunities enjoyed by the relatively few highly educated Indonesians for rapid career advancement. Investments in education by a growing proportion of the population should cause education-related wage differentials to continue to narrow. If so, the incentives for educated Indonesians to seek work abroad could increase in the future.

International migration is not very important for Indonesia. With a labour force of 80 million in 1991, the loss of a few hundred thousand workers a year to other countries does not make much difference one way or another to the Indonesian economy. Yet it is more important than is generally realised, since official figures exclude most of the largest flow — of mainly unskilled workers to neighbouring Malaysia. This largely illegal migration is of interest partly for political reasons (why do both governments normally turn a blind eye to it?), partly because of its implications for the Malaysian labour market (in relation to which it is far from small), and partly for what it tells us about the potential mobility of Indonesian unskilled workers (on persuading whom to transmigrate internally to undesired destinations millions of dollars have been spent). The other interesting aspect of Indonesian migration is brain drain: there is not any. Almost unique among economies at this level of average income, Indonesia manages to keep virtually all of its higher-educated and professional workers at home.

This paper discusses these and other aspects of the migratory process in Indonesia, examines government policies towards migration, and looks at the background to migratory movements provided by the economic reform programme. Finally, it assesses the prospects of durable alternatives to migration as wages rise and the comparative advantage of the economy changes.

The Migratory Process in Indonesia

Analysis of international migration from Indonesia is hampered by lack of reliable statistics. Official statistics on gross outflows of migrant workers, shown in Table 1, give only a partial picture of the numbers involved.

The export of labour from Indonesia is overseen by an Office for Overseas Employment in the Ministry of Manpower. Migrants, usually through registered recruitment agencies (of which there were 247 in 1991), are supposed to register with this office and obtain correct documentation. As can be seen from Table 1, the number of migrant workers passing through these official channels is small — fewer than 900 000 over the whole period of nearly twenty-five years. Three destinations account for 89 per cent of the official flows — Saudi Arabia, accounting for 63 per cent of the total, by far the most important destination, followed by Malaysia (20 per cent) and Singapore (6 per cent).

Table 1. **Number of Indonesian Workers Processed for Overseas Migration by the Ministry of Manpower, by Destination and Plan Periods, 1969/74-1989/94**

	1969/74	1974/79	1979/84	1984/89	1989/94*	Total
Saudi Arabia	0	3 817	55 976	223 573	259 702	543 068
Malaysia	12	536	11 441	37 785	118 528	168 302
Singapore	8	2 432	5 007	10 537	33 563	51 547
Netherlands	3 332	6 637	10 104	4 375	4 175	28 623
USA	146	176	2 981	6 987	9 541	19 741
Brunei	0	0	0	920	7 630	8 550
Hong Kong	144	1 297	1 761	1 735	3 304	8 241
Kuwait	0	0	1 210	952	2 930	5 092
Japan	292	451	920	395	2 274	4 332
Other	1 690	1 696	7 010	5 093	8 315	23 804
Total	5 624	17 042	96 410	292 262	449 962	861 300

* April 1989 to December 1992 only.

Source: Ministry of Manpower, Jakarta.

Table 2 gives an annual breakdown of official flows in the most recent development plan period, showing the fall in migration to Saudi Arabia at the time of the Gulf war and its subsequent revival, and the recent increase in official migration to Malaysia and Singapore.

Table 2. **Number of Indonesian Workers Processed for Overseas Migration by the Ministry of Manpower, by Destination and Gender, 1989/90-1992/93**

	1989/90	1990/91	1991/92	1992/93*	Total Number	% Female
Asia/Pacific	19 422	39 968	55 917	53 549	168 856	39.2
of which:						
Malaysia	11 130	29 240	40 401	37 757	118 528	29.8
Singapore	4 877	7 743	10 829	10 114	33 563	61.4
Middle East	60 456	41 810	89 244	72 631	264 141	87.3
of which:						
Saudi Arabia	60 389	41 466	77 401	71 594	250 850	91.4
Europe	1 961	2 033	1 882	1 467	7 343	1.6
America	2 235	2 453	2 739	2 195	9 622	0.4
Total	84 074	86 264	149 782	129 842	449 962	66.0

* April through December 1992 only.

Source: Ministry of Manpower, Jakarta.

The figures on gender reflect the differences in the nature of migration to different regions. Some 87 per cent of migrants to the Middle East, and 91 per cent of those to Saudi Arabia, are female, almost all of them housemaids. A larger proportion of migrants to Asia and the Pacific are male, but the figure for Singapore shows that movement of housemaids to other Asian countries is also growing in importance, while females represent only a tiny proportion of the very small number of official migrants to Europe and America.

Official figures understate migration to all regions. Some Indonesians working in the Middle East have entered as pilgrims rather than as official recruits through a registered agency. The biggest understatement, however, is in the case of Malaysia. Lin Lean Lim (1986:footnote 2) reports "generally accepted estimates" of the number of Indonesians in Malaysia of between 350 000 and 450 000 in the early 1980s. More recently Pillai (1992)[1] has estimated the approximate number of foreign workers in various sectors in Malaysia in 1991, shown in Table 3.

Hugo (1993b:45) comments on this table that "it would seem. .. that at the very least half a million workers are working in Malaysia and the number is almost certainly closer to 1 million". This is far more than the 320 000 who registered at the time of the "amnesty" for illegal Indonesian workers in Malaysia in June 1992, but that was recognised at the time to be a small proportion of the total. Employers prefer unregistered workers because they avoid the levy (ranging from $133 to $185 per year in 1991) on foreign workers, and employees may also prefer to escape close monitoring by the authorities[2].

Table 3. **Approximate Number of Foreign Workers in Various Sectors in Malaysia, 1991**

Economic Sector	Employment by Sector	Approximate % of Foreign Workers	Approximate Number of Foreign Workers
Agriculture and forestry	1 835 000	30	550 500
Construction	466 000	70	319 200
Non-government services	2 290 000	10	229 000
Manufacturing	1 374 000	3	41 200
Total	5 955 000	20	1 200 920

Source: Pillai (1992), quoted by Hugo (1993b).

At any rate these estimates suggest that the annual gross flow of migrant workers to Saudi Arabia, which including those through unofficial channels may approach 100 000, is far exceeded by flows to Malaysia, still almost entirely illegal. They suggest that international migration is more significant in relation to the Indonesian labour force (of 80 million in 1991) than is generally supposed. They also, incidentally, reveal the misconception at the heart of the government's huge, World-Bank-financed internal transmigration programme. Billions of dollars were borrowed in order to assist migrants from overcrowded Java to move to settlement areas in other parts of Indonesia where they would not otherwise have chosen to go to. Experience in Malaysia has shown that it is incentives, not assistance, that matters. Indonesian workers are very ready to move hundreds of miles, without any official assistance, to work on estates at wages that are below what local residents would accept but higher than they could get at home.

The vast majority of Indonesian migrant workers are relatively unskilled, with a low level of education. In 1986 only about 2 per cent of the country's migrants to the Middle East had completed secondary schooling (Juridico and Marius, 1987:25). Malaysia's 1980 census showed that 92 per cent of Indonesians working in Sabah state had only primary schooling or less, compared with 86 per cent of Filipino immigrant workers and 67 per cent of Malaysians (Colclough *et al.* 1984: Table 5.1).

Table 4 shows the sectors to which officially processed migrant workers went in the two most recent plan periods.

Together with Tables 2 and 3, Table 4 suggests that the most important categories of Indonesian overseas workers are: plantation workers (in Malaysia, particularly Sabah); construction workers (particularly in Peninsular Malaysia); housemaids (particularly in Saudi Arabia, and increasingly in Malaysia, Singapore and Hong Kong); and drivers.

Not only does Indonesian migration to the Middle East and Malaysia consist almost entirely of less educated, relatively unskilled workers. There is also a virtually complete absence of "brain drain", permanent or long-term overseas migration of those with higher education or professional skills. Almost uniquely among economies at this level of average income, Indonesia can expect most of its students to return from overseas studies, and its professionals to seek work at home.

Table 4. **Sector of Employment of Officially Processed Migrant Workers, 1984-93**

Sector	1984-89		1989-93*	
	Number	per cent	Number	per cent
Personal services	205 079	70.2	268 328	57.6
Plantations	34 398	11.8	119 482	25.6
Transport	41 438	14.2	66 108	14.2
Construction	4 409	1.5	381	0.1
Utilities	760	0.3	5 234	1.1
Hotels	958	0.3	111	..
Finance	5 189	1.8	..	..
Oil	19	..	3 346	0.7
Other	12	..	2 982	0.9
Total	292 262	100.0	465 972	100.0

* April 1989 to January 1993 only.
.. = Negligible.

Source: Hugo (1993a: Table 5).

In particular contrast to the countries of South Asia, Indonesians are also underrepresented in applications for jobs in international organisations. The reasons for this and for other aspects of the Indonesian migration pattern will be explored below.

Return Migration and Remittances

Even less information is available about return migration and migrants' remittances.

Contracts for migrant workers in Saudi Arabia and other Middle Eastern countries are of limited duration, usually two years, although new contracts are subsequently obtainable. In Sukabumi district in West Java, the Department of Manpower reported in 1987 that of the 37 male workers who had migrated to Saudi Arabia in the previous three years 35 per cent remained abroad, 43 per cent had gone back to Saudi Arabia after returning to Indonesia and 22 per cent were back in Indonesia; however, of the 212 female migrants from the district as many as 70 per cent had not yet left Saudi Arabia, 19 per cent had left and returned, and only 11 per cent were back in Indonesia (Wirutomo, 1987:6). These figures suggest that renewal of contract without return to Indonesia is common for housemaids.

In the case of Malaysia there is a mixture of temporary and permanent migration. Similarities of language and religion enable migrants to merge with the local population. Lin Lean Lim (1986:20) says that "the main aim of the majority of Indonesian migrants [in Malaysia] is to legalise their status, bring their families over and stay permanently". This may have happened particularly in the case of agricultural workers and particularly in East Malaysia. Hugo (1993b:61) describes these permanent settlers as "a significant proportion of all Indonesians in Malaysia"[3]. A second group of migrant workers, many without official documents, spend all or most of their working lives in Malaysia but keep their families at home and return home after retirement. A third category consists of those, mostly without documents, who have a series of spells, of two years or so, of work in Malaysia, and then return home. Hugo admits that it is impossible to measure the relative size of these three groups, but suggests that "there is a growing transition from temporariness to permanency in the movement" (p.61).

Juridico and Marius (1987) estimated total remittances from an estimated stock of 93 000 Indonesian workers in the Middle East in 1986 at only $39.2 million, based on an assumption of annual average earnings of $2 000 and average remittances per worker of $422. This compares with an estimate for the Philippines a few years earlier of $3 912 million, based on comparable assumptions of a stock of 1.1 million, average earnings of $4 900 and average remittances of $3 556.

A survey of 200 outgoing and 200 returning official migrants working in the Middle East was carried out in 1987 (Kelly 1987). It found the average annual **family** income of migrants before migration to have been equivalent to $462, reflecting the modest backgrounds from which they came. Returning migrants, on the other hand, reported that they had earned an average monthly wage rather higher than that assumed by Juridico and Marius — $173, or $230 for the 57 males in the sample and $150 for the 143 females. On this basis monthly remittable income (net of cost-of-living expenses) was estimated at $152 ($180 for men and $140 for women), or $1 824 per year. However, returning migrants reported remittances during their entire stay abroad of only $582 on average. This appears to reflect the practice of "batching" remittances, hoarding savings while abroad and bringing them home at the end of a contract or when on leave. If this is taken into account, the 1986 estimate quoted above of annual average remittances per worker of $422 looks to have been on the low side.

Official figures on remittances from migrant workers for the most recent plan period, shown in Table 5, suggest that they have increased considerably since the 1987 survey.

Table 5. **Official Remittances from Indonesians Working Overseas, April 1989 to December 1992**

Country of Destination	Remittances (US$ '000)
Saudi Arabia	777 629
United Arab Emirates	13 996
Qatar	136
Bahrain	474
Kuwait	6 887
USA	1 719
Malaysia	1 252
Singapore	1 014
Oman	87
Other	1 560
Total	804 756

Source: Hugo (1993a: Table 6).

The figure of $805 million in remittances for less than four years of the Fifth Five-Year Plan, although equivalent to less than one per cent of export earnings, is more than double the official estimate for remittances in the entire five years of the previous plan period. Yet it represents only part (and probably a relatively small part) of total remittances, which include those from illegal Indonesian workers in Malaysia.

Returning migrants were also asked, in the 1987 survey, about how they intended to use their funds. The most frequently mentioned item of family expenditure (30 per cent of total mentions) was education of a family member, followed by consumption goods (24 per cent), construction/repair of a house (23 per cent) and purchase of land (16 per cent). When asked specifically about their own plans, the most frequently mentioned use of funds was as business capital (23 per cent of total mentions), followed by land purchase (20 per cent), house construction/repair (20 per cent), education of a family member (18 per cent) and bank deposit (12 per cent). The most popular planned business venture, by far, was a shop or foodstall (65 per cent of the total), others being a repair shop (15 per cent), tailoring (9 per cent), livestock/fishing (6 per cent) and agriculture (6 per cent).

Migration Policies

Government policy towards overseas employment is positive. The target for the Fourth Five-Year Plan (1984-89) was an official outflow of 225 000, and Table 1 shows that this was easily exceeded. The target for the fifth plan (1989-94) was accordingly set at 500 000, and again is likely to have been exceeded.

It is not difficult to see why Indonesian planners are in favour of exporting labour. In addition to remittances of more than $200 million per year through official channels alone (spent only partly on consumer goods, mainly on assets of one kind or another including education of family members), benefits include fees for government and incomes for agencies, and costs are reduced by the fact that migrants (recruited from unemployment registers) would have contributed little to output if they had stayed in Indonesia.

Yet there is no denying the uneasiness felt by many, inside and outside government, about the nature of the trade. Indonesia is the only Islamic country in South/South-East Asia which allows recruitment of housemaids for work overseas. Cases of mistreatment (including sexual abuse) and bad working conditions are exposed in the press from time to time. As a result, the government banned the export of domestic servants to the Middle East between 1980 and 1982, and is under occasional pressure for reimposition of the ban. On the recommendation of an ILO project[4], the government has for several years been committed in principle to upgrading the average skill level of migrants, through more effective recruitment, selection, orientation and training. However, there is no evidence of any successful moves in this direction. Most Indonesians working overseas still have few skills and little education.

The other controversial issue in migration policy is the illegal movement of Indonesian workers to Malaysia. The two governments involved make intermittent attempts to regularise this migration. As Tables 1 and 2 show, the number of migrants going through official channels has increased in recent years, but they are still thought to represent a small proportion of the total. In the end, however, the interests of those who gain from this illegal migration — employers in Malaysia, the migrants themselves, the two governments[5] — tend to prevail over those who lose, namely Malaysian employees whose wages are lower than they would otherwise be, and, arguably, future generations of Malaysians who would benefit from a faster transition from an economy based on cheap labour to one based on skills and higher technology.

Development Strategy and Employment Creation: Background to Migratory Movements

The background to migratory movements since the mid-1980s is an extremely successful economic reform programme. Real GDP grew at an annual average rate of about 7 per cent between 1987 and 1991, the current account deficit was cut from 8 per cent of GNP in the early 1980s to 4 per cent by 1992, the overall public sector deficit was reduced from over 4 per cent in 1983 to less than 1 per cent in 1991, the inflation rate was held to below 10 per cent and fell to around 3 per cent in 1992, and the debt service ratio declined from 40 per cent in 1986 to 30 per cent in 1992. A revolution in land transportation turned Java virtually into a single urban area. Non-oil exports grew particularly fast and by 1991/92 were estimated to account for 64 per cent of total exports, compared with 21 per cent nine years earlier. Within non-oil exports manufacturing exports performed especially well, and a wide range of labour-intensive exports has emerged, with textiles, clothing and footwear recording the most spectacular growth.

The impact of the reform programme on the demand for labour is difficult to judge. The usual labour force survey measures are not very illuminating in a labour market as flexible as Indonesia's. With the unemployment rate never rising above 2.9 per cent in the 1986-90 period, the number working has been largely supply-determined and has grown at an annual average rate of 2.6 per cent — the same rate as the population in the economically active age group. Thus, inspection of total employment series tells us nothing about what is happening in labour markets.

The most significant labour force statistic is the annual average growth rate of nearly 5 per cent recorded by wage employment over the 1986-90 period — a sure sign of an improvement in the economy's demand for labour. Table 6 breaks down the growth by sector.

The table shows the very fast growth of wage employment in agriculture and manufacturing and the even faster growth in trade and restaurants, partly derived from growth in other sectors, partly reflecting the rapid expansion of international tourism. Female wage employment grew significantly faster than male during the 1980s — rising from 27 per cent of the total in 1980 to 31 per cent in 1990.

As wage employment has increased, at least until recently, real wages and labour costs have not tended to rise much. The Indonesian economy has apparently still been in the phase of development with unlimited supplies of labour, analysed by

Lewis (1954) and Ranis and Fei (1961), in which employers in the capitalist sector are faced with a perfectly elastic supply of labour. This is most easily illustrated for Indonesia by trends in the manufacturing sector, for which data on value added per worker are also available.

Table 6. **Wage Employment by Sector, 1986 and 1990 ('000)**

	1986	1990	1986-90 Annual average rate of growth (%)
Agriculture, Forestry etc.	3 531	4 876	8.4
Manufacturing	3 105	4 296	8.5
Trade & Restaurants	789	1 169	10.3
Public Services	7 283	7 300	0.1
Other	2 872	3 435	4.6
Total	17 580	21 076	4.6

Source: BPS, *Labour Force Survey*, 1986 and 1990.

Figure 1 shows what happened to real labour cost and value added per employee (deflated by producer prices) in manufacturing since 1986. As can be seen, as wage employment rose by 38 per cent between 1986 and 1990, value added per employee increased by 10 per cent, but real labour cost per employee fell by 1 per cent. Even if an extra year of rising real wages is added to the period, 1986-91 saw a 47 per cent increase in wage employment in manufacturing, accompanied by a 13 per cent increase in real productivity and a 9 per cent increase in real labour cost per employee — consistent with at least a relaxed definition of the unlimited-labour-supplies phase[6].

Figure 1. **Indonesia: real labour cost**

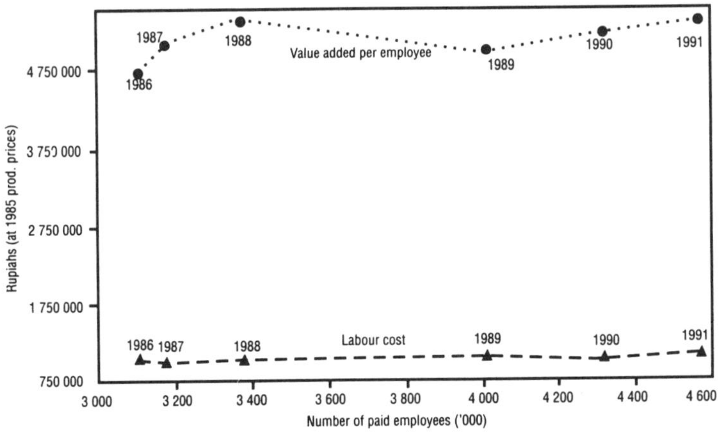

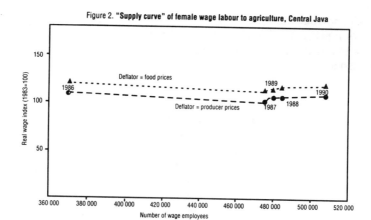

Figure 2. "Supply curve" of female wage labour to agriculture, Central Java

Figure 3. "Supply curve" of male wage labour to agriculture, Central Java

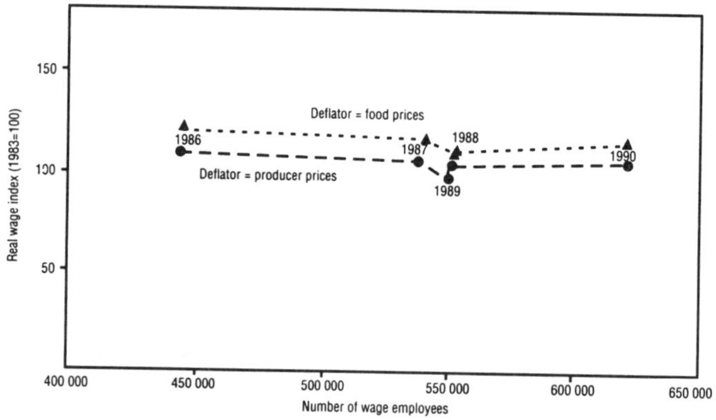

Wage and wage employment data from other sectors show a similar picture over the 1986-90 period. Figures 2 and 3, for instance, show what happened to the real wage index (deflated both by consumer food and by producer prices) for male and female employees in agriculture in Central Java, an important source of emigrant workers, as agricultural wage employment increased.

As can be seen, the increase in male and female wage employment was not accompanied by any substantial increase in either the real consumer or the real producer wage. The same was true of agriculture in East and West Java and of the construction sector in the main cities of Java[7].

Thus, as far as international migration is concerned, even though the demand for labour in Indonesia has increased fast since 1986, it had not, by the beginning of the 1990s, reached the point of exhausting the reserves of surplus labour. In the circumstances, the availability of large numbers of unskilled women and men for work as housemaids and drivers in the Middle East or as plantation and construction workers in Malaysia is not surprising.

An additional factor encouraging movement of labour has been exchange rate policy. Figure 4 shows how real effective exchange rates (which take into account

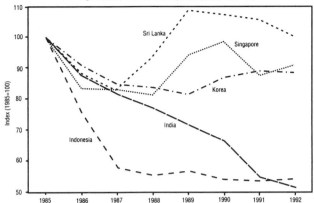

Figure 4. **Real effective exchange rate** (index, 1985=100)

inflation both in the country concerned and in its trading partners) have moved in five Asian countries since 1985.

The severity of Indonesia's real effective devaluation in recent years is apparent, overtaken only by India's enthusiastic adoption of this strategy in the 1990s. It has encouraged export of labour in two ways, on the supply side by increasing the rupiah equivalent of any given earnings figure in foreign currency, and on the demand side by reducing the foreign-currency equivalent of any given supply price in rupiahs, in practice enabling overseas employers to pay far less than would be necessary to attract most other nationalities, while enabling Indonesian migrants to earn far more than would be conceivable at home.

Table 7 illustrates the growing gap between hourly compensation costs in manufacturing in US dollars in various Asian countries, which provides the logic both for relocation of labour-intensive processes and for movement of labour from low to high dollar-wage economies.

Table 7. **Hourly Compensation Costs for Production Workers in US Dollars, Manufacturing, Selected Asian Economies, 1986-92**

	1986	1987	1988	1989	1990	1991	1992
Indonesia	0.36	0.31	0.33	0.35	0.37	0.43	..
Australia	8.49	9.40	11.28	12.33	12.89	13.36	12.94
Hong Kong	1.88	2.09	2.40	2.79	3.20	3.58	3.89
India	0.39	0.38	..	..	..	..	..
Japan	9.22	10.79	12.63	12.49	12.74	14.55	16.16
Korea	1.34	1.65	2.30	3.34	3.88	4.39	4.93
New Zealand	5.50	6.77	8.19	7.80	8.33	8.36	7.91
Pakistan	0.36	0.38	0.37	..	..	..	..
Singapore	2.23	2.31	2.67	3.15	3.78	4.39	5.0
Sri Lanka	0.29	0.30	0.31	0.31	0.31	0.35	..
Chinse Taipei	1.73	2.26	2.82	3.53	3.95	4.39	5.19

..   Data not available.

Sources: For Indonesia, *Survei Industri* and IMF, *International Financial Statistics*; for other countries, US Department of Labour, Bureau of Labour Statistics, Office of Productivity and Technology, *Hourly Compensation Costs for Production Workers in Manufacturing, 31 Countries or Areas*, March 1993.

Thus the combination of wage and exchange rate changes cut hourly US-dollar compensation costs in Indonesian manufacturing as a proportion of Singapore's from 16 per cent in 1986 to only 10 per cent five years later; as a proportion of Korea's the fall was even greater — from 26 to 10 per cent. Such changes in differentials represent a powerful incentive for a search for cheaper labour, and indeed the search has intensified, as labour shortages have emerged not only in Korea, Singapore, Chinese Taipei and Hong Kong, but also in Malaysia[8]. Even though migrants are paid less than host-country nationals, differentials are large enough to be extremely attractive. In the case of Malaysia, Hugo (1993b: Table 10) quotes recent estimates of wages obtained by Indonesian migrant workers that are between four times (for migrants from Semarang, Central Java, to Sarawak in 1991) and eight times (for migrants from Lombok to Peninsular Malaysia in 1990) what they could have obtained at home.

Wage figures also raise doubts about the logic of trying, at this stage, to upgrade the average skill level of Indonesian migrant workers. Table 8 shows what has happened to wage differentials by schooling and gender in Indonesia as output from the educational system has increased since 1977.

Table 8. **Wage Differentials by Level of Schooling and Gender, Indonesia, 1977-90**
(Indices, <Primary = 100)

	Male				Female			
	1977	1982	1987	1990	1977	1982	1987	1990
<Primary	100	100	100	100	100	100	100	100
Primary	151	142	128	122	149	151	128	126
Lower Secondary	275	203	170	158	396	290	225	203
Upper Secondary								
General	245	249	212	214	380	368	304	287
Vocational	328	262	214	209	483	375	348	319
Tertiary	1 033	410	372	366	1 428	582	551	508

Source: Manning (forthcoming: Table 3), from Central Bureau of Statistics, National Labour Force Surveys (SAKERNAS), 1977,1987, 1990, and National Social Economic Survey (SUSENAS), 1982.

As can be seen, such wage differentials have narrowed considerably, but they are still wide enough to represent substantial quasi-rents for the more educated, and to suggest a continuing comparative advantage in export of unskilled rather than skilled labour and its products. From the national point of view, the pay-off to exporting surplus unskilled labour still looks likely to be higher than that to exporting skilled labour.

This is presumably one of the reasons for the absence of long-term or permanent, as well as temporary, migration of those with higher education and professional skills. They are still in relatively short supply at home and able to obtain jobs that may not be highly paid by international standards but offer the chance of rapid promotion to positions of power and influence. There are other factors also. English is not spoken as widely and fluently in educated circles as it is, say, in South Asia and the Philippines. National higher educational and professional qualifications are not as internationally negotiable as are those of some other developing countries. International employers have reservations about the quality of Indonesian skilled and managerial labour[9]. Finally, maybe educated Indonesians just prefer to live at home, comfortable with their own culture and uneasy with those of others. Certainly none of these hypotheses will be put to the test until a surplus of international-quality Indonesian professionals emerges.

Prospects of Durable Alternatives to Migration

The prospects are good. Although achievements so far should not be exaggerated, the ground is apparently being laid for the transition from labour surplus to labour shortage, which begins in the unlimited-supplies-of-labour model when average product in the subsistence sector (on which the supply price of labour to the capitalist sector is based) starts to rise as a result of a fall in the number of workers in that sector. Capitalists then have to pay higher real wages along the now upward-sloping supply curve of labour.

In the real world an increase in the real producer wage, associated with an increase in productivity, may be taken as a sign that an economy is approaching this turning point. Figure 1 above showed that Indonesia, to judge by what happened to real labour cost and productivity in manufacturing as paid employment in the sector changed between 1986 and 1991, has not yet begun the transition. Nevertheless, the upward trend in manufacturing productivity and the beginnings of an upward trend in wages are at least interesting.

Even more interesting have been the recent signs of warming labour markets in other sectors of the economy. Figures 5 to 7, for instance, show what has happened to real producer wages, (i.e., agricultural real wages seen from the point of view of the producer), in Central, East and West Java over the past ten years[10].

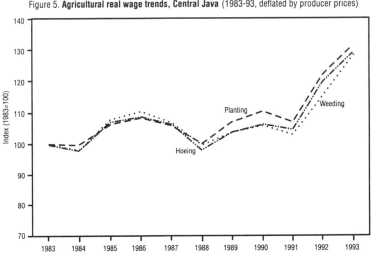

Figure 5. **Agricultural real wage trends, Central Java** (1983-93, deflated by producer prices)

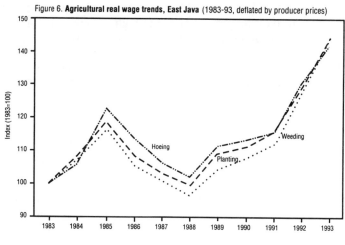

Figure 6. **Agricultural real wage trends, East Java** (1983-93, deflated by producer prices)

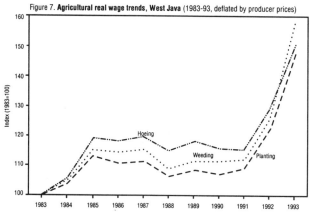

Figure 7. **Agricultural real wage trends, West Java** (1983-93, deflated by producer prices)

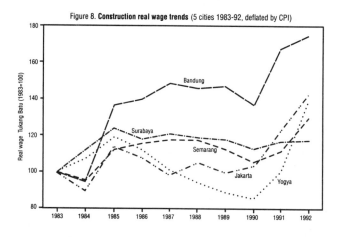

Figure 8. **Construction real wage trends** (5 cities 1983-92, deflated by CPI)

In all three provinces, as can be seen, employers were favourably placed between 1985 and 1991, with no signs of steep upward pressure on real wages so defined. However, employers faced a sharp rise in real wages in 1992 and 1993.

Regional producer price indices are not available for other sectors but, with wage data available for the construction sector, deflation by regional consumer price indices reveals some interesting trends. Figure 8 shows a similar upturn in real wages in 1991-92 in the construction industry, to judge from the BPS data on bricklayers' wages in five Javanese cities (selected to correspond with the provinces for which agricultural wage data have just been reviewed[11]).

In all cases except Bandung construction wages were lower in real terms in 1990 than they had been five years earlier. In all cases they have risen since then, steeply except in the case of Surabaya.

The influence of trade unions on what happens in Indonesian labour markets has been minimal. The official labour union, SPSI, is virtually an arm of government. However, workers have begun, in the last few years, to express their grievances over low pay and poor working conditions directly, by going on strike. In the first ten months of 1992 there were 177 such strikes, compared with 130 in the whole of 1991 and virtually none before 1990. Some non-government organisations have been advising workers, and new, as yet unrecognised, labour unions are beginning to emerge but, on the whole, these protests are local and spontaneous, involving mostly female workers.

The recent upturn in some wages, already noted, raises the question as to whether this increased militancy reflects feelings of greater bargaining power in a slightly improving labour market. The data, on labour productivity changes in particular, are not yet in to test this hypothesis. Most observers remain sceptical, however, about the evidence of sustainable improvement and place more emphasis on the more permissive political climate. The government has allowed a gradual demilitarisation of industrial relations, and since 1989 the Manpower Ministry has conducted a campaign against breaches of minimum wage regulations. These regulations are now to be revised, and will be based on minimum living needs rather than merely minimum subsistence needs.

To summarise the prospects for transition on the basis of the data reviewed so far, wage employment, particularly of women, has increased very fast since 1985. At least until the end of the 1980s employment expansion was not accompanied by an increase in real wages. Indonesia seemed to fit the classical model of economic development with unlimited supplies of labour. In the last few years, and especially in 1992, there have been some significant developments. Agricultural real wages appear to have turned sharply upwards in 1992 and 1993, while a similar steep upturn in construction wages in some cities seems to have started a year earlier. Manufacturing wage and labour cost data are not yet available beyond 1991, but there are some signs of upward pressure in that year.

It is much too early to judge whether these trends are evidence of a tightening of the labour market. Wages are still desperately low and labour is weak. Relevant data on labour productivity trends are not yet available. Most observers, interviewed in 1993, are sceptical of interpretations that presage the rising-real-wage turning point. They put this at least ten years in the future. This scepticism is reinforced by doubts about both the quality and quantity of Indonesia's more educated labour and of management[12]. Nevertheless, it is not too fanciful to suggest that, if political conditions are favourable (which will depend partly on sensitive handling of current labour unrest), Indonesia could join the ranks of the Newly Industrialised Economies in the first decade of the twenty-first century.

This does not mean that the pressure for migration will disappear, but its nature will probably change. As Indonesian wages rise, the forces underlying large-scale emigration of unskilled workers will weaken, as they did earlier in the case of migration from Korea and Malaysia. Although those already settled in Malaysia are likely to remain there, Indonesia will find itself undercut as a supplier of cheap labour by areas where labour is still in surplus.

As the quantity of more educated labour increases in Indonesia and quasi-rents are competed away, and as its quality improves, it will become more exportable. The "ethnocentricity" hypothesis about the reasons for the absence of brain drain from Indonesia will then be put to the test. As Indonesia moves up the labour import/export hierarchy, some movement of more skilled workers to urban jobs, particularly in other parts of Asia, can be expected. As long as internationally competitive growth continues, however, Indonesia should be able to avoid the fate of chronic reliance on exporting educated labour that has fallen to some other Asian countries, such as the Philippines and Sri Lanka.

Notes

1. Also quoted by Hugo, 1993a (his Table 4). The source of Pillai's percentages is a 1991 paper by Ching Cha Bo, Assistant Secretary (Research) of the Malaysian Trades Union Congress. According to Pillai, neither government nor private sector participants in the National Tripartite Seminar disputed these proposed percentages.
2. Lin Lean Lim (1986:7) reports that, of 100 Indonesian workers brought in under a government-to-government labour procurement deal for work on a plantation in October 1984, 65 had absconded by February 1985, leaving behind their work permit papers, identification documents, etc.
3. This is consistent with the findings of Guinness' study of a village in Johor which found that "two thirds of the sixty households in 1987 were of Indonesian origin, most of them with five to ten years of residence in Malaysia and holders of 'red identity cards', that is, papers of permanent residence, though few of them had these on first moving into the area".
4. Project for Overseas Employment Promotion, INS/87/003.
5. The fact that Indonesian immigrants share religion and language with the *bumiputera* population of Malaysia is politically significant. Whether or not this is the Federal government's intention, it is widely believed among the non-Malay population, particularly in Sabah state, that an official blind eye is being turned to immigration and the acquisition of citizenship by some, for future electoral purposes.
6. As attempts to make the Lewis model more rigorous (e.g. Ranis and Fei 1961) showed, the arithmetic of labour transfer is such that special assumptions are necessary to preserve the possibility of a perfectly horizontal labour supply curve, even where there is surplus labour in the subsistence sector, potentially available for employment at the going wage. This means that we should be fairly relaxed in allowing an economy with fluctuations in the supply-price of labour still to be defined as a labour-surplus economy, as long as those fluctuations are not occurring around a steeply rising trend.
7. See Godfrey (1993a, 1993b and 1994) for further discussion.
8. See Godfrey (1992) for further discussion.
9. See Godfrey (1994) for further discussion of these issues.
10. The data are from the Central Statistical Office's Farmers' Terms of Trade Survey.
11. Semarang and Yogyakarta are the cities closest geographically to the Central Javanese agricultural labour market, Bandung and Jakarta to that of West Java, and Surabaya to that of East Java.
12. See Godfrey (1994) for further discussion.

Bibliographical References

COLCLOUGH, Christopher, Martin GODFREY and Neil KEMP (1985), *Sabah Manpower Masterplan Study 1983/84*, British Council, London.

GODFREY, Martin (1992), "Labour Shortage as an Aim of Employment Strategy: an Overview of Trends and Prospects in Developing Asia", in *Employment and Labour Market Interventions*, Papers and Proceedings of the Fourth Meeting of Asian Employment Planners, ILO-ARTEP, Geneva.

GODFREY, Martin (1993a), *Labour Market Monitoring and Employment Policy in a Developing Economy: a Study of Indonesia*, ILO-ARTEP, Geneva.

GODFREY, Martin (1993b), "Employment Policy within the Context of Economic Reforms: a Case Study of Indonesia", *World Employment Programme Research, Working Paper, WEP 2-46/WP 39*, ILO, Geneva.

GODFREY, Martin (1994), "From Cheap Labour to Skill-based Competitiveness: Some Labour-Market Aspects of the Transition", paper for Workshop on Skill Development and International Competitiveness, Institute for Development Studies (IDS), Sussex, UK, March.

GUINNESS, Patrick (1992), *On the Margin of Capitalism: People and Development in Mukim Plentong, Johor, Malaysia*, Oxford University Press, Oxford.

HUGO, Graeme (1993a), "International Labour Migration", Chapter 7 in Chris Manning and Joan Hardjono (eds.), *Indonesia Assessment 1993: Labour: Sharing in the Benefits of Growth?*, Political and Social Change Monograph 20, Research School of Pacific Studies, Australian National University, Canberra.

HUGO, Graeme (1993b), "Indonesian Labour Migration to Malaysia: Trends and Policy Implications", *Southeast Asian Journal of Social Science*, 21:1.

JURIDICO, Elmor D., and Heino MARIUS (1987), "A Comparative Study of the Overseas Employment Practices of Asian Labour-Sending Countries: Alternatives for Indonesia", Project Discussion Paper, INS/82/013-09, ILO Jakarta.

KELLY, Terence (1987), "The Contribution of Overseas Employment to Indonesia's Growth Prospects", Project Discussion Paper, INS/82/013-08, ILO Jakarta.

LEWIS, W.A. (1954), "Economic Development with Unlimited Supplies of Labour", *Manchester School of Economic and Social Studies*, 22:2.

LIM, Lin Lean (1986), "Impact of Immigration on Labour Markets in Peninsular Malaysia", *NUPRI Research Paper Series No. 31*, Nihon University, Population Research Institute, Tokyo.

MANNING, Chris (forthcoming), "A Note on Wage Data and Trends in Indonesia 1970-1990", *Bulletin of Indonesian Economic Studies*.

PILLAI, P. (1992), *People on the Move: an Overview of Recent Immigration and Emigration in Malaysia*, Institute of Strategic and International Studies, Kuala Lumpur.

RANIS, G., and J.C.H. FEI (1961), "A Theory of Economic Development", *American Economic Review*, 51:4.

WIRUTOMO, Paulus (1987), "Area Survey: Case Studies on Migrant Workers in Three Areas of West Java, Indonesia", Project Discussion Paper, INS/82/013-14, ILO Jakarta.

PART III

MIGRATION, REMITTANCES AND RETURN: MACRO AND MICRO IMPACTS

Remittances, Inequality and Asset Accumulation: the Case of Rural Pakistan

by Richard H. Adams, Jr.*

Summary

Using a three-year panel data set, this essay examines the effects of migrant remittances on asset accumulation and income distribution in certain poor rural districts of Pakistan, comparing remittances from internal and international migration. Remittances from internal migration are found to have an equalising effect on rural income distribution and international remittances a negative one. This is because while internal migrants very often come from lower-income households relatively few international migrants do. International migration tends to be more selective of the better educated and richer members of the community, in large part because of the high entry costs. External remittances have a significant positive impact on the accumulation of income-generating assets, particularly on land and livestock holdings, while internal remittances have no such effect. This is mainly due to the fact that richer income groups, who tend to be the main recipients of external remittances, possess complementary assets like farm machinery and tend to have a higher propensity to invest than lower income groups.

The evidence suggests that external remittances can contribute significantly to rural development by stimulating investment in productive assets. On the other hand, internal remittances serve to mitigate income inequality while external remittances increase it. These results suggest divergent policies for growth-promotion and equity-enhancement: if the government would like to promote rural asset accumulation, one way would be to encourage international migration; if, on the other hand, its primary concern is to improve income distribution, then encouragement of internal migration is called for.

---

* International Food Policy Research Institute, Washington, D.C.
   The author is grateful to Jane He for valuable computer assistance

Introduction

Internal and international migration can have a profound impact upon the rural economies of most Third World countries. In many African, Asian and Latin American countries the bulk of the labour force still lives in the countryside. As the Harris-Todaro model (1970) has shown, in these countries it is the difference between expected rural and urban incomes that causes workers to migrate, either to urban centres or abroad. The remittances — defined as the money and/or goods sent home by migrant workers — can have a profound effect on income distribution and asset accumulation in these rural areas. For example, a large inflow of external remittances to rural households at the upper end of the income distribution could increase both income inequality and asset accumulation (e.g. land) by the rich. From an economic standpoint, these developments could doom those broader-based development efforts which depend on increasing the purchasing power of the rural poor. From a political standpoint, such developments could also shorten the life of an unpopular ruling elite.

Despite these considerations, there is still no general consensus about the effect of remittances on either income distribution or asset accumulation in the rural Third World. With respect to equity, Lipton (1980) argues that internal remittances in India worsen rural inequality because they are earned mainly by upper-income villagers. Gilani, Khan and Iqbal (1981) in Pakistan and Adams (1991b) in Egypt produce similar findings for external remittances. However, other studies of the equity effects of remittances suggest a very different outcome. For example, Oberai and Singh (1980) find that internal remittances in India have an egalitarian effect on rural income distribution. Stark, Taylor and Yitzhaki (1986, 1988) arrive at a similar conclusion for the impact of internal and external remittances in two Mexican villages[1].

While the welfare effects of remittances continue to be debated, many observers seem to have concluded that such income transfers have little or no impact on rural asset accumulation. In his review article on migration and remittances Lipton (1980) summarises prevailing opinion when he concludes that "everyday (consumption) needs often absorb 90 per cent or more of a village's remittances" and that "investment is only the fourth (and last) priority for remittances" (p. 12). Although more recent studies (Taylor, 1992; Adams, 1991a; Lucas, 1987) have questioned such pessimistic conclusions, most observers still remain convinced that the bulk of remittance monies is spent on personal consumption — and not on investment in income-producing assets[2].

This paper attempts to clarify and extend the debate over the effects of remittances on rural equity and asset accumulation by doing the following. First, it uses a three-year panel data set from rural Pakistan to pinpoint the effect of different sources of income — including internal and external remittances — on income inequality. This analysis reveals that remittances have a differential effect on equity: while internal remittances have an equalising impact on rural income distribution, external remittances have just the opposite effect. Second, the paper models the effect of internal and external remittances on various types of rural asset accumulation. This examination suggests that while internal remittances have no effect on the accumulation of income-producing assets, external remittances positively and significantly affect the level of landholdings and livestock holdings.

The analysis pursued in this paper is quite focused. Most notably, the study concentrates on the direct, first-order effects of remittances on income distribution and asset accumulation. While the author is quite aware of the second- and third-order effects of remittances on equity and assets through wage, employment and investment linkages[3], these issues are largely ignored. Given the confusion which surrounds the first-order effects of remittances, it seemed advisable to limit the scope of the investigation.

The study proceeds in five sections. The first presents the methodology for decomposing income inequality. The second discusses the data set. Next comes an analysis of the effect of internal and external remittances on income distribution. The following section analyzes the effects of internal and external remittances on rural asset accumulation. The final section summarises and discusses relevant policy conclusions.

The Decomposition of Income Inequality

In order to identify the effect of internal and external remittances on income distribution, it is useful to decompose one or more inequality measures. Such a decomposition exercise can answer the question: What is the contribution of any particular income source — like internal or external remittances — to overall inequality?

A number of different inequality measures have been proposed in the literature. Which one of these measures should be chosen for decomposition? According to Foster (1985), the selected inequality measure should have five basic properties: (1) Pigou-Dalton transfer sensitivity; (2) symmetry; (3) mean independence; (4) population homogeneity; and (5) decomposability.

Pigou-Dalton transfer sensitivity holds if the measure of inequality increases whenever income is transferred from one person to someone richer. Symmetry holds if the measure of inequality remains unchanged when individuals switch places in the income order. Mean independence holds if a proportionate change in all incomes leaves the measure of inequality unchanged. Population homogeneity holds if increasing (or decreasing) the population size across all income levels has no effect on the measured level of inequality.

The property of decomposability allows inequality to be partitioned either over sub-populations or sources. It is the latter type of decomposition that is the subject of this analysis. Ideally, an inequality measure can be regarded as source decomposable if total inequality can be broken down into a weighted sum of inequality by various income sources (e.g. internal and external remittances). However, since activities which influence a particular source of income are likely to have an impact on other activities from which total income is comprised, any inequality measure which is source decomposable must address covariance among the income sources.

Among the inequality measures which meet the five preceding properties are Theil's entropy index T, Theil's second measure L, the coefficient of variation and the Gini coefficient[4]. The two Theil measures, however, are not decomposable when sources of income are overlapping and not disjoint. While the need for non-overlapping groups is not restrictive when inequality is decomposed over regions, this restriction rules out using the two Theil measures in this study because many of the survey households receive income from several different sources. The decomposition analysis in this study is therefore based on the two remaining inequality measures: the coefficient of variation and the Gini coefficient.

The source decomposition based on the coefficient of variation can be developed following Shorrocks (1982, 1983) and Ercelawn (1984). Let total income, y, consist of income from k sources. The variance of total income, σ^2, can be written as the sum of variances of each source of income, σ_i^2, and of the covariances between sources of income, σ_{ij}:

$$\sigma^2 = \sum \sigma_i^2 + \sum_{i \neq j} \sigma_{ij} \qquad (1)$$

The contribution of the i-th source of income to total income variance consists of the i-th income variance and the part of the covariances allocated to the i-th source. According to Shorrocks (1982), the "natural" decomposition of the variance assigns to the i-th source exactly one-half of all covariances involving the i-th income source. This leads to the expression:

$$\sigma^2 = \sum \sigma_{iy} \qquad (2)$$

where the (absolute) contribution of the i-th source is measured by its covariance with total income, y. This relationship can be rewritten so as to express the contribution in relative terms. As is apparent, the relative contributions remain the same whether inequality is measured by the variance or by the coefficient of variation. Since the variance does not meet the axiom of mean independence (i.e. it is not invariant to proportional changes in all incomes), the coefficient of variation will be adopted here. The decomposition corresponding to the coefficient of variation can be further elucidated by defining the following terms:

$$\sum w_i c_i = 1 \; ; \; w_i = \frac{\mu_i}{\mu} \; ; \; c_i = \rho_i \frac{\sigma_i/\mu_i}{\sigma/\mu} \qquad (3)$$

where $w_i c_i$ is the so-called "factor inequality weight" of the i-th source in overall inequality; μ_i and μ are the mean income from the i-th source and from all sources, respectively; c_i is the relative concentration coefficient of the i-th source in overall inequality; and ρ_i is the correlation coefficient between the i-th source and total income.

The decomposition of the Gini coefficient can be developed as follows. Pyatt, Chen and Fei (1980) have shown that the Gini coefficient of total income, G, can be written as:

$$G = \frac{2}{n\mu} \, Cov(y, r) \qquad (4)$$

where n is the number of observations, y refers to the series of total incomes and r refers to the series of corresponding ranks. On this basis the Gini coefficient of the i-th source of income, G_i, can be expressed as:

$$G_i = \frac{2}{n\mu_i} \text{Cov}(y_i, r_i) \qquad (5)$$

where y_i and r_i refer to the series of incomes from the i-th source and corresponding ranks, respectively. Since total income is the sum of source incomes, the covariance between total income and its rank can be written as the sum of covariances between each source income and rank of total income. Equations (4) and (5) can then be used to express the total income Gini as a function of the source Ginis:

$$G = \sum \frac{\mu_i}{\mu} R_i G_i \qquad (6)$$

where R is the "correlation ratio" expressed as:

$$R_i = \frac{\text{cov}(y_i, r)}{\text{cov}(y_i, r_i)} = \frac{\text{covariance between source income amount and total income rank}}{\text{covariance between source income amount and source income rank}} \qquad (7)$$

The decomposition corresponding to the Gini coefficient can then be expressed by defining the following terms:

$$\sum w_i g_i = 1 \; ; \; w_i = \frac{\mu_i}{\mu} \; ; \; g_i = R_i \frac{G_i}{G} \qquad (8)$$

where $w_i g_i$ is the "factor inequality weight" of the i-th source in overall inequality; and g_i is the relative concentration coefficient of the i-th source in overall inequality.

An income source can be defined as inequality-increasing (inequality-decreasing) on the basis of whether an enlarged share of that income source leads to an increase (decrease) in overall income inequality. From the decomposition equations (3) and (8), it follows that the i-th income source is inequality-increasing or inequality-decreasing according to whether c_i (or g_i) is greater than or less than unity[5].

Data Set

Data come from a three-year survey (1986-87 to 1988-89) of 727 households in three provinces in rural Pakistan[6]. This survey was *not* designed either as a migration/remittances study or as one which would be representative of rural Pakistan as a whole. Rather, the purpose of the study was more limited, namely, to analyze the determinants of rural poverty in Pakistan. To these ends, the "poorest" district in each Pakistani province was selected for surveying, with poverty being defined on the basis of a production and infrastructure index elaborated by Pasha and Hasan (1982). The selected districts included Attock (Punjab province), Badin (Sind province) and Dir (Northwest Frontier province). Since rural poverty also exists in more prosperous areas, a fourth district Faisalabad (Punjab province) was also added to the survey[7].

Table 1 presents summary data for the seven sources of income in the survey:

(1) *Non-farm* — Includes wage earnings from non-farm labour, government and private sector employment plus profits from non-farm enterprises;

(2) *Agricultural* — Includes net income from all crop production including imputed values from home production and crop by-products plus wage earnings from agricultural labour;

(3) *Livestock* — Includes net returns from traded livestock (cattle, poultry) plus imputed values of home-consumed livestock plus bullock traction power;

(4) *Rental* — Includes rents received from ownership of assets such as land, machinery and water;

(5) *External remittances* — Includes income (money and goods) received from an international migrant;

(6) *Internal remittances* — Includes income (money and goods) received from an internal migrant in Pakistan;

(7) *Other* — Includes pensions (government), cash and zakat (alms payments to the poor).

All income figures in Table 1 are in net terms. This means that the remittance figures are calculated net of any household-to-migrant flows and direct migration costs. However, it should be noted that the remittance figures in this table refer *only* to the income and goods that households reported receiving from migrants. Remittance figures in Table 1 do *not* include the value of savings held outside the household by migrants. In all likelihood, this data limitation tends to underestimate the actual value of remittances — defined as money, goods *and* savings — received by migrant households.

According to Table 1, external and internal remittances account for relatively small shares of household income. Depending on the year, external remittances account for between 6.6 and 9.2 per cent of mean annual per capita household income, while internal remittances account for between 3.6 and 7.1 per cent of such income.

As calculated from Table 1, the Gini coefficient for three-year mean per capita household income is 0.381. While this Gini is slightly higher than that (0.327) which can be calculated from the rural portion of the 1987-88 Pakistan Household Income and Expenditure Survey (HIES)[8], it is well within the range of Gini coefficients for household income recorded for other Asian countries[9].

In Table 2 the seven sources of income are presented by quintile group based on three-year mean per capita household income. The results are instructive because they reveal the very different effects of internal and external remittances on income distribution. While the share of mean per capita household income from internal remittances falls steadily with income group, the share of such income from external remittances rises with income group. Thus, while households in the lowest quintile group receive over 10 per cent of their mean per capita income from internal

Table 1. **Summary of Income Data from 1986-87, 1987-88 and 1988-89 Surveys in Rural Pakistan**

Source of Income	1986-87		1987-88		1988-89	
	Mean Annual Per Capita Household Income[a] in Rupees[b]	Standard Deviation	Mean Annual Per Capita Household Income[a] in Rupees[b]	Standard Deviation	Mean Annual Per Capita Household Income[a] in Rupees[b]	Standard Deviation
Non-farm	1 007.39	1 158.40	1 204.65	1 364.28	959.54	1 086.19
Agricultural	763.75	2 170.35	851.39	2 188.16	832.90	2 048.37
Livestock	534.88	641.98	444.21	832.35	435.05	718.71
Rental	425.07	1 429.80	405.46	1 357.63	473.84	1 610.71
External remittances	289.11	1 448.68	319.50	1 391.91	202.94	928.83
Internal remittances	232.79	493.39	197.56	664.68	109.79	347.85
Other[c]	32.11	139.29	56.29	419.70	56.65	642.71
Total	3 285.10	3 015.60	3 479.06	3 288.21	3 070.71	3 107.57

N = 727 households

a. Mean income figures include negative source incomes recorded for some households in various years.
b. In 1986, 1 Pakistani Rupee = US$ 0.062. All Rupee figures in constant 1986 terms.
c. Other income includes government pensions, cash and zakat (payments to the poor).

Table 2. **Sources of Income Ranked by Three-Year Mean Annual Per Capita Household Income Quintile Group**

Per Cent of 727 Households Ranked by Three-Year Mean Annual Per Capita Income	3 Year Mean Annual Per Capita Income[a] in Rupees[b]	Per Cent from Non-Farm Income	Per Cent from Agricultural Income	Per Cent from Livestock Income	Per Cent from Rental Income	Per Cent from External Remittances	Per Cent from Internal Remittances	Per Cent from Other Income[c]
Lowest 20%	1 008.47	49.9	6.8	24.5	4.9	1.0	10.7	2.2
Second 20%	1 818.35	48.4	9.3	23.5	5.3	3.6	8.4	1.5
Third 20%	2 536.99	43.6	14.3	18.3	8.7	7.3	6.4	1.4
Fourth 20%	3 638.61	42.7	21.4	15.6	7.6	6.4	4.1	2.2
Highest 20%	7 353.50	16.8	36.5	8.8	20.8	11.6	4.5	1.0
Total	3 271.18	40.3	17.7	18.2	9.4	6.0	6.8	1.6

N = 727 households

a. Mean income figures calculated by averaging household income over the three years and then dividing by average household size.
b. In 1986, 1 Pakistan Rupee = US$ 0.062. All Rupee figures in constant 1986 terms.
c. Other income includes government pension, cash and zakat (payments to the poor).

remittances, these same households receive only 1 per cent of such income from external remittances.

Why do external remittances go mainly to upper-income households? One of the main reasons has to do with the high "entry costs" to international migration in Pakistan. In this study most international migrants went to work in the Arab Gulf (e.g. Saudi Arabia, United Arab Emirates, Kuwait)[10]. For these international migrants the average costs of migration were 21 000 rupees ($1 300). These costs, which include travel expenses (8 000 rupees) plus fees paid to a Pakistani agent for visa, work permit and other documentation (13 000 rupees), were too onerous for many lower-income households. Poorer households with a desire to send a member outside of their rural communities were thus forced to pursue internal migration, where the entry costs were lower because there was no need to hire an agent. However, the wages (and remittances) received for work in Pakistani cities like Karachi or Quetta were also much lower than those from abroad.

Table 3 presents data on these issues. Here households are classified according to whether they receive no remittances, internal remittances or external remittances.

Table 3. **Selected Characteristics of Non-Migrant, Internal Migrant and External Migrant Households, Based on Three-Year Mean Data**

Item	Households with No Remittances	Households Receiving Internal Remittances	Households Receiving External Remittances
Migration and Remittances			
1. Number of households	181	487	146
2. Three-year mean annual per capita income (Rupees)	3 148.31	3 214.78 (0.29)	3 730.67 (1.88)
3. Three-year mean annual per capita remittances (Rupees)	-	409.98	1 537.99
Socio-Economic			
4. Mean land owned (acres)	6.78	9.38 (2.08)*	5.71 (0.34)
5. Mean landholdings (land rented and owned) (acres)	6.12	7.91 (2.34)*	4.62 (-1.89)
6. Mean household size	9.06	9.15 (0.23)	10.84 (3.39)**
7. Mean number of males over 15 years in household	2.29	2.80 (3.88)**	3.37 (5.91)**
8. Mean education of males over 15 years in household (one in middle school or higher, zero otherwise)	0.23	0.23 (-0.11)	0.38 (3.69)**

Notes: N = 727 households. 1 Rupee = US$ 0.062.
Sum of households in row (1) exceeds 727 because some households receive both internal and external remittances.

Numbers in parentheses are t-statistics (two-tailed), which measure differences between non-migrant households and internal migrant or international migrant households.

*   Difference significant at the .05 level.
**   Difference significant at the .01 level.

In terms of income, row (2) shows that households receiving internal remittances *are* indeed poorer than those receiving external remittances. However, the results suggest that poverty should not be just defined in terms of income; households receiving internal remittances are also "poorer" than those receiving external remittances in terms of human capital. Households receiving internal remittances are smaller than external migrant households with respect to both household size [row (6)] and number of males over 15 years of age [row (7)].

Even more importantly, row (8) of Table 3 shows that the quality of human capital differs: households receiving internal remittances have lower mean levels of educational attainment than households receiving external remittances. Unlike other Third World rural areas, there are evidently positive rewards to schooling for external migration in rural Pakistan. For example, while in rural Mexico and rural Egypt it is the less educated who tend to migrate abroad[11], in rural Pakistan it is the more educated who pursue external migration. One reason for this may be that many rural Pakistanis find jobs as clerks and small business operators in the Arab Gulf, positions for which some educational skills are appropriate. As a result, in this sample external remittances to households with at least one middle-school educated male are twice as large, on average, as external remittances to households with no educated males. This difference is significant at the 0.05 level. Since upper-income households are more educated[12], the fact that external migration in Pakistan contains a large, positive reward to education may help to explain why the share of income from external remittances rises with income group.

Remittances and Income Distribution

Decomposing the coefficient of variation and the Gini coefficient provides two ways of measuring the contribution of any income source to overall income inequality. First, it can be asked whether inequality in an income source serves to increase or decrease overall income inequality[13]. Second, it is possible to identify how much of the overall inequality is due to any particular income source.

Table 4 reports the decomposition results for the relative concentration coefficients based on three-year mean per capita income. The decompositions of the coefficient of variation (c) and of the Gini coefficient (g) both confirm that external remittances represent an inequality-increasing source of income. This means that, *ceteris paribus*, additional increments of external remittance income will increase overall income inequality. Both decompositions also agree that internal remittances represent an inequality-decreasing source of income. With everything else held constant, additional increments of internal remittances will reduce overall income inequality.

Table 4 also presents the decomposition results for relative factor inequality weights of source incomes. The data show that external remittances make a moderate contribution to income inequality, accounting for between 11.9 and 12.7 per cent of overall income inequality. By contrast, internal remittances account for a very small share — between 2.8 and 2.9 per cent — of income inequality[14]. Among the seven sources of income, only "other income" accounts for a smaller percentage of overall income inequality.

Table 4. **Decomposition of Overall Income Inequality Based on Three-Year Mean Per Capita Household Income**[a]

	Relative Concentration Coefficients		Factor Inequality Weights	
Source of Income	c	g	wc	wg
Non-Farm	0.195	0.436	0.063	0.141
Agricultural	1.804	1.619	0.449	0.403
Livestock	0.272	0.435	0.039	0.063
Rental	2.223	1.701	0.295	0.226
External remittances	1.442	1.543	0.119	0.127
Internal remittances	0.513	0.528	0.028	0.029
Other[b]	0.553	0.807	0.008	0.012
Total	-	-	1.000	1.000

N = 727 households

$$w_i c_i \text{ where } w_i = \frac{\mu_i}{\mu}, \; c_i = p_i \frac{\sigma_i / \mu_i}{\sigma / \mu}$$

$$w_i g_i \text{ where } w_i = \frac{\mu_i}{\mu}, \; g_i = R_i \frac{G_i}{G}$$

a. All estimates based on three-year mean per capita household income expressed in constant 1986 terms.
b. Other income includes government pensions, cash and zakat (payments to the poor).

Why do external remittances make a much larger contribution to income inequality than internal remittances? This question can be answered by analyzing the three elements of the Gini decomposition procedure (1) source income weight; (2) source Gini (G_i); and (3) correlation ratio between source income and total income (R). These three elements of the Gini decomposition are shown in Table 5.

Row (1) of Table 5 reveals that both external and internal remittances have relatively small source income weights. However, row (2) shows that the two types of remittances have very different source Ginis. Among the seven sources of income, only "other income" has a higher source Gini than external remittances. External remittances is a very unevenly distributed source of income because in any given year less than 12 per cent of households receive external remittances and the standard deviation of external remittance income is between four and five times the mean of such income (see Table 1). By contrast, internal remittances has a much lower source Gini. In any given year between 23 and 58 per cent of households receive internal remittances, and the standard deviation of such income is only two to three times the mean (Table 1).

Row (3) of Table 5 reports the correlation ratios between source income and total income. As might be expected, external remittances has a much higher correlation ratio with total income than internal remittances. Of the seven sources of income, internal remittances has the lowest correlation ratio with total income.

The data in Table 5 serve to explain the factor inequality weights reported above. External remittances has a moderate factor inequality weight because it has a high source Gini and is strongly correlated with total income. By comparison, internal remittances makes a much smaller contribution to overall income inequality because it has a low source Gini and is poorly correlated with total income.

Table 5. **Decomposition of Overall Income Inequality Using Gini Coefficient and Based on Three-Year Mean Per Capita Household Income**[a]

1. Source income weight	Non-Farm	0.322
	Agricultural	0.249
	Livestock	0.144
	Rental	0.133
	External remittances	0.083
	Internal remittances	0.055
	Other[b]	0.015
		1.000
2. Source Gini (G_i)	Other[b]	0.943
	External remittances	0.936
	Rental	0.876
	Agricultural	0.844
	Internal remittances	0.763
	Livestock	0.580
	Non-Farm	0.510
3. Correlation ratio between source income and total income (R)	Rental	0.740
	Agricultural	0.731
	External remittances	0.628
	Non-Farm	0.326
	Other[b]	0.326
	Livestock	0.286
	Internal remittances	0.264
N = 727 households		

$$G_i = \frac{2}{n\mu_i} \text{cov}(y_i, r_i), \quad R = \frac{\text{cov}(y_i, r)}{\text{cov}(y_i, r_i)}$$

a. All estimates based on three-year mean per capita household income expressed in constant 1986 terms.
b. Other income includes government pensions, cash and zakat (payments to the poor).

Remittances and Rural Asset Accumulation

Following Taylor (1992), the effect of external and internal remittances on the accumulation of income-producing rural assets can be estimated using the following model:

$$x_3 = \beta_0 + \beta_1 x_1 + \beta_2 y_1 + \beta_3 z_1 \tag{9}$$

where
x_3 = asset holding in year 3
x_1 = asset holding in year 1
y_1 = total mean per capita household income in year 1
z_1 = remittances (internal, external) received by household in year 1

In this study equation (9) can be estimated for five different types of rural assets/land owned; landholdings (land owned plus land rented in minus land rented out); livestock holdings (number of local cows, male and female buffalo, bullocks); agricultural capital (value of tubewell, tractor and machinery); and non-farm assets (value of vehicle, shop or business and building outside of village)[15].

Table 6. **Means of Variables for Rural Asset Accumulation Model**

Variable	Year 1 (1986-87)	Year 3 (1988-89)	T-Statistic (Two-tailed)
Land owned (acres) (LNDOWN)	8.55 (19.49)	8.38 (18.44)	0.18
Landholdings (land rented and owned) (acres) (LNDHLD)	7.03 (11.10)	7.13 (10.18)	-0.18
Livestock holdings (number of local cows, male and female buffalo, bullock) (LIVE)	3.90 (3.43)	3.79 (3.54)	1.47
Agricultural capital (value of tubewell, tractor, machinery) (Rupees)[a] (AGRCAP)	8 544.32 (29 910.16)	9 904.51 (41 227.00)	-0.67
Non-farm assets (value of vehicle, shop, building) (Rupees) (NONFARM)	11 091.82 (60 974.70)	7 271.00 (44 581.06)	1.36
Internal remittances (Rupees)[a] (INTREMIT)	232.79 (493.39)	109.79 (347.85)	5.49**
External remittances (Rupees)[a] (EXTREMIT)	289.11 1 448.68	202.94 (928.83)	1.35
Total mean per capita household income (Rupees)[a] (TOTINC)	3 285.10 (3 015.60)	3 070.71 (3 107.57)	1.33

N = 727 households

Note: Standard deviations in parentheses.

a. In 1986, 1 Pakistan Rupee = US$ 0.062. All Rupee figures in constant 1986 terms.

** Difference is significant at the 0.01 level.

One obvious problem with this model is the relatively short time lag — two years — between receipt of remittances (in year 1) and the change in rural asset holdings (in year 3) being measured. Given the longer time lag usually needed for investment in "lumpy" assets (like land) it would have been preferable to estimate the model over a longer time period. However, this was impossible given the nature of the data set.

Table 6 presents means and standard deviations for the variables in the model. The only variable whose mean value is significantly different between years one and three is internal remittances. Between 1986-87 and 1988-89 the mean level of internal remittances fell by over 50 per cent The reasons for this sharp decline are unclear.

The model was estimated by three-stage least squares on 727 households in years one and three of the sample. The 3SLS method of estimation was chosen because it takes account of potential cross-equation error correlations and it produces consistent estimates of the equation parameters.

Table 7. 3SLS Regression to Estimate Rural Asset Accumulation: Landowned and Landholdings

Variable	(1) Regression Coefficient	(2) Regression Coefficient
(a) Dependent Variable: LNDOWN (Year 3)		
INTREMIT (Year 1)	-0.045	-
	(-0.261)	
EXTREMIT (Year 1)	-	0.001
		(0.748)
LNDOWN (Year 1)	0.849	0.850
	(16.825)**	(45.393)**
TOTINC (Year 1)	0.002	0.001
	(0.288)	(0.349)
CON	3.914	0.644
	(0.293)	(1.232)
D-W Stat.	1.95	1.90

Variable	(3) Regression Coefficient	(4) Regression Coefficient
(b) Dependent Variable: LNDHLD (Year 3)		
INTREMIT (Year 1)	-0.078	-
	(-0.548)	
EXTREMIT (Year 1)	-	0.002
		(2.849)**
LNDHLD (Year 1)	0.893	0.744
	(2.415)*	(26.344)**
TOTINC (Year 1)	0.004	-0.001
	(0.566)	(-1.704)
CON	6.766	2.240
	(0.717)	(4.925)**
D-W Stat.	1.93	1.83

Notes: N = 727 households. Numbers in parentheses are t-statistics (two-tailed). Variables are defined in Table 6.

* Significant at 0.05 level.
** Significant at 0.01 level.

Table 7 presents the results of the model for two types of rural assets/ land owned (LNDOWN) and landholding (LNDHLD). Controlling for land owned in year one, part (a) of the table reveals that neither type of remittances has a statistically significant effect on the accumulation of land owned in year three. One obvious explanation exists for this finding. The high price of land in the sample — for example, an estimated 55 000 rupees ($3 420) for an acre of irrigated land in Punjab province — makes it very difficult for migrants to accumulate enough funds within the space of two years to buy more land.

Part (b) of Table 7 reports the results of the model for landholdings (land owned plus land rented in minus land rented out) (LNDHLD). The findings show that internal remittances received in year one have no effect on the accumulation of landholdings in year three. However, external remittances *do* have a positive and significant effect on the accumulation of landholdings in year three. While the size of the coefficient for external remittances (EXTREMIT) is quite small (0.002), and the equation (4) itself is dominated by the coefficient for year one landholdings (LNDHLD), these results suggest that external remittances play a significant role in the accumulation of landholdings over time.

Table 8. 3SLS Regression to Estimate Rural Asset Accumulation: Livestock Holdings and Agricultural Capital

Variable	(1) Regression Coefficient	(2) Regression Coefficient
(a) Dependent Variable: LIVE (Year 3)		
INTREMIT (Year 1)	-0.031	¾
	(-0.594)	
EXTREMIT (Year 1)	¾	0.001
		(3.269)**
LIVE (Year 1)	0.845	0.742
	(3.032)**	(25.697)**
TOTINC (Year 1)	0.001	-0.001
	(0.610)	(-2.094)*
CON	2.667	0.995
	(0.811)	(5.320)**
D-W Stat.	1.96	1.75
(b) Dependent Variable: AGRCAP (Year 3)		
Variable	(3) Regression Coefficient	(4) Regression Coefficient
INTREMIT (Year 1)	-18.119	¾
	(-0.021)	
EXTREMIT (Year 1)	¾	0.086
		(0.023)
AGRCAP (Year 1)	0.738	0.757
	(0.844)	(19.406)**
TOTINC (Year 1)	2.505	1.610
	(0.061)	(2.078)*
CON	-1 633.80	-3 081.20
	(-0.024)	(-1.537)
D-W Stat.	2.03	1.98

Notes: N = 727 households. Numbers in parentheses are t-statistics (two-tailed). Variables are defined in Table 6.

* Significant at 0.05 level.
** Significant at 0.01 level.

This is an important finding, one that bolsters the view that remittances *do* have a positive impact on development. It is thus useful to speculate on the reasons for the differences in model results for land owned and landholding (land rented and owned). Two issues need to be considered. First, as noted above, the high price of land coupled with the relatively moderate levels of external remittances may well prevent external migrants from buying the main income-producing asset in rural Pakistan: land. However, international migrants still do not "waste" their overseas earnings. Rather than buying land, they choose to rent it, simply because the rental prices for land — for example, 1 200 to 1 500 rupees ($74 to $93) per acre per year for irrigated land in Punjab province — are more reasonable. Second, as shown above, external remittances in this sample go mainly to upper-income households. It is these richer households who possess those complementary assets — capital equipment, education and managerial expertise — that make it profitable to rent in more land. By way of contrast, internal migrant households lack both the funds and the complementary assets needed to rent in more land.

Table 8 reports the model results for livestock holdings (LIVE) and agricultural capital (AGRCAP). Controlling for livestock holdings in year one, part (a) of the table shows that internal and external remittances have different effects on livestock holdings in year three. While receipt of internal remittances in year one has no statistical effect on livestock herds, receipt of external remittances does positively and significantly affect the level of such herds in year three. Again, the size of the coefficient for external remittances is quite small (0.001), and the equation is dominated by the coefficient for the size of year one livestock holdings (LIVE). Despite these caveats, the findings suggest that external remittances have a positive effect on the accumulation of livestock over a relatively short two-year time span. It is likely that such remittances would have an even greater impact on the level of livestock holdings if the model could be estimated over a longer time period.

Part (b) of Table 8 reports the results of the model for agricultural capital (value of tubewell, tractor, machinery) (AGRCAP). The findings show that neither type of remittances has a statistically significant effect on the accumulation of agricultural capital in year three. This outcome may be caused by the relative reluctance of survey households to invest in agricultural equipment, like tubewells and tractors[16].

Table 9 reports the model results for non-farm assets (value of vehicle, shop or business, and building outside of village) (NONFARM). The findings show that internal remittances received in year one have no statistically significant effect on the level of non-farm assets in year three. These findings also hold for external remittances at the 95 per cent level of confidence. However, the external remittances variable (EXTREMIT) is significant at the 90 per cent level. This suggests that the level of external remittances received in year one has at least some effect on the accumulation of non-farm assets in year three.

Table 9. 3SLS Regression to Estimate Rural Asset Accumulation: Non-Farm Assets

Variable	Dependent Variable: NONFARM (Year 3)	
	(1) Regression Coefficient	(2) Regression Coefficient
INTREMIT (Year 1)	808.615	-
	(0.195)	
EXTREMIT (Year 1)	-	9.835
		(1.680)
NONFARM (Year 1)	0.722	0.171
	(0.256)	(5.961)**
TOTINC (Year 1)	-38.457	-0.648
	(-0.190)	(-0.541)
CON	-63 200.00	4 655.32
	(-0.190)	(1.502)
D-W Stat.	1.95	1.78

Notes: N = 727 households. Numbers in parentheses are t-statistics (two-tailed). Variables are defined in Table 6.
*   Significant at 0.05 level.
**   Significant at 0.01 level.

Conclusions and Policy Recommendations

This paper has used three-year panel data from 727 households to examine the effects of two types of remittances — internal and external — on income distribution and asset accumulation in rural Pakistan. It has focused on evaluating the direct, first-order effects of remittances on equity and assets; no attempt has been made to analyze the second- and third-order effects of these income flows on wages and employment. With these caveats in mind, the main findings of the study appear to be in conflict with one another because they suggest that there are important tradeoffs between equity and growth for internal and external remittances.

With respect to equity, the study finds that internal remittances have a positive effect on income distribution, and that external remittances have a negative effect. Internal remittances are earned mainly by lower-income groups and represent an important component of the incomes of households in the bottom income quintile. As a result, internal remittances account for only a small proportion of overall income inequality: less than 3 per cent. Among the seven sources of income identified in this study, only "other income" accounts for a smaller share of overall income inequality. On the other hand, because of the high "entry costs" to external migration in Pakistan, external remittances are earned mainly by upper-income groups. As a result, external remittances represent an inequality-increasing source of income and account for a moderate share (12 per cent) of overall income inequality.

From an equity standpoint, then, Pakistani policy makers should encourage internal migration. Policy makers could do this by subsidising transportation (bus, train) to Karachi and Quetta, and by offering temporary housing for rural migrants in these (and other) Pakistani cities.

With respect to rural asset accumulation, however, the findings of this study suggest very different policy conclusions. On the basis of the asset accumulation model estimated here, internal remittances in year one have *no* effect on the accumulation of rural income-producing assets in year three. However, the same model shows that external remittances have a positive and statistically significant effect on the accumulation of two types of rural assets: landholdings (land owned plus land rented in minus land rented out) and livestock holdings. These are important findings because they show that external migration income can and *does* play a key role in asset growth and rural development.

From the standpoint of rural development, then, Pakistani policy makers should take steps to encourage external migration. External remittances provide the capital needed for rural asset accumulation; internal remittances, however, fail to do this.

The main policy findings of this study are thus at variance with one another. With regard to equity, the results suggest that policy makers should emphasize internal migration. However, with regard to rural asset formation, the findings suggest that these same policy makers should stimulate external migration, and de-emphasize internal migration.

In a theoretical sense, one way to resolve these conflicting findings is to consider the issue of marginal propensities to invest. In this study internal remittances go mainly to lower-income groups, which on the whole have a lower marginal propensity to invest increments of income in assets. By contrast, higher income groups, like those who receive external remittances, generally have a higher marginal propensity to invest increments of income in assets like landholdings and livestock. Viewed from this perspective, it is little wonder that external remittances — and not internal remittances — positively affect the accumulation of rural assets.

In any event, this study shows quite clearly that remittances — both internal and external — have important effects on the rural economy. In the future researchers need to do more work on evaluating the equity and growth effects of internal and external remittances in different Third World contexts, and policy makers need to pay more attention to the possibly divergent impacts of these two sources of incomes on the rural economy.

Notes

1. Stark, Taylor and Yitzhaki (1986, 1988) find that the distributional impact of internal and external remittances varies for different periods in a village's migration history. In their study internal remittances have an equalising impact on income distribution in one village, and external remittances have a equalising effect in another village.
2. See, for example, Chandavarkar (1980), Amin and Awny (1985) and Kayser (1972). See also the review contained in Russell (1986: 686-688).
3. Unfortunately, few works analyze the second- and third-order effects of remittances on employment and investment. For notable exceptions, see Taylor (1992) and Stahl and Habib (1989).
4. For a review of these four inequality measures, see Anand (1983: 89-92).
5. This analysis ignores feedback effects, that is, the effects that a change in any source income share might have on distribution within any source income. Of course, such an assumption might be quite unrealistic for large changes in any source income share.
6. This study was undertaken by the International Food Policy Research Institute (IFPRI) working in collaboration with Pakistani research institutes — Applied Economic Research Centre (University of Karachi), Punjab Economic Research Institute (Lahore), the University of Baluchistan (Quetta) and the Center for Applied Economic Studies (University of Peshawar). See Adams (1993b).
7. The 727 households were distributed as follows: 148 from Attock District (Punjab province), 239 from Badin District (Sind province), 193 from Dir District (Northwest Frontier province) and 147 from Faisalabad District (Punjab province).
8. This 1987-88 Household Income and Expenditure Survey (HIES) was a national-level survey which included 9 760 rural Pakistani households.
9. The Gini coefficients of household income recorded for ten Asian countries in Lecaillon, Paukert, Morrisson and Germidis (1984: Table 4) range from a low of 0.351 (Korea) to a high of 0.561 (Iran). It should, however, be noted that the Gini coefficients for these Asian countries are based on the distribution of *overall* (i.e. rural and urban), while the Ginis used in this study are based on *rural* household income. In theory, one would expect the distribution of rural household income to be more egalitarian than that of overall household income.
10. For an overview of Pakistani international migration to the Arab Gulf states, and the effect of such migration on the Pakistani economy, see Addleton (1992).
11. In rural Mexico, Stark, Taylor and Yitzhaki (1986, 1988) found that the economic rewards to schooling were higher for internal than external migrants. In rural Egypt Adams (1993a) found that the *least* educated had the highest propensity to pursue external migration.

12. In this data set education and income are highly correlated: a simple correlation between mean level of household education and total three-year mean per capita income is positive and significant at the 0.01 level.
13. In analyzing whether an income source is inequality-increasing or -decreasing, it is assumed that additional increments of that income source are distributed in the same fashion as the original units.
14. Decomposition results based on annual mean per capita income data yield identical results. In each year of the study, external remittances represent an inequality-increasing source of income and internal remittances represent an inequality-decreasing source. Depending on the year, external remittances account for between 7.2 and 18.4 per cent of overall income inequality, and internal remittances account for between 0.8 and 4.7 per cent of such inequality.
15. Taylor (1992) uses a similar model to examine the effect of remittances on rural asset accumulation in Mexico. He finds that remittances (mainly external remittances) have a positive and significant effect on the accumulation of livestock assets, but no effect on family education.
16. Because there are no tubewells in two (Attock and Badin) of the four districts in the sample, less than 5 per cent of the 727 households own a tubewell. Similarly, less than 5 per cent of the survey households own a tractor.

Bibliographical References

ADAMS, Jr., Richard H. (1991a), "The Economic Uses and Impact of International Remittances in Rural Egypt." *Economic Development and Cultural Change* 39 (July): 695-722.

ADAMS, Jr., Richard H. (1991b), *The Effects of International Remittances on Poverty, Inequality and Development in Rural Egypt*, Report 86, Washington, D.C.: International Food Policy Research Institute.

ADAMS, Jr., Richard H. (1993a), "The Economic and Demographic Determinants of International Migration in Rural Egypt", *Journal of Development Studies*, 30 (October): 146-167).

ADAMS, Jr., Richard H. (1993b), "Sources of Income Inequality and Poverty in Rural Pakistan", Draft manuscript, Washington, D.C.: International Food Policy Research Institute.

ADDLETON, Jonathan S. (1992), *Undermining the Center: The Gulf Migration and Pakistan*, New York: Oxford University Press.

AMIN, Galal and Elizabeth AWNY, (1985), International Migration of Egyptian Labor: A Review of the State of the Art, Manuscript Report IDRC-MR108e, Ottawa, Canada: International Development Research Centre.

ANAND, Sudhir (1983), *Inequality and Poverty in Malaysia: Measurement and Decomposition*, London: Oxford University Press.

CHANDAVARKAR, A. B. (1980), "Use of Migrants' Remittances in Labor-Exporting Countries." *Finance and Development* 17 (June): 38-40.

ERCELAWN, Aly, (1984), "Income Inequality in Rural Pakistan: A Study of Sample Villages", *Pakistan Journal of Applied Economics* 3 (Summer): 1-28.

FOSTER, James, (1985), "Inequality Measurement", In *Proceedings of Symposia in Applied Mathematics*, Vol. 33, ed. H. Peyton Young, Providence, Rhode Island: American Mathematical Society.

GILANI, Ijaz, M. Fahim KHAN, and Munawar IQBAL, (1981), *Labor Migration from Pakistan to the Middle East and Its Impact on the Domestic Economy*, Research Report No. 126, Islamabad: Pakistan Institute of Development Economics.

Government of Pakistan, (1988), *Household Income and Expenditure Survey, 1987-88*, Islamabad, Pakistan.

HARRIS, John and Michael TODARO, (1970), "Migration, Unemployment and Development: A Two-Sector Analysis", American Economic Review 60 (March): 126-142.

KAYSER, Bernard (1972), *Cyclically-Determined Homeward Flows of Migrant Workers and the Effects of Emigration*, Paris: Organisation for Economic Co-operation and Development.

LECAILLON, Jacques, Felix PAUKERT, Christian MORRISSON and Dimitri GERMIDIS (1984), *Income Distribution and Economic Development: An Analytical Survey*, Geneva: International Labour Office.

LIPTON, Michael (1980), "Migration from Rural Areas of Poor Countries: The Impact on Rural Productivity and Income Distribution", *World Development* 8 (January)1-24.

LUCAS, Robert E. (1987), "Emigration to South Africa's Mines", *American Economic Review* 77 (June): 313-330.

OBERAI, A. S. and H. K. SINGH (1980), "Migration, Remittances and Rural Development: Findings of a Case Study in the Indian Punjab." *International Labour Review* 119: 229-241.

PASHA, Hafiz and Tariq HASAN (1982), "Development Ranking of Districts of Pakistan", *Pakistan Journal of Applied Economics* 1 (Winter): 157-192.

PYATT, Graham, Chau-nen CHEN and John FEI (1980), "The Distribution of Income by Factor Components", *Quarterly Journal of Economics* 95 (November): 451-473.

RUSSELL, Sharon S. (1986), "Remittances from International Migration: A Review in Perspective", *World Development* 14 (June): 677-696.

SHORROCKS, A. F. (1982), "Inequality Decomposition by Factor Components", *Econometrica* 50 (January): 193-211.

SHORROCKS, A. F. (1983), "The Impact of Income Components on the Distribution of Family Income", *Quarterly Journal of Economics* 98 (May): 311-326.

STAHL, Charles W. and Ahsanul HABIB (1989), "The Impact of Overseas Workers' Remittances on Indigenous Industries: Evidence from Bangladesh." *The Developing Economies* 27 (September): 269-285.

STARK, Oded, J. Edward TAYLOR, and Shlomo YITZHAKI (1986), "Remittances and Inequality", *The Economic Journal* 96 (September): 722-740.

STARK, Oded, J. Edward TAYLOR, and Shlomo YITZHAKI (1988), "Migration, Remittances and Inequality: A Sensitivity Analysis Using the Extended Gini Index", *Journal of Development Economics* 28 (May): 309-322.

TAYLOR, J. EDWARD (1992), "Remittances and Inequality Reconsidered: Direct, Indirect and Intertemporal Effects." *Journal of Policy Modeling* 14 (April): 187-208.

International Return Migration and Remittances in the Philippines

by Edgard R. Rodriguez and Susan Horton[*]

Summary

Migration plays an important role in the economy of the Philippines, as in recent years migrant outflows have absorbed the equivalent of the annual increase in the labour force and official remittances have represented roughly one-fourth of export earnings. The Philippines is one of the largest migrant-sending countries in the world. Using household income and expenditure survey data, this paper sheds light on the characteristics of Filipino migrants and explores the determinants of both remittances and return migration. There are significant differences between temporary and permanent migrants with respect to age, sex and other chracteristics: the former are on average younger and more often male. Both types of migrants have above-average educational attainment and come disproportionately from urban areas. Returnees are more often household heads and tend to be slightly less educated than those still abroad. The most important determinant of return, however, is the length of stay abroad, with the former showing an inverted-U relationship to the latter; the expectation of return also influences levels of remittances, which therefore have a similar functional form. It is also found that the likelihood of a migrant's return is inversely and significantly related to the unemployment rate in the region of origin. Remittances have an adverse effect on income distribution, since migrants tend to be from better educated and better off urban households.

With regard to policy, the experience of the Philippines suggests that permissive rather than coercive policies are apt to be more effective in attracting remittances and that the private sector can be relied upon to organise migrant outflows, though government needs to monitor private operators to discourage abusive practices. In any attempt to maximize the benefits from migration, policy makers would need to consider the impact of length of stay abroad on the propensity to remit and to return home.

---

[*] Department of Economics, University of Toronto

Introduction

For anyone who leaves his or her place of origin, the possibility of returning home, whether temporarily or permanently, remains. For some, the return may never occur; for others, it may be closer than expected. For instance, the unanticipated invasion of Kuwait in 1990 forced migrant workers, including many Filipinos, to leave this small country in the Gulf and to return home immediately. Soon after the war ended, the number of Filipino workers going to Kuwait resumed its pre-war levels. Under normal circumstances, thousands of Filipinos do return home year after year. Each year the Philippines receives overseas workers on holidays who will return abroad to continue their contracts, as well as workers who have finished their contracts and who may stay while looking for another contract overseas. Those who stay face an economy with a GNP per capita that has declined on average every year over the last decade (-1.2 per cent per annum between 1980-91; World Bank, 1993a). Available evidence suggests that return migrants have high rates of unemployment and they do not use their remittances productively, which has limited migrants' contribution to economic development[1]. Not surprisingly, the Philippine government and the International Labour Office (ILO) have expressed their concern about the prospects for the returnees (Amjad, 1991; ILO-DOLE, 1993: 149).

In this paper, we aim to provide a systematic description of international return migrants from the Philippines, using recently available national surveys. This descriptive effort represents a pre-requisite for further research on the consequences of return migration in the Philippines. In the background section, we provide information about migration trends, using published data from the Philippines and from host countries. This section also examines the data available on remittances, and compares sources. The next section draws profiles of migrants (temporary and permanent) and non-migrants. Following a profile of returned migrants versus absent migrants, regression analysis is used to examine the determinants of return migration. Further econometric analysis shows the influence of the pattern of return on total remittances. The section closes by examining the distributional impact of remittances in the Philippines. In the next section we discuss policy issues concerning return migration and remittances, and conclusions follow. Further information on the data used in this study is given in the appendices.

Background: International Migration and Remittances

Trends in Migration and Labour Markets

Whether temporary or permanent, emigration reflects the labour market conditions in the source country. Although labour migration has helped ease pressure from unemployment in the Philippine economy, the emergence of a new sector (i.e. the overseas labour market with its own barriers to entry and highly paid jobs for those who can bypass them) may have also accentuated the dualistic structure of the Philippine labour market.

Since the 1950s, labour markets in the Philippines have shown little dynamism in terms of employment and real wages. Taking unemployment rates in the Philippines from 1956 to the present[2], we can observe two major periods (Figure 1): a decline from 1956-80 and a sharp increase in the 1980s (peaking in 1985). Real minimum wages[3], another indicator of the labour markets, do not show an improvement either (also Figure 1). With a rapid increase in the size of the labour force in the 1970s and 1980s (more than 4 per cent per annum; World Bank, 1993b: 373), real minimum wages declined in the face of a stagnant economy. Industrialisation policy exacerbated problems of labour absorption, since macro-economic and trade policies favoured the capital-intensive importables sector. Although labour supply growth will slow down towards the year 2000, the Philippines still needs to create approximately 650 000 jobs a year, which may entail introducing overdue changes in its economic policies with greater emphasis on liberalisation (World Bank, 1993b).

Figure 1. **Real wages and unemployment rate** — Philippines, 1951-1992

Sources: BLES (1991, 1993); NSO (1992c).

Emigration has helped to reduce the pressure on domestic labour markets by creating a segment of workers with overseas appointments. In 1991, 665 123 migrants left the Philippines as permanent migrants (emigrants) and temporary workers (land-based and sea-based contract workers) (Table 1). Between 1982 and 1991, the number of migrants grew at an average annual rate of 5 per cent. The growth in the category of emigrants (most of whom were bound for North America) was only 1.5 per cent per annum, probably reflecting the increasing difficulty to migrate under the category of "permanent resident" to industrialised countries. The growth was the largest for sea-based contract workers (an annual average rate of 7 per cent). However, most of the migrants are still land-based contract workers in the Middle East and other Asian countries. While the most important destination in the Middle East (Saudi Arabia) has experienced lower oil prices and has faced a decline in GNP per capita since the early 1980s, labour shortages in East Asia have turned it into the fastest-growing market for Filipino labour, increasing at 15.6 per cent annually and comprising by 1991 almost 20 per cent of the outflow of all Philippine migrants. If this trend continues, by the end of the century the numbers of Philippine migrants leaving for Asian countries would equal those leaving for the Middle East. Although statistics regarding migrants leaving the country are now readily available, it is more difficult to find information about the reverse flow[4].

Table 1. **Composition of the Outflow of Philippine Nationals, 1982-91**

Migration	1982	%	1985	%	1991	%
Emigrants	53 953	13.3	45 269	10.8	62 671	9.4
Americas[a]	49 336	12.1	40 750	9.7	51 214	7.7
Oceania[b]	2 931	0.7	3 458	0.8	5 728	0.9
Other	1 686	0.4	1 061	0.3	5 729	0.9
Landbased[c]	289 065	71.0	320 494	76.7	476 693	71.7
Africa	1 098	0.3	1 977	0.5	1 964	0.3
Asia	31 011	7.6	52 838	12.6	132 592	19.9
Americas	3 707	0.9	3 744	0.9	13 373	2.0
Europe	1 465	0.4	4 067	1.0	13 156	2.0
Middle East	210 283	51.6	253 867	60.7	302 825	45.5
Oceania	683	0.2	953	0.2	1 374	0.2
U.S. Trust Territories	1 148	0.3	3 048	0.7	11 409	1.7
Other	39 670	9.7		1.0		
Seabased[c]	64 169	15.8	52 290	12.5	125 759	18.9
WORLD	407 187	100.0	418 053	100.0	665 123	100.0

a. Canada and the US.
b. Australia.
c. Processed files for 1982.

Sources: Commission for Filipinos Overseas (CFO), data on emigrants; Philippine Overseas Employment Administration (POEA), data on landbased and seabased contract workers.

As migrants move back and forth, it is difficult to calculate the number abroad. In Table 2, we present a crude estimate of 1.7 million Philippine nationals living overseas in the early 1990s. Using mainly data from the censuses in the host countries, we are able to draw together information about the numbers of Filipinos overseas. In some cases, this information includes illegal migrants. Most permanent migration has been to the United States, Canada and Australia, and these countries account for over three-quarters of the estimated stock of Filipinos abroad. Almost 87 per cent of the whole Filipino community overseas is concentrated in the United States, Saudi Arabia and Canada. Between 1980-1990, the Philippine-born community has grown significantly in these countries. By 1990, it had doubled in the United States (representing around 60 per cent of the Filipino community worldwide), it had more than quadrupled in Saudi Arabia (where 19.6 per cent of the Filipino community abroad resided), and it had less than doubled in Canada (7.3 per cent of the worldwide community lived in Canada in 1991). Our estimates consider as Filipino migrants (temporary or permanent resident) all individuals born in the Philippines but living abroad. While the United States, Australia, Canada, New Zealand and Singapore enumerate their residents by place of birth, countries such as Hong Kong and Japan report residents by nationality (see Appendix 2 for details). Although we do not use them, Canada and the United States have additional criteria to identify Filipino migrants, such as language[5] or race[6]. When information on place of birth (or any other criterion) is not available like in Saudi Arabia, we use the flows of Filipinos entering and leaving the country to calculate the stock of Filipinos. As the population of Filipinos in Saudi Arabia was negligible before 1970, we obtain a stock of migrants by compiling net entries since 1970.

Table 2. **Estimated Stock of Philippine-Born Population[a] Worldwide: 1980-90**

Country	Estimated Stock 1980[b]	Estimated Stock 1990[c]	Stock in Per cent	% Change 1980-1990
USA	501 000	998 000	58.70	99.20
US Trust Territories[d]		39 947	2.35	
Guam	16 998	(24 545)	(1.44)	44.40
American Samoa	38	(380)	(0.02)	900.00
Saudi Arabia	65 195	334 013	19.64	412.33
Canada	66 460	123 295	7.25	85.52
Australia	15 400	73 700	4.33	378.57
Japan	5 547	49 092	2.89	785.02
Hong Kong		60 340	3.55	
Spain	2 878	7 416	0.44	157.68
New Zealand	405	4 185	0.25	933.33
Sweden	1 258	3 380	0.20	168.68
Singapore	5 826	2 609	0.15	-55.22
Switzerland	1 769	2 424	0.14	37.03
Macau	345	1 879	0.11	444.64
Other Countries	4 291			
Total Population Overseas	687 410	1 700 280	100.00	148.60
Total Population in the Philippines	48 098 460	60 703 206		26.21

a. Philippine-born residents in the US, the US Trust Territories, Canada, Australia, New Zealand and Other Countries. For the rest of the countries, see Appendix 2.
b. 1981: Canada, Australia, New Zealand, Switzerland and Macau.
   1985: Sweden.
c. 1991: Canada, Australia, Hong Kong, New Zealand and Macau.
   1992: Sweden.
d. Guam, American Samoa, Commonwealth of the Northern Marianas and the Republic of Palau.

Sources: Appendix 2.

Worldwide, the estimated stock of Filipinos overseas represents 2.8 per cent of the total population living in the Philippines in 1990. It corresponds to a higher percentage of the Philippine labour force (4.4 per cent) (coincidentally this figure is similar to the percentage of Philippine-born residents in the labour forces of the United States[7] and Saudi Arabia). This crude estimate of the economically active population overseas gives a total population of 1 060 743 Philippine-born individuals of working age (15-65 years old). We assume a participation rate of 50 per cent for the United States, Canada, Australia and New Zealand as entire families have settled there, including family members who are not in the labour force. For Saudi Arabia and the other countries, we assume a participation rate of 100 per cent since almost all these migrants are contract workers. Adjusting the stock of Filipinos by labour participation rates increases the significance of Filipino migrants in the Middle East and Asia in comparison to the large stock of Filipinos in North America (especially given that migration to the Middle East and Asia is mainly temporary). For instance, Filipino migrants in Saudi Arabia represent a third of all working-age Filipinos abroad (31.6 per cent) although they represent just a fifth of the population of overseas Filipinos worldwide.

Trends in Remittances

This section reviews the magnitude of international transfers. Although the Central Bank of the Philippines (CBP) normally reports figures on remittances, several studies have attempted to provide estimates of migrants' remittances in the belief that official figures are underestimated. Extending back to the early 1980s, the CBP time series is the longest available, but it appears that the CBP series imputes the category of personal income from abroad to contract workers' remittances. These data, collected from individual banks, are based on remittances via banks but likely include remittances from permanent migrants. This misclassification is evident when remittances are broken down by country of origin. As Abella (1989) notes, although the number of contract workers in the United States or Canada is negligible, the CBP reports significant remittances from these countries. Further, since the CBP only reports official transfers, transfers received by households via courier, mail or in person are excluded. Although liberalisation in the early 1990s has helped to increase official remittances, household surveys may give a better indication of the receipts from abroad, even if they too are subject to under-reporting (Abrera-Mangahas, 1989).

A second source of information on remittances is the National Statistics Office (NSO) of the Philippines which undertakes family income and expenditure surveys (FIES) that include a category for income transferred from abroad since 1985. Also the NSO provides a third data source for remittances: since 1991, it has administered the survey of overseas workers (SOW), which includes information on the remittances from individual migrants (mainly contract workers). The major limitation for the comparison of the latter survey with the first two sources (CBP and NSO-FIES) is that it includes only migrant workers working overseas in the last 6 months and their remittances during that time (April-October 1991)[8]. Table 3 shows that the NSO-FIES data tended to be about twice as large as the CBP data before the 1990s liberalisation, and thereafter about 50 per cent larger (NSO-FIES-reported remittances represented a quarter of all Philippine exports in 1985 and 1991). The NSO-SOW data are somewhere in between the other two sources.

Figure 2 shows the evolution of total remittances as well as the transfers from the United States and Saudi Arabia sent by land-based migrants (who sent most of the official remittances). Despite the well-known underestimation of the official figures, we observe two trends in remittances: the growing importance of remittances from the United States, together with the rise and decline of remittances from Saudi Arabia during the 1980s. According to these aggregate figures (and also according to estimated remittances per migrant which we do not report), remittances from the United States rose during the last decade, together with the stock of Filipino migrants and the recovery of the US economy. In Saudi Arabia, despite the significant increases in the stock of migrants, total remittances (and average remittances) from migrants in this country peaked in 1985 but declined thereafter. This pattern of remittances contrasts with the evolution of the Saudi economy whose peak occurred before 1985 (between 1970-80, Saudi Arabia grew at 10.1 per cent but -0.2 per cent between 1980-91; World Bank 1993a). However, a number of other factors could have also influenced this evolution in remittances, including the economic crisis in the Philippines in the mid-1980s. If the CBP figures are correct, they suggest the increasing importance of permanent migrants (who doubled their numbers in the United States over the decade) and the reduction in remittances from Filipino workers in Saudi Arabia (also increasing in number but facing a weaker Saudi economy). After 1988, estimated remittances per migrant in the United States surpass transfers from migrants in Saudi Arabia when we use the CBP data, which normally gives estimates well below $2 000 per year[9].

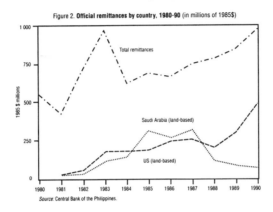

Figure 2. **Official remittances by country, 1980-90** (in millions of 1985$)

Source: Central Bank of the Philippines.

Table 3. **Total Remittances from Abroad 1978-92**
($ million, per year)

	Central Bank of the Philippines (CBP)[a]	Family Income-Expenditure Survey - National Statistics Office (FIES-NSO)[b]	Survey of Overseas Workers-National Statistics Office (SOW-NSO)[c]
1978	290.9		
1979	364.7		
1980	421.3		
1981	357.7		
1982	649.8		
1983	895.2		
1984	602.9		
1985	687.2	1 380.2	
1986	680.4		
1987	791.9		
1988	856.8	1 513.7	
1989	973.0		
1990	1 181.1		
1991	1 628.3	2 400.0	1 775.8
1992	2 202.4		

a. Total for landbased and seabased sources.
b. Includes income from contract workers, other family members abroad and gifts from overseas.
c. The total remittances of 24.4 billion pesos for the last six months (NSO, 1992a) before the survey are doubled to obtain an annual estimate.

Source: Central Bank of the Philippines (CBP); National Statistical Office (NSO).

Other estimates of per capita remittances are generally higher (above $3 000) than those estimates based on official figures. However, using samples of re-migrating workers, the 1981 Overseas Employment Development Board (OEDB) survey and the 1982 Institute of Labour and Manpower Studies (ILMS) survey[10] contain an upward bias to estimated remittances, as these migrants tend to be more "successful" in their overseas postings. Also, these estimates may be subject to over-reporting due to the self-reporting by migrants themselves. Further, it is not clear if these average remittances include cash brought home in addition to the regular stream of remittances the migrant sends while he or she is away.

Finally, no long series of average remittances is available; however, data from national surveys provide useful benchmarks. Survey data give more representative average remittances from migrants to the Philippines: higher than estimates based on the CBP figures and lower than the estimates from surveys based on re-migrating migrants. According to the 1991 NSO-SOW, annualised average total transfers per remitting worker (mainly contract workers) are below $3 000 (lower if we exclude cash brought home, $1 825) (NSO, 1992a). Alternatively, according to the 1991 NSO-FIES, the average remittances that households received from contract workers were $1 601 a year and $1 293 from "other migrants" (non-contract workers and permanent migrants).

Returnees and Remittances

Profile of Migrants: Temporary Versus Permanent

How different are temporary migrants from permanent emigrants? Table 4 shows differences in destination, sex, age, occupation and education between these two groups of migrants. First, the United States is still the major destination for permanent migrants and Saudi Arabia for temporary migrants. Japan and Canada attract both types of migrants. Second, regarding the gender of the migrants, about 60 per cent of the permanent migrants are women and about 60 per cent of the temporary workers are male. More temporary migrants are male as Filipinas working as domestic helpers are outnumbered by the predominantly male labourers and crew members. In the case of permanent migrants, a substantial number leave as fiancees or spouses of foreign nationals (they represented 28.8 per cent of all emigrants in 1991, CFO, 1991b).

Third, the age distribution of both types of migrants differs (Table 4). On the one hand, almost 70 per cent of all temporary workers concentrate in the prime age group (25-44 years old), more than in the Philippine labour force. On the other hand, permanent migrants are more similar in distribution to the non-migrant population residing in the Philippines, but migrants are on average older. For instance, 17.9 per cent are under 14 years old whereas 39.8 per cent of the population in the Philippines is under this age. Actually, Filipinos overseas appear older than the population in host countries. In the United States, the stock of Filipinos has a smaller proportion of the very young and a similar proportion of people over 65 years old (Table 5).

Table 4. **Profile of Permanent Versus Temporary Migrants 1991**
(in per cent)

		1990 Census (NSO)	1991 Labour Force (NSO)	Permanent Migrants (CFO)	Temporary Migrants (NSO-SOW)
Destination	US			70.2	3.6
	Saudi Arabia				43.2
	Canada			11.5	1.7
	Japan			6.3	9.3
Sex	Male	50.2	62.5	39.6	59.6
	Female	49.8	37.5	60.4	40.4
Age	14<	39.8		17.9	
	15-24	20.5	26.4	22.0	16.5
	25-34	15.1	24.3	25.0	40.4
	35-44	10.4	21.1	11.9	28.8
	45>	14.2	28.3	23.1	14.3
Occupation	Professional		5.3	12.0	12.7
	Managerial		1.1	0.7	0.4
	Clerical/Sales	59.4	16.6	9.0	5.0
	Service		8.2	3.1	37.1
	Agriculture		39.6	2.2	0.5
	Production		19.1	4.9	44.4
	Unemployed	7.0	10.6	15.7	
	Out of labour force[a]	33.6		52.7	
Education	No Education		3.8		0.2
	Primary		44.9		9.1
	High School		31.1		34.9
	College		8.9		27.2
	University		11.3		28.2

a. Includes housewives, retirees, students, minors and armed forces.

Source: 1992 Philippine Yearbook (NSO, 1992c); Commission for Filipinos Overseas (CFO, 1991b); Survey of Overseas Workers (NSO, 1992a).

Also, regarding occupation and education, there are significant differences between the group of temporary and permanent migrants and the non-migrant population in the Philippines (Table 4). The breakdown by occupation reveals that the distribution is essentially not different between permanent and temporary migrants at the 1-digit level for the first four categories (professional, managerial, sales and clerical) despite differences at the 2-digit level. The major differences are that more temporary migrants are concentrated in services and production whereas a high proportion of permanent migrants are out of the labour force (52.3 per cent) and unemployed (15.7 per cent). Note that permanent migrants leaving the Philippines report their occupation before migration. The emphasis on family reunification in host countries explains the large proportion of permanent migrants out of the labour force (housewives, students, minors and retirees), which represents an "echo" migration of relatives of those who left before. A closer examination of the characteristics of the stock of permanent migrants overseas shows that they are extremely well represented in professional occupations. For example, the proportion of Philippine-born professionals in the United States is 20.1 per cent, much higher than any other group (foreign or US-born, Table 5). On the other hand, 12.7 per cent of all temporary workers in the Middle East and Asia have professional occupations,

Table 5. **Characteristics of the US Population by Selected Country of Birth — 1980 Census**
(In Per Cent)

Country of Birth		Total	Age		Education[a]		Occupation[c]		Median Household Income
		('000)	<15 yrs	65 yrs>	High School	University[b]	Professional	Service	(1979 US$)
Total		226 546	22.6	11.3	66.5	16.2	12.3	12.9	16 841
US Born		212 466	23.5	10.6	67.7	16.3	12.3	12.7	17 010
Foreign Born[d]		14 080	8.8	21.2	53.1	15.8	12.0	16.1	14 588
Asia	**Philippines**	**501**	**11.3**	**10.4**	**74.0**	**41.8**	**20.1**	**16.2**	**22 787**
	Korea	290	24.2	2.6	77.8	34.2	14.7	17.0	18 085
	China	286	3.8	14.8	60.0	29.5	16.8	24.4	18 544
Americas	Mexico	2 199	14.7	7.6	21.3	3.0	2.5	16.6	12 747
	Canada	843	4.9	29.3	61.8	14.3	16.2	11.4	15 953
	Cuba	608	4.1	13.8	54.9	16.1	9.2	12.2	16 326
Europe	Germany	849	4.7	27.9	67.3	14.9	13.4	14.1	15 790
	Italy	832	2.1	44.5	28.6	5.3	6.1	16.3	13 736
	England	442	6.2	26.8	74.6	16.4	17.4	12.2	16 006

a. For persons 25 years old and over.
b. Completed 4 years or more of university.
c. Employed persons 16 years old and over.
d. Includes other countries not shown in this table.

Sources: US Bureau of the Census (1986).

while only 5.3 per cent of non-migrant members of the labour force in the Philippines are professionals (Table 4). With respect to education, the differences are equally striking: among temporary workers, fully 55 per cent have college or university education, while the figure for the Philippine labour force is only 20 per cent.

Higher education and professional occupations have contributed to make Filipinos living overseas a prosperous community, not only in the United States but also in Australia and Canada[11]. In 1980, Table 5 shows that annual median household income of Filipino-born residents in the United States ($22 787) exceeded that of US-born residents and of all other foreign-born groups (excluding India-born). In Australia, Filipinos had similar median incomes to Australia-born residents in 1986 (BIPR, 1991). Data on income and ethnicity are not available for Canada.

Determinants of Return Migration: Who Returns and When

Many studies have explored the determinants of migration following Harris and Todaro (1970), whereas fewer studies have addressed the determinants of return migration. In this section, we examine the characteristics of returnees using two alternative data sets (the 1991 SOW mentioned above, and the 1988 National Demographic Survey) to explain the pattern of return to the Philippines. First, return migration could represent a change in the perception of the net benefits of migration; thus, "over-optimistic" migrants become dissatisfied and return (Yezer and Thurston, 1976). An alternative explanation often put forth is that the return to a previous place of residence or birthplace indicates an accumulation of location-specific human capital (DaVanzo, 1983). This human capital can be close family ties or aspirations to inheritance, which migrants value and decide to keep by returning. Finally, exogenous factors can also explain the return of migrants through deportations, sickness, war in the host country, etc. The latter seems particularly applicable to international migration, where institutional obstacles hinder the free movement of labour across borders.

At this point, we need to define what is meant by a returnee. Here, we use two samples with different definitions of returnees. One is the 1991 Survey of Overseas Workers (1991 SOW) which asks the household "is there a family member who is working or has worked abroad during the past 6 months — from April to September 1991? (including only those who used to live with this household or are now here with this household)". Households are asked "If still abroad, when is the worker expected to return to the Philippines?" (excluding holidays). For overseas workers who have already returned, there is a specific code which allows us to identify workers who arrived home between April-September 1991. The sample size was 1 653 migrants, of whom 252 were returnees. The sample represents more than 700 000 overseas workers, of whom more than 100 000 returned (NSO, 1992a). Table 6 presents the characteristics of these returned migrants and of those migrants who stay away, according to this survey.

Also Table 6 includes in brackets an additional definition of both groups of migrants. The National Demographic Survey of April 1988 (1988 NDS) asks "in the last five years — from 1983 to 1988 — has any member or former member of this

Table 6. **Philippine Migrants: Migrants Away Versus Returned Migrants in the 1991 SOW and the 1988 NDS**
(in per cent)

	Migrants Away 1988 NDS	Migrants Away 1991 SOW	Returned Migrants 1988 NDS	Returned Migrants 1991 SOW
Male (%)	55.8	62.6	77.6	54.6
Age (in years)	33.1	33.9	36.5	34.1
Head or Spouse (%)	44.1	40.5	63.5	42.2
Urban (%)	67.1	76.5	64.8	65.5
Contract Workers (%)	79.5	96.2	90.6	92.2
Time Spent Away (in years)	1.2	2.7	1.6	3.2
Regional Unemployment 1980-91[a] (%)	10.8	12.3	12.2	10.8
Estimated Monthly Wage[b] (US$)	n.a.	436	n.a.	452
Average Total Remittances (US$)	n.a.	2 813	n.a.	8 589
Education (%)				
No Education	0.5	0.1	0.8	0.2
Primary	6.4	8.7	9.1	9.1
High School	35.2	34.4	39.8	34.9
College	19.3	27.9	19.1	27.2
University	32.0	28.6	26.0	28.2
Occupation[c] (%)				
Professional	16.2	14.1	12.4	13.6
Administrative	0.7	0.6	0.8	0.5
Clerical	6.5	5.0	4.4	4.6
Sales	5.8	1.2	5.4	1.1
Services	10.0	32.6	8.5	34.3
Production	32.9	45.9	48.7	42.3
Destination (%)				
Middle East[d]	40.3	47.2	52.2	32.6
Asia[e]	28.5	32.0	27.6	39.5
Europe	6.3	7.2	5.6	10.5
Americas	20.1	2.4	9.9	8.5
Other	4.8	11.2	4.7	8.9

a. Unemployment rates (BLES, 1991).
b. Estimates from POEA contracts.
c. For the 1988 NDS, "Occupation" refers to occupation at home.
d. Saudi Arabia (1988 NDS).
e. Other countries in Asia, including other Middle Eastern countries (1988 NDS).

Source: 1991 Survey of Overseas Workers (SOW); 1988 National Demographic Survey (NDS).

household left for abroad and been away or intends to stay away for one year or more?" For those that answered this question in the affirmative, the household is then asked if the person has returned since he or she left, and if so, when. Including contract workers and other workers as well as emigrants (excluding tourists, students and miscellaneous), we obtained a sample of 1 587 migrants. Of these, 387 were returnees.

There are two major differences between these alternative definitions of returnees. First, in the 1991 SOW, the screening question emphasizes that the person is working abroad and excludes people who left to live abroad but who do not work. The returnees in this data set are recent returnees (within the past 6 months) and almost all are contract workers (96 per cent). The 1988 NDS does not restrict the definition to working migrants and it includes a wider range of migrants (12 per cent of the sample are permanent migrants). A second main difference between these two samples refers to the reference period. The 1988 NDS restricts both the date of departure and return of the migrant to the last 5 years prior to the survey (i.e. 1988). While, in SOW 1991, there is no restriction on the date the family member left for the first time, the date of return is restricted to the last 6 months prior to the survey (April-October 1991). With a longer period to return (1983-88), the 1988 NDS gives a higher rate of returnees (24.2 per cent) than the 1991 SOW (14.8 per cent). On the other hand, the longer time horizon in the 1991 SOW (i.e. no restriction on the original date of departure) gives a longer average stay overseas among migrants (3.2 years among returned migrants to the 1988 NDS's 1.6 years). Using both surveys, Figure 3 depicts the pattern of return among migrants, by showing the percentages of returnees with respect to the year migrants left (i.e. the ratio of returned migrants to all the migrants who left the same year). Regardless of the sample used, the figure exhibits a quadratic pattern. In the 1988 NDS, the highest rates of returnees occur among migrants who left 2 to 3 years before and, in the 1991 SOW, rates are highest among those who left 3 to 6 years before the survey. Although we also observe high rates among returnees who had been away for 6 years (NDS) or 9 years or more (SOW), they represent a small number of migrants. Note that neither sample is a random sample of all migrants or all returnees, but both are truncated depending on the reference period used.

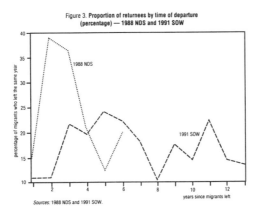

Figure 3. Proportion of returnees by time of departure (percentage) — 1988 NDS and 1991 SOW

Sources: 1988 NDS and 1991 SOW.

Table 6 shows that returned migrants are (not surprisingly) slightly older than migrants still away, have less education, are more likely to be in service occupations (SOW) or production (NDS) and less likely to be professional workers. They are more likely to be the head of the household or their spouse and to have come from regions in the Philippines with low unemployment rates. Using both samples of returnees (1991 SOW and 1988 NDS), we examine the effects of migrants' and migrants' household characteristics on return using probit analysis (Table 7). First, the amount of time spent overseas shows a statistically significant quadratic relationship with the probability of return, even after controlling for other characteristics. The coefficients for time spent overseas are smaller with the 1991 sample (which contains migrants with longer migration periods) than with the 1988 sample.

Table 7. **Return Among Filipino Migrants (Standardized Probit Estimates)**

	1991 SOW		1988 NDS	
Migrants away	1 418 (85.2%)		1 202 (75.8%)	
Returnees	247 (14.8%)		385 (24.2%)	
Age	-0.105		0.063	
Age Squared	0.132		0.151	
Sex ('Female' is omitted variable)				
Male	0.028		0.286	**
Relationship to Head ('Other' is omitted variable)				
Spouse or Head	0.043		0.183	**
Son or Daughter	-0.028		0.027	
Marital Status ('Other' is omitted variable)				
Married			-0.122	*
Education ('No Education' is omitted variable)				
Primary	-0.08		-0.072	
High School	-0.138		-0.098	
College	-0.211		-0.093	
University	-0.166		-0.154	
Destination ('Other' is omitted variable)				
Middle East	-0.156	**	-0.014	
Asia	-0.025		0.06	
Europe	0.022		0.005	
Americas			-0.041	
Occupation ('Production workers' is omitted variable)				
Professional	-0.102	*	-0.012	
Artist	0.046		0.038	
Administrative & Related	-0.087	*	-0.044	
Domestic Helper	-0.019		-0.082	
Other Services	0.036		-0.002	
Transportation	-0.029		0.014	
Urbanity ('Rural' is omitted variable)				
Urban	-0.055		0.006	
Visa ('Other' is omitted variable)				
Contract Worker	-0.088	**	0.0004	
Emigrant			-0.182	**
Time Away				
Away	0.487	**	1.315	**
Away Squared	-0.507	**	-1.143	**
Characteristics of Head				
Head-Age	0.329		0.084	
Head-Age Squared	-0.313		-0.225	
Head-Male	0.019		0.445	**
Head-Married	-0.007		-0.334	**
Head-Single	0.083	*	0.053	**
Head-Primary	-0.173	*	-0.041	
Head-High School	-0.18	*	0.053	
Head-College	-0.055		0.003	
Head-University	-0.129		0.113	
Labour Markets at Home				
Average Regional Unemployment 1980-91	-0.201	**	-0.118	**
-2 Log Likelihood (Chi-Square for covariates)	109.5 (32 d.f.)		376.9 (35 d.f.)	

* Indicates at least 90 per cent significance.
** Indicates at least 95 per cent significance.

Source: 1991 Survey of Overseas Workers (SOW); 1988 National Demographic Survey (NDS).

Another important correlate with the likelihood of return is regional unemployment (in the migrant's region of origin). This variable represents average unemployment from 1980 to 1991 in the area of origin and, for both samples, a 1 per cent increase in unemployment reduces the probability of return by 12 per cent to 20 per cent. Also, having an emigrant visa as opposed to a contract-worker visa unsurprisingly reduces the probability of return in the 1988 NDS sample. In the 1991

SOW sample, having a contract visa reduces the probability of return, most probably because the reference group is workers who are not under contract (i.e. mostly illegal workers or *tago-nang-tago*[12]). Some characteristics of the sending household are also significant.

Determinants of Remittances

Temporary migrants might be expected to remit more than permanent migrants as they retain closer ties due to expectations of return[13] (although permanent migrants also transfer funds to their relatives in the Philippines). From the 1988 NDS and the 1991 SOW, only the latter contains information about remittances and we use it to compare the characteristics of remitting and non-remitting migrants and their households[14] (Table 8). The SOW 1991 has information about transfers (either cash or in-kind) made in the 6 months prior to the survey (April-September 1991). In the 1991 SOW, 83.6 per cent of the migrants remitted. Compared to the non-remitters, the migrants who sent money home are on average older, slightly better educated, less commonly in occupations related to services (like domestic help) and more frequently either the head or spouse of the head of household. At home, the heads of the households with remitters are on average younger and more educated. Our estimates differ from the preliminary estimates published by the NSO, mainly because we also include the category of "cash brought home"[15].

Table 9 examines the determinants of total transfers (including cash brought home and remittances in kind). The first column indicates the incidence of total transfers in the sample. To measure the probability of being a remitter, we have used probit estimates. As we expected, time spent away influences positively the probability of remitting and has a quadratic effect. Age exhibits a similar effect on remittances. That is, the older the migrants and the longer they stay abroad, the more likely they will remit although this incidence decreases for long absences or older migrants. The duration of the migration has a larger coefficient than age (for the linear term the coefficient is 70.8 per cent for duration and 42.5 per cent for age; the latter variable has a smaller effect in the quadratic term). Also Table 9 (column 1) shows that being a member of the nuclear family (i.e. head, spouse or child) increases the chances of remitting. The probability is 15.3 per cent higher for spouses or heads and 10.3 per cent for children, either son or daughter, as opposed to other more distant members. Finally, being a contract worker increases the incidence of remittances very modestly (7.6 per cent) and so does being an artist (10 per cent). After controlling for the rest of the migrants' characteristics, migrants from the Middle East have a 13.5 per cent lower probability of remitting compared to the other destinations, which may reflect the less favourable economic conditions in oil exporting countries where most contract workers go.

To estimate amounts of remittances from migrants, we use Tobit analysis to avoid the biased and inconsistent estimates we would obtain by ignoring families that report zero transfers but that have migrants working abroad. Under three different specifications for the dependent variable (in Table 9, columns 2, 3 and 4 correspond to the regressions for total remittances, per capita remittances and remittances as a percentage of the migrant's estimated wage overseas[16]), we find that

Table 8. **Philippine Migrants: Remitters Versus Non-Remitters - 1991 SOW**
(in per cent)

	All Migrants	Non-Remitters	Remitters
Total	751 317	127 887	623 430
Male	61.4	52.3	63.1
Age (in years)	33.9	31	34.5
Urban	74.8	67.5	76.2
Education			
No Education	0.2	0.4	0.01
Primary	9.1	11.6	8.7
High School	34.9	34.7	35
College	27.2	27.8	27.1
University	28.2	25.3	28.7
Occupation Overseas			
Professional	13.7	10.4	14.2
Administrative, Clerical & Sales	6.2	5.4	6.3
Services	34.3	43.7	32.5
Production	45.3	39.0	46.5
Destination Overseas			
Middle East	45	44.8	45
Asia	33.1	33.6	33.1
Europe	7.7	10.1	7.2
Americas	3.3	1.8	3.6
Other	10.9	9.7	11.1
Type of Visa			
Contract workers	95.6	92.8	96.2
Other	4.4	7.2	3.8
Other Characteristics			
Time Away if Overseas (in years)	2.8	1.7	3
Estimated Monthly Wages (US$)	438	403	445
Conditions at Home			
Head or Spouse of Head	40.5	29.6	48.3
Children of Head	45.3	51.6	38.4
Family Size-All[1]	5.3	5.3	5.3
Family Size-Children under 10[1]	1.1	1.1	1.1
Female-Headed Families[1]	48.2	34.3	51.5
Age of Head (in years)[1]	48.2	50.1	47.7
Heads w/No Education[1]	3	4.3	2.9
Heads w/Primary[1]	34.8	42.2	33.3
Heads w/High school[1]	33	30	33.6
Heads w/College[1]	13.6	11.6	14
Heads w/University[1]	15.5	11.9	16.2
Unemployment in the Region 1980-91[2]	12.3	11.5	12.4
Average Remittances (US$)			
Remittances in Last 6 Months	3 670		3 670
¾ Cash Remittances	954		954
¾ Remittances in Kind	498		498
¾ Cash Brought Home	2 623		2 623

a. From 1991 October Labour Force Survey (characteristics of the head).
b. From the 1991 Yearbook of Labor Statistics (unemployment).

Source: 1991 Survey of Overseas Workers (SOW).

the amount of remittances is mainly explained by two factors, namely, the time the migrant has spent away and the location of the migrant's household in an urban area. Note again that the sample is *only* one of migrants, i.e. it examines the amount of remittances conditional on the household having a migrant.

First, urban households receive larger remittances (Table 9), which implies that international remittances could increase inequality in the Philippines (see next section). Second, the time spent away represents an indication of the likelihood of the migrant's return, which follows a quadratic pattern as we have already observed. This inverted-U probability of return also affects remittances in a similar fashion.

Hence, although more time abroad represents more experience and higher earnings, remittances do not increase continually because ties with the household at home weaken among those migrants who have stayed away longer. Because time spent abroad represents such a significant factor in explaining remittances, time should be taken into account in any study on the benefits of emigration for the source country[17]. Earlier we observed that probability of return increases with low regional unemployment[18] and when the migrant is a member of the nuclear family. In Table 9, these variables also increase remittances (only statistically significant under two of the three specifications). Lower unemployment in the region of origin increases the migrant's remittances, and migrants who are sons or daughters tend to remit more to their households (but households with older heads receive smaller transfers from international migrants). Again, other demographic characteristics of the migrants and their households do not appear significant, except being an artist which had a positive but insignificant effect on the probability of return and which also has a positive and statistically significant effect on the amount of remittances.

Remittances and Income Inequality

A remaining issue is to determine whether or not remittances increase inequality in the Philippines, where income distribution appears to have worsened since the 1960s[19]. According to some studies, international remittances increase income inequality in the rural areas. In a rural province of Egypt, Adams (1989) finds an increase in inequality when international remittances are included (a 14.8 per cent increase in household income inequality and a 21.3 per cent increase using per capita household income). For rural Pakistan, the same author reports opposite effects of domestic and international remittances (the former reducing and latter increasing inequality) (Adams, 1992). In the Philippines, the number of families receiving income from international sources has increased (especially among rural households), but urban families still receive a larger share of income from abroad than rural families (Figure 4). In 1991, 17.2 per cent of all Philippine households reported having received some income from abroad (around 8 per cent of the total income of Philippine households comes from abroad). Most of this income came from contract workers (52.5 per cent of total income from abroad), income from relatives who are not contract workers overseas (26.8 per cent), cash gifts from other relatives (who would not be part of the household if they were in the Philippines) and private institutions abroad (16.5 per cent), and pensions or dividends from overseas (4.2 per cent). Whereas earlier we discussed the characteristics of households with remitting and non-remitting migrants, here the FIES data allow us to compare households with migrants who remit and those households that do not have any migrants or remittances (Table 10). The former group is predominantly urban and has higher total income and expenditure than households with no remittances. Table 10 also indicates that the heads of households receiving remittances are slightly older and more likely to be female, and, although they are less likely to be employed, they also have more education than heads of non-recipient households. These figures already suggest that migration may exacerbate inequality since migrants come from better educated, wealthier, urban households. Using these data from the 1991 FIES and following a similar

Table 9. **Total Remittances: Incidence (Standardized Probit Estimates) and Amounts**
(Tobit Estimates)

	Incidence of Total Remittances[a]		Amount of Total Remittances		Amount of Total Remittances Per Capita		Total Remittances as % of Estimated Annual Wages	
Mean	83.6%		98 374 Pesos		23 847 Pesos		76.4%	
Constant			-217 227		-28 671		-118	
Characteristics of Migrant								
Age	0.425	**	10 135		1 889		8.9	
Age Squared	-0.314	*	-105		-20		-0.09	
Sex ("Female" is omitted variable)								
Male	0.006		13 668		6 358		-2	
Relationship to Head ("Other" is omitted variable)								
Spouse or Head	0.153	*	-13 013		2 084		-52.7	
Son or Daughter	0.103	*	76 497		27 093	*	84.6	**
Education ("No Education" is omitted variable)								
Primary	-0.102		-72 934		-12 365		-53.1	
High School	-0.065		13 394		4 336		4.9	
College	-0.088		54 709		12 729		41.3	
University	-0.067		41 945		9 159		31.1	
Destination ("Other" is omitted variable)								
Middle East	-0.135	**	32 785		10 642		65.4	
Asia	-0.05		19 976		74		-22.1	
Europe	-0.074		-80 892		-20 713		-64.7	
Occupation ("Production Workers" is omitted variable)								
Professional	0.005		-21 437		2 733		-36.9	
Artist	0.1	**	421 276	**	100 599	**	128.1	
Administrative & Related	0.038		-44 168		-10 035		-38.9	
Domestic Helper	-0.037		6 973		5 420		65.4	
Other Services	-0.033		-50 375		-10 905		-29.3	
Transportation	-0.039		6 190		9 042		53.8	
Urban ("Rural" is omitted variable)	0.038		37 769		19 606	**	80.2	**
Contract Worker ("Other" is omitted variable)	0.076	**	95 127		22 795		52.5	
Time Away								
Time Away	0.708	**	24 124	**	8 175	**	34.2	**
Time Away Squared	-0.538	**	-405		-319	*	-1.4	**
Characteristics of Head								
Head-Age	-0.347		9 932		-3 640	*	-12.5	**
Head-Age Squared	0.285		73		30	*	0.09	
Head-Male	-0.056		-31 224		-5 252		-26.4	
Head-Married	-0.009		79 349		11 756		81.8	
Head-Primary	-0.042		77 330		21 321		69.1	
Head-High School	-0.005		21 406		13 746		52.3	
Head-College	-0.02		18 442		11 589		45.2	
Head-University	-0.021		81 826		35 350		104.4	
Labour Markets at Home								
Average Regional Unemployment 1980-91	0.042		-5 230		-1 850	*	-5.5	*
-2 Log Likelihood (Chi Square for covariates)	140.2 (31 d.f.)							
Log Likelihood for Normal			-20 710.1		-18 826.4		-10 882.8	

a. 1 392 remitters and 273 non-remitters in the sample.
* Indicates at least 90 per cent significance.
** Indicates at least 95 per cent significance.

Source: 1991 Survey of Overseas Workers (SOW).

methodology to the one used by Adams (1989, 1992), Rodriguez (1994) calculates the effect of remittances from international migrants on the income distribution of the Philippines. The study shows that income inequality increases by 7.7 per cent for the whole country (the Gini coefficient increases from 0.297 to 0.320 with remittances from international migrants), and the increase is greater in urban areas (8.8 per cent). These findings need to be considered when evaluating the contribution of migrants (returnees or not) to the Philippines.

Table 10. **Characteristics of Households Receiving Income from Abroad: FIES 1991**

	Non-Recipient Households	Income from Abroad Excl. Pensions & Dividends[a]	Contract Workers	Other Migrants	Cash Gifts from Abroad	Pensions & Dividends from Abroad
Number	20 529	4 260	1 808	1 176	1 643	182
Age of Head (years)	46.0	48.6	47.9	50.6	48.6	58.5
Head-Male	0.885	0.704	0.607	0.690	0.816	0.709
Head-Married	0.845	0.800	0.831	0.753	0.791	0.648
Head-Single	0.031	0.041	0.034	0.050	0.043	0.044
Household Size (persons)	5.281	5.257	5.246	5.258	5.279	5.022
Member under 1 year	0.119	0.095	0.088	0.089	0.107	0.049
Member under 7 years	0.850	0.698	0.705	0.659	0.705	0.516
Members under 15 years	1.151	1.078	1.082	0.969	1.132	0.764
Members under 25 years	0.983	1.133	1.187	1.170	1.060	1.005
Members over 25 years	2.179	2.252	2.184	2.371	2.276	2.687
Urban	0.596	0.690	0.698	0.690	0.693	0.698
Head-Has a Job	0.890	0.679	0.626	0.628	0.748	0.429
Head-Primary	0.504	0.330	0.338	0.301	0.335	0.313
Head-High School	0.276	0.333	0.348	0.301	0.338	0.319
Head-College	0.082	0.151	0.148	0.156	0.156	0.143
Head-University	0.082	0.159	0.142	0.217	0.141	0.198
Head-Public Employee	0.075	0.094	0.084	0.109	0.093	0.093
Head-Private Employee	0.304	0.224	0.209	0.195	0.256	0.121
Head-Employer	0.051	0.043	0.043	0.054	0.036	0.027
Head-Self-Employed	0.425	0.283	0.259	0.235	0.326	0.165
Head in Agriculture	0.432	0.224	0.220	0.179	0.254	0.137
Head in Mining	0.008	0.004	0.004	0.002	0.006	0.016
Head in Manufacturing	0.086	0.065	0.065	0.063	0.064	0.022
Head in Utilities	0.006	0.004	0.003	0.006	0.005	0.000
Head in Construction	0.063	0.043	0.038	0.032	0.050	0.027
Head in Wholesale	0.087	0.090	0.086	0.094	0.086	0.077
Head in Transport	0.065	0.062	0.051	0.053	0.077	0.016
Head in Finance	0.017	0.024	0.020	0.027	0.026	0.022
Head in Personal Services	0.126	0.163	0.139	0.172	0.181	0.110
Owner of House and Lot	0.606	0.595	0.593	0.577	0.605	0.566
Total Household Income (pesos)	70 829.8	112 304.1	116 241.3	134 283.9	98 554.6	134 751.3
Total Wages (pesos)	30 569.7	33 905.7	31 239.5	38 885.4	33 195.3	30 722.4
Total Entrepreneurial Activities (pesos)	22 224.9	17 608.2	13 698.2	20 428.9	19 760.4	13 737.3
Total Income from Abroad (pesos)	0.0	33 628.7	46 766.2	39 497.7	20 161.2	13 064.2
% of Income from Abroad in Total Income		29.2	39.1	29.7	19.8	22.5
Income from Contract Workers (pesos)	0.0	18 343.5	43 220.9	3 251.2	3 004.3	5 630.2
Income from Other Migrants (pesos)	0.0	9 640.5	1 851.1	34 992.3	2 521.2	5 685.0
Cash gifts from Abroad (pesos)	0.0	5 644.7	1 694.3	1 324.2	14 635.7	1 748.9
Other Income from Abroad (pesos)	243.0	515.0	248.1	1 177.8	543.9	39 466.0
Total Expenditure (pesos)	54 669.7	91 902.8	94 594.0	108 207.8	82 508.8	108 218.4

a. Income from abroad can include income from contract workers, other migrants and gifts.
Note that some households receive remittances from more than one source.

Source: FIES 1991.

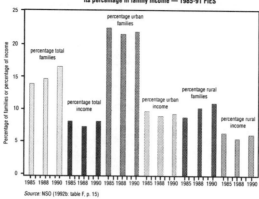

Figure 4. **Percentage of families with income from abroad and its percentage in family income — 1985-91 FIES**

Source: NSO (1992b: table F, p. 15)

Policy on Return Migration and Remittances

The contribution of returned migrants and remittances to the economic development of the Philippines has been considered disappointing (Abella, 1992). Earlier we mentioned Vasquez's (1992) findings that indicate return migrants are mostly unemployed, and their savings or remittances are consumed rather than invested in small businesses. These findings have become the predominant view on the impact of international migration in the Philippines (ILO-ARTEP-DOLE, 1993) and they echo similar experiences in other countries like Mexico, Central America and the Caribbean (Diaz-Briquets and Weintraub, 1991). Can regulation bring more remittances to the country, stimulate temporary return or give remunerative employment to permanent returnees? Most of the programmes aimed to increase official remittances will not meet their goals if they do not consider sufficiently the factors governing the decision to remit or return. Some policies have proved to be feasible and even profitable for the government (e.g. the "Balikbayan" programme — "returnee" in Tagalog — has increased business at the government-run duty free shops), whilst some others may have a more limited success (e.g. the Participatory Debt Reduction Certificate, retirement programmes or simpler immigration procedures). Some of these are discussed in more detail below.

Several government entities run or sponsor programmes that aim to favour international migrants in the Philippines, including the Commission for Filipinos Overseas (CFO), the Overseas Workers' Welfare Agency (OWWA) and the Philippine Overseas Employment Agency (POEA). According to the Commission for Filipinos Overseas (CFO), in 1990, 4 per cent of all visitors to the Philippines were "balikbayans". Approved in 1989, the "Balikbayan" programme offers to returning Filipinos (including former Filipino citizens) tax-free shopping up to $1 500, visa-free entry for a year, travel tax exemptions, and special areas in the ports of entry to expedite the processing of documents[20]. Another programme aimed to Filipino returnees is the Philippine Retirement Authority (PRA), a government agency currently implementing a national scheme offering incentives to retirees who choose the Philippines for their retirement. Since 1987, however, only 1 207 retirees have enlisted in the programme[21].

The Overseas Workers' Welfare Agency (OWWA) has a number of programmes aimed specifically at contract workers. Some of these programmes lend money to contract workers or their families [the Expanded Livelihood Development Program, the Pre-Departure Program — which gives up to 5 000 pesos (or roughly $200) and the Family Assistance Loan]. For protection, the OWWA offers legal assistance, repatriation of workers, life and death/disability insurance (less than $1 000). In addition, there are Training Grants for Seamen's Career Development, Training Loans for Filipino Seamen and a Skills-For-Employment Scholarship Program[22].

No information is available about the actual impact of any of these programmes (CFO or OWWA) either in terms of funds spent or number of beneficiaries. The POEA does however publish statistics about four groups of cases handled by the POEA and the OWWA: illegal recruitment cases, legal recruitment cases, recruitment regulation cases and welfare cases (Overseas Employment Statistical Compendium, 1982-1991). The last group, under the auspices of the OWWA, represented 5 386 welfare cases in 1991, of which only 2 397 were resolved in the same year. In 1991, the POEA's activities included handling 712 cases concerning illegal recruitment (down from 1 671 in 1984) and 2 564 cases of disputes concerning legal recruitment (down from 2 694 in 1984). Of these, the number of cases settled and workers who benefited was 39 for illegal and 698 for legal recruitment cases in 1991. Considering the size of the outflow of contract workers (almost half a million in 1991), these figures may not appear impressive.

When we examine the legislation on the remittances of contract workers, we continue to observe the strong involvement of the Philippine government. In 1982, an inter-agency body formed by the Central Bank, the Ministry of Foreign Affairs and the Ministry of Labour and Employment, issued Executive Order (EO) 857 which provided for the mandatory remittance of 50-70 per cent of overseas workers' salaries. As sanctions, the government would not renew the worker's passport or approve new employment contracts. After complaints from contract workers, the EO 1021 of 1985 repealed the punitive provisions of EO 857, but the remittance target figure continues in effect until now, although it is not widely observed. It is difficult to implement except for a subgroup of contract workers — the seamen — who get paid by their contractors in the Philippines. But in the case of seamen, there is less difficulty complying with the government target due to the nature of their work (most of their expenses are covered aboard the ships). For the majority of contract workers, permanent migrants or Filipinos with a new citizenship, the government cannot possibly enforce this policy.

Instead of imposing restrictions, the government has started to give incentives to remitting migrants by means such as the Overseas Workers Investment programme, approved in 1991. Again, we have no information about the success of this programme. Other minor programmes have tried to facilitate remittances by providing alternative channels. For instance, the OWWA has a remittance assistance service for Filipinos overseas which takes deposits abroad and delivers the money in 24 hours in Manila or 72 hours in the provinces. Many Philippine banks offer similar services.

The change of policies from more punitive to more supportive probably indicates the difficulty of increasing remittances through the use of legislation.

Although lifting restrictions reduces transaction costs, the economies of the host countries, the prospects of return of the migrants and the strength of family ties are the most significant forces determining remittances. Reducing transaction costs and offering a market rate for the hard currency increases the amounts transferred through legal channels without necessarily increasing total remittances.

Conclusions

The paper has reviewed the basic statistics on international migration and remittances in the Philippines. Statistics on remittances from previous micro studies tend to be unrepresentative of the entire country, and were often not clearly defined. The regularly published national data from the Central Bank under-report the value of remittances in the aggregate (by a factor as large as 50 per cent). At the beginning of the 1990s, the estimated stock of Filipinos residing abroad represented 2.8 per cent of the total population resident in the country and 4.4 per cent of the labour force and they contributed remittances equivalent to a quarter of the country's total exports. The two major groups of migrants are contract workers in Saudi Arabia and permanent migrants in the United States, but contract workers in the rest of Asia are a rapidly growing group.

Compared to the population, permanent migrants from the Philippines are on average older and are more often female. More than half are out of the labour force before leaving the Philippines. This reflects in part the "echo" migration fostered by family reunification. Almost a third of permanent migrants from the Philippines leave as "fiancées and spouses of foreign nationals". On the other hand, temporary migrants are in their prime working years and are more likely to be men, working mainly in services (including domestic help) and production (which includes transport). Both permanent migrants and contract workers are on average more educated than the non-migrant employed population in the Philippines. Abroad, Filipinos outperform the populations of the host countries in terms of qualifications, occupation and income.

Return migrants are an interesting group in terms of impact on the domestic economy. Our study, based on previously little-used microdata sets, presents two alternative definitions of returnees and examines what determines their pattern of return. A profile of return migrants reveals that they are slightly older than migrants still away, have less education, and are more likely to be service or production workers. When we control for demographic characteristics, two factors explain the probability of return. First, migrants coming from areas with high average unemployment delay their return. Second, time spent overseas is associated with an inverted-U pattern in the probability of return which is also manifested in the pattern of remittances, of which cash brought home by visiting or returning migrants is a substantial fraction. Data on households that receive remittances indicate that these families are more likely to be urban, have more educated heads, and higher incomes (even excluding overseas income). Hence, remittances from international migrants exacerbate income inequality.

Finally, we review some policies affecting remittances. Permissive policies have generally been more successful than coercive ones, although the impact of some programmes aiming to increase remittances has not yet been adequately documented.

Notes

1. Studies that report high unemployment among returnees do not control for the difference between those who will eventually leave again and those who will finally adjust. The latter group seems to be the most interesting, but no data are available except studies based on small (rather unrepresentative) samples, often of very recently-returned migrants. Vasquez (1992) acknowledges this limitation in his study that includes 240 workers in the province of Pampanga. Fifteen per cent of them were return migrants and had an unemployment rate of 76 per cent. Another survey of 506 returning contract workers reports that more than half of the returned migrants had not found local employment at the time of the survey (Arcinas, 1991). Most of the remittances were used to increase consumption (Arcinas, 1991; Vasquez, 1992). Even when some investment occurred, the study by ILO-POEA-CEC (1991) shows that the results were very modest. The latter study used a sample of 373 returning migrants and their relatives, who became self-employed with funds obtained overseas.

2. There are changes in definitions. From 1956-76 and 1987 onwards the reference period is the "past week" while this period changed to the "past quarter" between 1977-86. There was no labour survey conducted in 1979. Further, before August 1976, the definition of labour force includes people over 10. After 1976, it changes to include those over 15 years old.

3. The World Bank documents the lack of a long series of wages (World Bank, 1993b: 372-384); it constructs a series for 1965-91 which does not differ much from the one we could draw for 1951-92, by converting to real terms the legal minimum wage for non-agriculture in the National Capital Region.

4. The Department of Tourism has figures on Philippine nationals arriving and leaving. This information is interesting as it can provide some indirect evidence on the number of returning Filipinos. In 1990, the number of arrivals of Filipinos reached 130 757, of which 73.7 per cent declared they were visiting friends and relatives or just having a holiday (short-term returnees). Only 4.8 per cent claimed to be on business, leaving 14.8 per cent of Philippine nationals under the category of "others". This latter class (19 352 Filipinos) could include those migrants returning to the Philippines permanently, although distinction between "visiting" and "returning permanently" might be difficult (NSO, 1992c).

5. The Canadian 1991 census collects information on the mother tongue of the population. While the criterion of mother tongue gives 110 435 residents who speak Tagalog, the 1991 Census indicates 123 295 residents were born in the Philippines which would include Chinese-Filipinos who do not report Tagalog as mother tongue.

6. In the United States, data classify residents by race, giving a number of 1.4 million residents under the racial category of "Filipino". However, this figure includes

American residents descended from Philippine-born parents, and excludes the significant Chinese Filipino community living in North America who are not of Filipino descent.

7. In some of the US Trust Territories, Filipinos comprise a large share of the population: for example, 31.3 per cent of the population in the Mariana Islands and 18.4 per cent in Guam but only 9.7 per cent in Palau.

8. In 1992, the same survey changed the screening question to comprise any family member — not only workers — who had left for abroad between October 1987 and September 1992, giving a much broader definition of Filipinos overseas.

9. Also using CBP remittances and assuming that they are sent by an estimated stock of contract workers abroad, Canlas and Tan (1989) estimate per capita remittances between 1980-86 (below $2 000). These estimates have two opposite biases. They are underestimated because they exclude cash brought home by migrants (or sent through other non-official channels). At the same time, they also include income sent from emigrants and non-contract workers.

10. The 1981 OEDB survey contains 480 re-migrating workers and reports remittances of $3 477. The 1982 ILMS survey has 798 re-migrating workers with estimated annual remittances of $4 734 (Canlas and Tan, 1989: Table 8.13).

11. Although Philippine migrants in Canada commonly appear as domestic helpers (15 per cent of all migrants from the Philippines in 1989 and half of all the domestic helpers entering Canada that year), they also enter the country as "investing" immigrants. Since 1986, the Canadian Immigration grants a special class to investors that have a net worth of at least half a million dollars and invest between $150 000-500 000 in Canada. In 1992, 2.5 per cent of the 2 196 principal applicants as investors were from the Philippines (87.5 per cent were from either Chinese Taipei or Hong Kong), according to Employment and Immigration Service, Canada (1993).

12. Also known as TNT, this Tagalog expression means "hiding and hiding".

13. For Germany, Mekle and Zimmermann (1992) find empirical evidence that migrants' expectations about return to their country of origin affect remittances positively.

14. The information on heads of household comes from the Labour Force Survey which the National Statistics Office administered at the same time as the Survey of Overseas Workers (October 1991). So the information corresponds to the matched household.

15. If we use all the observations in the sample, we find that "cash brought home" represents 71 per cent of the total average remittances from international migrants, and the latter figure is heavily influenced by a few migrants in the sample who report large sums of money brought home. Therefore, it is important to clarify whether the definition of remittances includes only the regular cash flow (i.e., monthly transfers), or also includes lump-sum transfers upon return of the migrant. If we include the latter then the transfers in the last 6 months could reach $3 670, using the 1991 SOW (an annual estimate would have to consider that the cash brought home could occur only upon return of the migrant, for holidays or for permanent return). If cash brought home is not included in the calculation, then our figures are closer to those published by the NSO (regular cash transfers of $954 for a 6-month period).

16. The 1991 SOW does not give any information on migrants' earnings so that we use 1993 data on wages in US dollars as a proxy for overseas wages according to the characteristics of migrants in our sample. The overseas earnings equation was estimated, using data from more than 100 000 contracts registered during the second quarter of 1993 at the Philippine Overseas Employment Administration (POEA), which has to approve the overseas contracts before allowing the migrant to leave the Philippines as a contract worker.

17. Goldfarb *et al.* (1984) show that large flows of remittances from Philippine-born physicians living in the United States would compensate the Philippines for the loss of doctors. The study does not account for the decline in remittances over time which may be steeper among permanent migrants.
18. The country is divided in 13 regions. The regions with higher unemployment (above 10 per cent) between 1980 and 1991 were the National Capital Region (18.8 per cent), Central Luzon (13 per cent), Southern Tagalog (10.2 per cent) and Western Visayas (10.1 per cent).
19. Boyce (1993: 13-53) suggests that household survey data understate the incomes of the rich and that data on real wages provide a strong case for an increase in inequality in the Philippines.
20. Even the private sector supports the programme with the issuing of a Balikbayan Plus Card that gives discounts at stores, banks, hotels, and on transport fares and overseas phone calls (CFO, p.2, 1991).
21. The requirements are to be over 50 years old (no age limit for Filipinos or former Filipino citizens) and a deposit of $50 000 ($30 000 for Filipinos). The benefits mainly include a special resident retiree's visa and $7 000 exemption from customs duties. In general, the government has aimed to simplify immigration procedures for overseas Filipinos returning to the Philippines. For instance, no visa is required for visits up to a year and for longer stays a non-quota immigrant visa can be obtained. However, returning Filipinos who have renounced their Philippine citizenship can buy land only for residential purposes in the Philippines.
22. Also the OWWA offers other programmes such as the Social Reintegration Programme Development (part of the OWWA's Integrated Return Programme for Contract Workers), Value Formation Programme and "Hatid-Saya" (or "Deliver Joy") project which brings entertainment to the overseas jobsites.

Bibliographical References

ABELLA, Manolo (1989), "Policies and Practices to Promote Migrants' Remittances" in *Philippine Labour Review: Improving Remittance Inflows*, Vol. 13, No. 1, January-June.

ABELLA, Manolo (1992), "International Migration and Development" in Battistella, G. and A. Paganoni (eds.), *Philippine Labour Migration: Impact and Policy*, Quezon City, Scalabrini Migration Center.

ABRERA-MANGAHAS, Maria Alcestis (1989), *Overseas Workers' Remittances: Not a Leak, but a Bypass*, SWS Occasional Paper, Quezon City, Social Weather Stations, Inc.

ADAMS, Richard Jr. (1989), "Worker Remittances and Inequality in Rural Egypt", *Economic Development and Cultural Change*, Vol. 38, pp. 45-71.

ADAMS, Richard Jr. (1992), "The Effects of Migration and Remittances on Inequality in Rural Pakistan", *The Pakistan Development Review*, Vol. 31, pp. 1189-1206

AMJAD, Rashid (1989), "Economic Impact of Migration to the Middle East on the Major Asian Labour Sending Countries — An Overview" in R. Amjad (ed.), *To the Gulf and Back: Studies on the Economic Impact of Asian Labour Migration*, UNDP, ILO-ARTEP.

ARCINAS, F.R. (1991), "Asian Migration to the Gulf Region: The Philippine Case" in G. Gunatilleke (ed.), *Migration to the Arab World: Experience of Returning Migrants*, Tokyo, United Nations University Press.

BOYCE, James K. (1993), *The Philippines: the Political Economy of Growth and Impoverishment in the Marcos Era*, London, MacMillan Press and OECD Development Centre.

BUREAU OF IMMIGRATION AND POPULATION RESEARCH (1991), *Community Profiles: Philippines*, Canberra, BIPR.

BUREAU OF LABOUR AND EMPLOYMENT STATISTICS (BLES) (1991), *1991 Yearbook of Labour Statistics*, Department of Labour and Employment, Manila.

BUREAU OF LABOUR AND EMPLOYMENT STATISTICS (BLES) (1993), *Current Labour Statistics*, Department of Labour and Employment, Manila.

BUREAU OF THE CENSUS (1986), *The Statistical Abstract of the US 1986*, Washington, D.C., Bureau of the Census.

CANLAS, Dante and Edita TAN (1989), "Migrants' Saving Remittance and Labour Supply Behaviour: The Philippines Case" in R. Amjad (ed), *To the Gulf and Back: Studies on the Economic Impact of Asian Labour Migration*, UNDP, ILO-ARTEP.

COMMISSION ON FILIPINOS OVERSEAS (CFO) (1991a), *Handbook for Filipinos Overseas*, Manila.

COMMISSION ON FILIPINOS OVERSEAS (1991b), *1991 Annual Report*, Manila.

DAVANZO, Julie (1983), "Repeat Migration in the United States: Who Moves Back and Who Moves On?", *Review of Economics and Statistics*, Vol. 65, pp. 552-9.

DIAZ-BRIQUETS, Sergio and Sidney WEINTRAUB, (eds.) (1991), *Migration, Remittances and Small Business Development : Mexico and Caribbean Basin Countries*, Westview Press.

GOLDFARB, R., O. HAVRYLYSHYN and S. MANGUM (1984), "Can Remittances Compensate for Manpower Outflows?: The Case of Philippine Physicians", *Journal of Development Economics*, Vol. 15, pp. 1-17.

ILO-POEA-Commission of the European Communities (1991), *Migrant Savings and Entrepreneurship: A Summary Report on the Socio-Economic Baseline Study of the Entrepreneurship and Migrant Earnings Project*, Manila, Scalabrini Migration Center.

ILS-DOLE-ILO-ARTEP (1993), *Philippines: Towards an Employment Strategy in the Successor Plan (1993-98)*, Manila, Institute of Labour Studies — Department of Labour and Employment — International Labour Organisation — Asian Regional Team for Employment Promotion.

MEKLE, Lucie and Klaus ZIMMERMANN (1992), "Savings and Remittances: Guestworkers in West Germany" in Zimmermann, K. (ed.), *Migration and Economic Development*, Berlin, Springer-Verlag.

NATIONAL STATISTICS OFFICE (NSO) (1992a), *Highlights of the October 1991 Survey on Overseas Workers*, Special Release, Office of the Administrator, May, Manila.

NATIONAL STATISTICS OFFICE (NSO) (1992b), *Highlights of the 1991 Family Income and Expenditures Survey: Preliminary Results*, Special Release, Office of the Administrator, May, Manila.

NATIONAL STATISTICS OFFICE (NSO) (1992c), *1992 Philippine Yearbook*, Manila.

RODRIGUEZ, Edgard (1994), *Social Welfare and International Migration in the Philippines*, Department of Economics, University of Toronto, mimeo.

VASQUEZ, Noel (1992), "Economic and Social Impact of Labour Migration" in Battistella, G. and A. Paganoni (eds.), *Philippine Labour Migration: Impact and Policy*, Quezon City, Scalabrini Migration Center.

WORLD BANK (1993a), *The World Development Report 1993*, New York, Oxford University Press.

WORLD BANK (1993b), *The Philippines: An Opening for Sustained Growth*, Report No. 11061-PH, Washington, D.C., The World Bank.

YEZER, Anthony and Lawrence THURSTON (1976), "Migration Patterns and Income Change: Implications for the Human Capital Approach to Migration", *Southern Economic Journal*, Vol. 42, pp. 693-702.

Appendix 1

Data Sets on International Migrants and Remittances in the Philippines

In this paper, we have used four data sets that the National Statistics Office (NSO) has collected:

1. 1991 Family Income-Expenditure Survey (FIES)

This survey aims to gather data on family income and family living expenditures and related information affecting income and expenditure levels and patterns in the Philippines. Also it determines the sources, distribution and levels of income and spending patterns of Philippine families. The latter is used to estimate the weights in the estimation of the consumer price index. Similar surveys have been undertaken in 1956-57, 1961, 1965, 1971, 1975, 1979, 1985 and 1988.

The 1991 survey we use in this paper includes interviews with more than 20 000 households at two separate times (June 1991 and January 1992) so the reference period was the last six months — except food and other items — making it easier to avoid memory bias on the part of the respondents. This data set includes information on remittances received but not on the number of migrant workers. Although in theory it is feasible to match the FIES and the LFS, in practice the match has proven problematic and is not feasible at present.

2. Labour Force Survey (LFS)

The NSO administers the LFS quarterly; however, data on salaries are only collected in the survey of the third quarter, along with information about each member of the household at the moment of the survey. The survey used in the paper corresponds to the third quarter of 1991 (October 1991) and it covers more than 25 000 households. The survey asks a question about migrant workers overseas (not reported in the questionnaire) which is used to draw the subsample for the SOW.

3. Survey of Overseas Workers (SOW)

The SOW was undertaken at the same time as the October LFS. These two surveys have been matched to provide more information about the household of the migrant workers. The SOW has information on 1 713 migrants working overseas and includes information on remittances. The reference period is the last six months before the survey (April to September 1991) that took place in October 1991.

4. The National Demographic Survey (NDS)

The NDS was undertaken in April 1988. It is a quinquennial nationwide survey and started in 1968 with the aim of collecting data on fertility, mortality, migration and social mobility. The 1988 round of the NDS covered 19 897 households nationwide. The latest NDS was in 1993 (that is still not available). In the paper, we have used two modules of the 1988 NDS: the household information to obtain the information about the heads of the households (module 1) and the information on contract workers, other workers and emigrants from the module on international migration (module 2). The survey has no information on migrants' earnings and remittances. The survey records stays overseas during the last 5 years (January 1983 to April 1988). Although in theory it is feasible to match the 1988 LFS and NDS, in practice it proved problematic to link the April NDS to the October LFS so that matched information is not available at present.

Appendix 2

Notes and Sources to Estimate the Stock of Philippine-Born

United States: Philippine-born population in censal years. *Statistical Abstract of the United States 1992*, Table 46, published by the Bureau of the Census.

US Territories: Philippine-born population in censuses. Bureau of the Census. *Social, Economic and Housing Characteristics: Guam* (1990), *Social, Economic and Housing Characteristics: Commonwealth of the Northern Mariana Islands* (1990), *Social, Economic and Housing Characteristics: Republic of Palau* (1990), *Social, Economic and Housing Characteristics:—American Samoa* (1990). For 1980, the *UN Demographic Yearbook 1989*, Table 32 (censuses of Guam and American Samoa only).

Saudi Arabia: Cumulative estimate of foreigners by nationality according to arrivals and departures from 1970 until 1990. *Statistical Yearbook* (several issues) published by the Ministry of Finance and National Economy. Original source from the Ministry of the Interior.

Canada: Philippine-born population in censuses. *Immigration and Citizenship: The Nation* (1992), Table 2 and *Place of Birth, Citizenship and Period of Immigration* (1984), Table 1b, published by Statistics Canada.

Australia: Philippine-born population in censal years. Shu, J. et al. (1994) *Australia's Population, Trends and Prospects*, AGPS: Canberra, Table 5.3. Original source from the Australian Bureau of Statistics.

Japan: Foreigners by nationality registered as of the end of the year in accordance with the Aliens Registration Law. *Japan Statistical Yearbook 1991*, Table 2-15, published by the Statistics Bureau. Original source from the Judicial System and Research Department, Minister's Secretariat, Ministry of Justice.

Hong Kong: Working population by nationality. *Hong Kong 1991 Population Census: Main Tables*, Table 20c, published by the Census and Statistics Department, Hong Kong.

Spain: Resident aliens by nationality. *Espāna-Anuarío Estadístico* (1991 and 1992), Table 3.2.1., published by the Instituto Nacional de Estadística. Original source from the Direccion Nacional de la Policía.

New Zealand: Philippine-born residents. *1991 Census of Population and Dwellings: National Summary*, Table 2, and *New Zealand Census of Population and Dwellings 1981.— Volume 7: Birthplaces and Ethnic Origin*, published by the Department of Statistics.

Singapore: Philippine- and Thai-born residents. *Singapore Census of Population 1990: Demographic Characteristics*, Table 10, and *Census of Population 1980 Singapore: Geographic Distribution*, Table 22, published by the Department of Statistics.

Sweden: Philippine-born residents (1985) and Philippine-born and Philippine nationals (1992). 1992 estimate from *Statistical Yearbook of Sweden 1994*, Table 60, published by SCB Befolkningsstatistik. For 1985, *UN Demographic Yearbook 1989*, Table 32.

Switzerland: Residents by nationality. *Annuaire Statistique de la Suisse* (1992, Table 1.30, and 1994, Table 1.9), published by the Office Fédéral de la Statistique. Original source from the Office Fédéral de la Statistique, Évolution de la Population.

Macau: Balance of foreigners with legal residence and non-resident workers as of December (1991) and the cumulative estimate of foreigners who legalised their residence in the territory (between 1975-81). *Anuario Estatistico* (several issues), published by the Direccao de Servicos de Estatistica e Census de Macau.

Other countries: Philippine-born residents. In 1980, Philippine-born residents appear in the population census of Malaysia (424), the Bahamas (63), Panama (38), Puerto Rico (290) and "Pacific Islands" — not specified — (1 899). In 1981, Philippine-born residents also appear in the population census of Belgium (522) and Denmark (976). In 1985, Finland's census only records 79 Philippine-born residents. *UN Demographic Yearbook 1989*, Table 32.

Labour Migration from South Asia: Patterns and Economic Implications

by Béatrice Knerr*

Summary

Although under-researched, the macroeconomic consequences of migration on migrant sending countries can be quite significant. Examining the effects on national labour markets and macroeconomic aggregates, this paper argues that labour outflows in South Asian countries have contributed positively to economic growth through the remittance inflows they generate. The effect of out-migration on domestic labour markets, notably for unskilled workers, has been quite limited. In the case of skilled labour, however, there are instances where migration-created shortages have driven up domestic wages. Perhaps a more serious but more difficult to measure impact has been the depletion of the stock of master craftsmen who provide valuable on-the-job training to domestic workers. In some cases, migration has opened employment opportunities for women who were not previously in the labour force. The elasticity of labour supply and regional and occupational mobility of labour remain crucial determinants of how easily domestic labour markets can adapt to migrant outflows.

As to remittances, whose officially recorded value is far below actual amounts, they represent as much as 30-100 per cent of merchandise exports and 3-5 per cent of GDP. They stimulate demand for non-tradeable like construction and services, which tend to grow fast but also to shrink soon after migration tapers off. Agricultural output is also stimulated by remittance inflows, given the high income elasticity of demand for food products in these low income countries. While remittances can alleviate foreign exchange constraints, high import propensities out of remittances limit these benefits. In none of the countries examined have remittances had a noticeable effect on real exchange rates.

---

* University of Hohenheim, Stuttgart. This is an abridged version of the paper presented at the OECD Development Centre's workshop on *Development Strategy, Employment, and Migration*, 11-13 July, Paris.

Although migrant sending governments have only limited control over the size of migrant outflows, the scope for efficient policy to capture macroeconomic benefits from migration can be large. A stable macroeconomic environment, with a competitive exchange rate and real interest rates that encourage savings, is perhaps the most important consideration for encouraging migrant remittances. Since remittances inflows can be highly volatile, governments are advised not to depend too heavily on them for foreign exchange. Governments should continue to promote diversification of sources of foreign exchange revenues even during a migration boom. Fortunately, in the South Asian context at least, they are not seriously hindered in this task by the onset of "dutch disease symptoms".

Introduction

Since the early 1970s, labour export has been a decisive factor in South Asia's economic development. Workers' remittances over the last two decades have been a major source of foreign exchange and foreign labour markets have provided a convenient outlet for growing domestic labour surpluses. The question, however, of whether large-scale contract migration1 promotes economic development is still widely debated. Due to varying conditions in receiving countries, the nature of short-term migrant contracts and monopolistic demand in the international labour market, labour export and remittance flows are highly variable. Furthermore, governments have only a marginal influence on the process of out-migration.

This study examines the patterns and consequences of international labour migration from India, Pakistan, Bangladesh and Sri Lanka. In broad terms, it assesses the labour market effects of out-migration from these labour exporting economies (LECs). It also analyses some of the macroeconomic implications of remittance inflows for the South Asian LECs, weighing them against certain hypotheses derived from "dutch disease" economics. The effects of remittances on overall GDP growth as well as on sectoral GDP growth are examined, as is their effect on imports. Given the sizeable impact which labour remittances appear to have on certain key macroeconomic aggregates in labour sending countries, migration policy deserves to be integrated into their overall development planning. Furthermore, given the links that migrants and their remittances create between countries of origin and of destination, labour receiving countries could find it useful to be aware of the implications of migration for the source countries.

Based on "dutch disease" economics and the standard neo-classical assumptions about the behaviour of production functions, utility functions and economic agents, the present analysis starts from the hypotheses that:

— If labour is still in completely elastic supply in the domestic market, remittance-induced additional demand will be satisfied by domestic production. The demand for tradeables will be satisfied by the world market. Wages and the real exchange rate will remain unchanged while the production of tradeables will stagnate.

— If labour becomes scarce, wages will increase and labour will be reallocated from the tradeables to the non-tradeables sector. The production of non-tradeables will expand; that of tradeables will decline, depending on the wage increases and on elasticities of demand and supply. The real exchange rate will fall. Net imports will thus increase at the expense of domestic production of tradeables. Symptoms of "dutch disease" would then be expected. The factor reallocations occurring over a remittance boom are often difficult to revise once the boom is over. A decline of the tradeable sectors is particularly harmful for the low-income South Asian LECs as they tend to have a vulnerable export sector. Furthermore, a contraction of sectors which may earn or save foreign exchange makes the economy dependent on further labour export. In particular, sectors like agriculture which face low income elasticities of demand will lag behind the aggregate growth of the economy.

The paper is organised as follows. The first section provides background information on the determinants and patterns of labour export from India, Pakistan, Bangladesh and Sri Lanka. Next comes an analysis of the flows of out-migrants and an investigation of their labour market implications[2]. There follows a description of the patterns of remittance behaviour and the allocation of remittance income. The next section summarises findings on the quantitative impacts of remittance inflows on certain macroeconomic aggregates in South Asian LECs. The final section summarises the main findings, draws conclusions and formulates some policy recommendations.

Determinants, Dimensions and Patterns of International Labour Migration from South Asia

Since the 1950s, professionals and highly skilled workers from South Asia have moved to industrialised countries, mainly the United Kingdom, the United States, Canada and Western Europe. Today a large number of South Asians are settled in the United Kingdom. Migration to the Middle East began to increase rapidly in the mid-1970s and, since the early 1980s, migration to other regions has become marginal in comparison. The quadrupling of oil prices in 1973 and their doubling in 1975 initiated a demand for manpower in the Middle Eastern oil-exporting countries which could not be met locally and thus led to large-scale imports of labour. After the first oil boom, a large share of the oil exporters' wealth was spent on the construction of ambitious infrastructural projects for which large numbers of unskilled foreign workers were recruited.

When the supply from neighbouring Arab countries became increasingly inelastic, the reservoir of cheap South Asian manpower was discovered. South Asian workers were particularly attractive given that they accepted low wages, were hard working and disciplined, and did not get involved in the political issues of host countries. Their recruitment through organised labour agencies kept information and transportation costs low while facilitating employers' planning. Furthermore, many were Muslims like the rest of the population in receiving countries (Knerr 1990a).

As priority in Middle Eastern countries shifted from infrastructural to industrial development, the demand for foreign labour shifted to higher skill workers, to the detriment of South Asians. Since the early 1980s, South Asians were increasingly replaced by East and South-East Asians, in particular Koreans and Filipinos, who migrate within well-organised "turn-key" company packages[3]. Migrants from Sri Lanka, many of them women, have been less affected by changes in foreign labour demand since they were mainly employed in the more stable service sector. The decline of oil prices in the mid-1980s brought a stagnation in the number of aliens employed in the Middle Eastern oil-exporting countries, and the Gulf war in 1991 further reduced their number. However, although receiving countries have tried to reduce the number of expatriate labour, it is generally expected that the Middle East oil-exporters will remain dependent on labour imports for the foreseeable future (Knerr, 1990a).

India and Pakistan were the first to respond to labour demand in the Gulf. Historical links with the Gulf states and a tradition of migration and labour force mobility have provided favourable conditions for manpower exports from these two countries. In 1981, the peak of its emigration, India exported 280 000 migrants (see Figure 1) while Pakistan's outmigration peaked a year earlier at around 170 000. Flows from Bangladesh and Sri Lanka gathered momentum by the time of the second oil shock, having been encouraged and organised by numerous recruitment agencies. Over the 1980s, the number of Bangladeshi workers who left for employment abroad continued to increase while those from Pakistan and India sharply declined after 1980/81 (see Figure 1). Although a latecomer in the supply of guestworkers to the Middle East, Sri Lanka was able to secure a significant share of the region's labour market by specialising in the export of housemaids, an occupation for which women from Arab and most other Muslim countries (with the exception of Indonesia) are not available. About one-half of Sri Lanka's out-migrants during the 1980s have been women; 70 per cent of them have been contracted as housemaids.

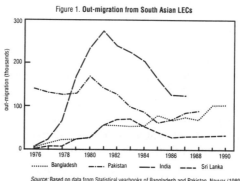

Figure 1. Out-migration from South Asian LECs

Source: Based on data from Statistical yearbooks of Bangladesh and Pakistan, Nayyar (1989), Rodrigo and Gayatissa (1989).

Large income differences have provided strong incentives for individual labour migration. The salaries of Kerala's migrants, for example, were 600 to 800 per cent higher than what was offered on the local labour market (Noman 1991: 83). For Sri Lankan manual worker migrants, foreign salaries were 6 to 10 times higher than those offered at home (ILO 1988: 8). Migration has also been stimulated as a result of the large-scale unemployment, under-employment and high growth rates of the

Table 1. **Share of South Asian Population Abroad**

Country	Per Cent of Population Abroad	Total Number of Migrants	Year	Remarks
India	0.13	957 000	1987	Middle East only
Pakistan	0.70	500 000	1975	
	2.12	1 700 000	1979	
	1.87	1 800 000	1985	
Bangladesh	0.00	5 900	1976	
	0.22	252 000	1989	
Sri Lanka	1.26	200 000	1985	Labour force in Middle East only

Source: Calculated with data from Nayyar (1989), Gilani *et al.* (1981), Manpower Division Pakistan, Mahmud (1989), World Bank, *World Tables*.

Table 2. **Skill Composition of Labour Outflow from India**
(In Per Cent)

	1981	1985	1986
High-skilled Technicien	1.9	3.8	4.2
Unskilled Construction	41.7	31.5	34.6
Unskilled Farm/Household	1.3	2.7	5.5
Others	8.4	5.0	1.2
White Collar Workers	3.6	3.5	6.5
Skilled Services	19.5	24.4	25.5
High Skilled Medical	1.3	0.7	1.0
Skilled Construction	22.3	28.4	21.5
Total Number	205 922	163 035	113 649

Source: Based on data from Nayyar (1989).

Table 3. **Skill Composition of Labour Outflow from Pakistan During 1981-85**
(In Per Cent)

	1981	1982	1983	1984	1985
Unskilled	50.6	45.8	41.4	45.2	45.1
Semi-skilled	3.7	3	3	2	3.32
Skilled	39.5	44.2	48.4	44.9	45.24
Highly Skilled	4.6	5.4	5.4	4.9	5.16
Highly Qualified	1.6	1.6	1.8	1.5	1.18

Source: Based on data from Pakistan Bureau of Emigration and Overseas Employment.

labour force. In the case of Pakistan and Bangladesh, labour force grew at 3 per cent per annum in the 1980s (UNDP 1993).

Government policy has supported labour export from Pakistan, Bangladesh and Sri Lanka. Under the government of Zulkifur Ali Bhutto in Pakistan, labour exports to the Middle East were a means to the end of forging stronger links with other Islamic countries, especially Saudi Arabia, the UAE and Kuwait. Migrant labour from Pakistan has become the object of bilateral state agreements. In Pakistan and Sri Lanka governments provide vocational and other training programmes designed to improve the skill levels of potential overseas workers. The Indian government's policy towards international migration is the least interventionist. "The policy regime in India offers neither carrot nor stick to sustain or increase the inflow of remittances" (Nayyar 1987: 72).

Labour Market Implications

The extent of out-migration does not say much about resulting labour shortages. The fact that out-migration usually is concentrated in certain occupations and regions may lead to frictions in domestic labour markets. Labour market implications of out-migration are essentially determined by rates of out-migration from different occupations and regions, occupational and regional mobility of the labour force, and length of stay abroad.

Skill Composition

South Asia migrants to the Middle East tend to be mainly unskilled. Between 1984 and 1986, 35 to 45 per cent of the total outflow of Indian and Pakistani labour consisted of unskilled workers, most of them contracted for work in the construction sector (Tables 2, 3, 4). Thousands of highly qualified Indian professionals are also working in the Middle East, in the United States and in many other countries (Nayyar 1989: 99). In the case of Pakistan the number of out-migrating professionals has displayed a clear downward trend, from 2 923 in 1977 (corresponding to 2.1 per cent of the out-migrants) to 664 in 1988 (or 0.8 per cent of the out-migrants). By contrast, service workers represented 22.1 per cent of total migrants in 1988, up from 8.1 per cent in 1977. The number of agricultural worker migrants has also increased; they accounted for 8 per cent of all migrants outflows in 1988.

Little is known about the occupational status of Indian out-migrants before their departure. A case study by Nair (1986) indicates that about half of them were unemployed before they left, having been underemployed members of peasant households, unemployed landless agricultural labourers, or underemployed/ unemployed casual wage labourers (Nayyar 1989: 114). Under these circumstances it can be readily assumed that out-migrants can be replaced easily from the stock of unemployed, and thus the export of labour is hardly felt on India's labour markets. In the case of Pakistan, almost half of the out-migrants from 1981 to 1985 were unskilled workers, and 44 per cent were classified as semi-skilled or skilled, with a

Table 4. Occupational Distribution of Pakistani Out-Migrants
(In Per Cent)

Category	1977	1978	1979	1980	1981	1982	1983	1984	1985	1986	1987	1988
Professional Workers	2.08	1.57	1.29	1.53	1.46	1.38	1.40	1.39	0.90	1.11	1.00	0.74
Administrative Workers	1.64	1.60	1.45	1.10	1.68	1.55	1.74	0.98	1.26	1.02	0.92	0.95
Clerical Workers	3.07	2.85	2.60	2.24	2.44	4.88	2.70	2.33	2.15	3.42	3.08	2.88
Service Workers	8.84	10.28	11.15	10.71	11.43	11.61	14.53	16.53	18.54	21.26	19.13	20.19
Agricultural Workers	2.03	1.79	1.49	2.43	2.91	3.91	4.26	5.13	3.52	9.03	8.13	7.32
Production Workers	69.33	74.64	77.10	75.34	78.13	75.81	68.99	66.80	66.71	69.81	62.82	59.40
Others	13.01	7.30	4.91	6.64	1.95	0.81	6.38	6.84	6.93	5.48	4.93	8.52
Total Number	140 445	129 533	118 439	118 407	153 081	137 535	128 146	100 407	88 461	62 641	69 619	89 140

Source: Based on data from Bureau of Emigration and Overseas Employment, Pakistan.

large share of them being construction workers. More than half of Sri Lanka's out-migrants are unskilled, and 45 per cent were housewives before migration, with half of those having never joined the labour force (Marga Institute 1986). The overwhelming share of Bangladeshi out-migrants are classified as workers (94 per cent in 1990); currently, only a small percentage are professionals though in the mid-1980s medical personnel and other professionals constituted roughly 10 per cent of outmigrants (Table 5).

Regional Concentration

Out-migration displays a high regional concentration. Private social networks resulting in chain migration and the economies of scale involved in recruiting migrants from specific areas help explain this pattern. About 50 per cent of Indian migrants come from Kerala state (ILO 1988), with the rest originating mostly from Karnataka, Goa, Maharashtra, Gujarat, and Punjab. Due to their high literacy rate and their reputation for industriousness, Keralites traditionally have been demanded as guest-workers both within India and outside. Historically, large-scale population movements were common, first within the state, then within the country and eventually abroad. Since the early 1970s, demand from the Middle East has offered migration opportunities, particularly to the unskilled and chronically unemployed. In 1987, 682 060 migrants from Kerala worked outside the state; 44.1 per cent were in the Gulf countries, 4.2 per cent in other foreign countries, and the rest in other states of India (Government of Kerala 1990: 16).

In Pakistan, about 70 per cent of the migrants come from the Punjab, representing 1.9 per cent of the region's labour force in 1988. Sind and the North-West Frontier Province are also major migrant sending regions. In Bangladesh, the districts of Chittagong, Noakhali, Comilla, Sylhet and Dhaka have the highest rates of out-migration (Ali et al. 1981: 36). Some 90 per cent of the migrants come from regions with a per capita income higher than the national average, while economically backward regions are hardly involved in the migration process (Knerr 1990b). Rates of out-migration are particularly high from areas with high population densities. In Sri Lanka, about one half of all migrants come from the district of Colombo and another 15 per cent from Gampaha (Rodrigo and Jayatissa 1989: 14). These two regions are the most densely populated in the country and are among the most economically developed ones. About 80 per cent of Pakistan's and 78 per cent of Bangladesh's international migrants come from rural areas (de Kruijk and van Leeuwen 1985: 416; Mahmud 1988: 1).

Impact on Labour Markets

Looking at India, labour outflows would seem to have a marginal effect on the national labour market. The share of out-migrants in the country's total labour force never exceeded 0.2 per cent in the 1980s (Figure 2). Even in the peak year of out-migration in 1981, the number of out-migrants was at 270 000, or roughly one-fortieth of the incremental labour force of that year (UNDP 1993; ILO 1993). At the regional level, effects may be more pronounced. Kerala for example had 12 per

Table 5. **Occupational Composition of Labour Outflow from Bangladesh**
(In Per Cent)

	Vehicle Drivers	Engineers	Medical Personnel	Professionals	Catering Workers	Miscellaneous	Workers	Technicians	Construction Workers	Total Outflow (n)
1977	3.61	2.05	3.87	5.32	3.12	42.90	18.43	9.32	11.40	15 725
1978	5.73	3.19	1.67	2.06	4.41	13.50	34.31	25.18	9.93	22 809
1979	7.96	0.87	0.60	0.30	4.59	22.36	35.90	19.02	8.38	24 485
1980	3.50	0.63	0.90	1.26	6.01	7.43	57.91	13.89	8.47	30 573
1981	4.62	0.42	0.49	3.41	4.76	5.23	56.43	1.57	6.08	55 787
1982	6.23	0.30	0.39	4.87	4.52	5.34	60.56	13.19	4.59	57 575
1983	3.23	0.12	0.85	5.79	3.82	1.42	69.43	10.50	4.84	58 200
1984	2.55	0.11	3.53	6.76	2.29	2.55	66.76	8.80	6.66	56 753
1985	3.82	0.20	0.25	2.85	1.60	2.03	56.84	17.28	15.12	77 724
1986	5.30	0.17	1.32	4.33	3.45	0.28	62.38	13.95	8.82	68 658
1987	5.25	0.10	0.21	2.69	4.15	4.12	66.70	7.24	9.53	74 017
1988	6.22	0.08	0.28	3.55	6.50		74.28	6.99	2.09	68 122
1989							98.50	1.50		97 859
1990							94.45	5.55		103 554

Source: Based on data from Bangladesh Bureau of Statistics.

cent of its labour force out of the region in 1981. For decades, Kerala has been affected by chronic and increasing unemployment at all skill levels. While participation rates have consistently declined, the number of job seekers has steadily increased (Government of Kerala 1990: 14-15). Surveys indicate that about 38 per cent of Kerala's migrants were unemployed before they left for the Middle East. Even so, out-migration has led to shortages of skilled and semi-skilled labour and to wage increases. The wages of skilled construction workers have risen especially fast (particularly from 1973 to 1983), reflecting the combination of a high incidence of out-migration, the large share of migrants' remittances spent on construction (notably for housing), and the existence of an administered labour market which reduces labour mobility (Nair 1989).

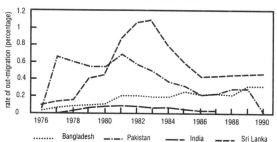

Figure 2. **Percentage of out-migrating labour force in total labour force of South Asian LECs**

Source: calculated with data from statistical yearbooks of Pakistan and Bangladesh, UNDP Human Development Report, Government of Pakistan (1990), Nayyar (1989) and World Tables.

In Pakistan, out-migration has represented a more significant share of the increase in the labour force: in 1981, the number of out-migrants was 168 403, while the incremental labour force was 943 748 (UNDP 1993; ILO 1993). The boom years of labour export were accompanied by rising real wages at all skill levels, especially in the construction sector and (to a lesser extent) in large-scale industry. Real wages increased on average by almost 25 per cent from 1978 to 1986. In construction, masons' real wages rose by 41 per cent, carpenters' by 47 per cent, and unskilled workers' by 70 per cent (ILO/ARTEP 1987). In the agricultural sector, wages for casual workers displayed an upward trend, but the average wage of all agricultural workers did not increase (Khan and Lee 1984).

Out-migration of unskilled workers has not resulted in serious domestic shortages due to the huge reservoir of under-utilised labour in the agricultural sector, the integration between rural and urban labour markets, and the high geographic mobility of labour (Mahmud 1989: 89). These factors have been particularly apparent in Bangladesh and Sri Lanka. By contrast, the withdrawal of a large number of skilled workers within a short time, in Pakistan for example, has led to serious shortages in certain occupational categories such as carpenters, electricians, and plumbers (Ahmed 1982; Gilani 1981). In addition, the out-migration of skilled workers in the late 1970s and early 1980s led to a deterioration of the quality of the labour supply, because the great majority of Pakistan's workers receive their skills informally through on-the-job training. The loss of the economy's master craftsmen and trainers has depressed the level of skills acquired by new entrants into the labour market (Ahmed 1982). In the case of highly skilled professionals, Pakistan is thought to have lost 50-76 per cent of its medical school graduates between 1973 and 1978 (Ahmed 1982). In Bangladesh and Sri Lanka the loss of skilled and professional labour was all the more significant given their short supply of such skills (World Bank, 1985). In Sri Lanka, for example, more than 2 000 medical doctors were graduated between 1971 and 1981, but only 318 joined the domestic labour market. There has also been a problem of brain drain from the state services to employment abroad (Rodrigo and Jayatissa 1989).

Labour outflows could cause a shift in the earning structure in favour of blue-collar jobs. As a consequence of the composition of out-migration from Pakistan, the upward wage trend was comparatively stronger for production and service workers than for professionals, in spite of higher supply elasticities of the first group (Gilani et al. 1981). At the same time, the wage gap between the highly educated and the less educated, and between the formal and the informal sector, narrowed. The shift of the wage structure in favour of "blue collar jobs" as compared to "white collar jobs" induced many new entrants into the labour market to choose "blue collar" qualifications, and others to shift to such occupations. In Bangladesh, by contrast, such a development did not occur. Real wages have declined markedly over the last decades, and the gap between the wages of skilled and unskilled workers has consistently increased from 1.29 to 1.42 between 1974-84. The coexistence of a large surplus labour force and a persistent shortage of technical personnel at all skill levels has meant that income differentials could not be easily adjusted by migration.

The shortages of skilled labour eased after the peak of out-migration was crossed, both because net migration of these skills declined, and because the domestic labour supply adapted to the changing market conditions. In some cases, large-scale out-migration caused a shift to more capital-intensive production (Noman 1991). This was particularly pronounced in Pakistan's construction sector where migration-related skill shortages were most acutely felt. The increasing technological bias in favour of more capital was a response to growing labour shortages as well as to the lower efficiency of workers who were employed to replace out-migrants (Noman 1991: 82). Also, the export of certain skills has led to an increase in the supply of such labour through additional domestic training. From the late 1970s onwards, Bangladesh's educational system expanded its annual output of professionals and technicians at a time when these categories of labour were highly demanded in the Middle East (Mahmud 1989: 91). Vocational training facilities for those skills which display a high incidence of out-migration were substantially expanded in all South Asian countries, in particular for skilled construction workers and engineers, vehicle maintenance, drivers and catering workers (Rodrigo and Jayatissa 1989). In addition, a reorientation of school-leavers away from the traditional aversion against manual skilled jobs as compared to white collar jobs has been initiated by the improved employment opportunities overseas for vocationally and technically qualified categories. A similar behaviour leading to increased labour supply has been observed in the sector of medical personnel (physicians, nurses, etc.).

After the peak of labour export had been crossed, the growth of employment slowed down in all sectors in Pakistan, except for services where it accelerated from an average rate of 2.7 per cent per annum between 1971 and 1978, to 5.3 per cent per annum from 1979 to 1985. Employment opportunities first of all deteriorated for unskilled urban workers. From 1982 onwards, wages in the construction sector and in large-scale industry and of skilled workers more generally declined along with the declining trend of out-migration (Irfan and Ahmed 1985: 428). Surveys conducted in 1986 indicate that firms in the manufacturing and construction sectors did not find it difficult to employ additional skilled workers (ILO/ARTEP 1987, Vol. VII).

Returnees

For lack of systematic data collection, the labour supply effect of return migration is more difficult to assess. In general, skilled and qualified migrants tend stay longer abroad than unskilled workers. According to ILO-ARTEP surveys[4], 90 per cent of the Pakistani returnees in 1985 were production workers, workers from the transport sector, equipment operators and labourers (ILO-ARTEP 1987, Vol. IV). Oftentimes, returnees remain unemployed for a considerable time. Half of Pakistan's return migrants remain unemployed for more than six months. This might not seem surprising given that the average unemployment rate in South Asian countries is estimated at around 20 per cent (World Bank 1985, Betz 1982), but returning migrants appear to have higher unemployment rates than others. For instance, 49 per cent of Kerala's returning migrants are unemployed after their return, while this share was only 36 per cent before migration; on the other hand, 24 per cent of the returnees become self-employed, against a share of only 19 per cent before out-migration, their preferred investments being in retail shops, restaurants, and transport services (Batzlen 1994). In the case of Pakistan, while 36 per cent of returnees had been employed before departure, only 11 per cent find regular jobs after their return (ILO-ARTEP 1987, Vol. VI). Unemployment among returnees in rural areas of Pakistan is much lower than in urban regions: in rural areas, 27 per cent of the returnees went into regular employment after their return but 63 per cent had been regularly employed before their departure. In Bangladesh, rural returnees face slightly higher unemployment than urban ones: 42 per cent of returnees in rural areas were unemployed compared with 7 per cent before departure; the shares in urban areas were 39 and 8 per cent respectively. In the case of Sri Lanka, the Marga Institute (1986) estimates that unemployment among returned males was 74 per cent and among females 28 per cent.

There is a positive relationship between level of education, skills, and financial savings on the one hand and unemployment on the other. Returned professionals and technical workers had higher rates of unemployment than unskilled workers, as they could draw on their high savings while looking for a suitable job (Kazi 1989). For instance, in Pakistan, about 30 per cent of returned migrants with college or university education in urban areas were unemployed after their return, but only 15-16 per cent of those from the group with primary and middle school education[5]. However, hard-core unemployment extending to more than two years after return is more frequent among the unskilled: in Pakistan, 25 per cent of all returned unskilled workers belong to this group.

Extent, Determinants and Patterns of Remittances

Remittances to India and Pakistan peaked in the early to mid-1980s and, in the case of Pakistan, displayed a downward trend thereafter. Remittances to Bangladesh and Sri Lanka began to rise from a low level in the latter half of the 1980s (Figure 3). Remittances from the Middle East are particularly high in comparison to other regions. Given that the majority of South Asian migrants are contract workers who migrate without their families and often live in shared cheap accommodations in receiving countries, their saving rates are particularly high. Remittances, however, are not always transmitted through official channels. Migrants often prefer to use informal channels that tend to be more efficient and reliable than official banking channels, as well as offering more favourable exchange rates (Noman 1991). Available estimates of the share of undocumented remittances to Pakistan puts them at 43 per cent of the total (ILO 1988).

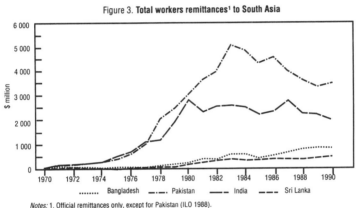

Figure 3. **Total workers remittances¹ to South Asia**

Notes: 1. Official remittances only, except for Pakistan (ILO 1988).
Sources: Based on data from World Bank, World Tables and ILO 1988 (Pakistan).

Patterns of Remittances

Pakistan registered the highest amount of remittances over the Middle East migration boom, with almost $5 billion in 1983, followed by India. Pakistan's population also received the highest volume of remittances per capita (almost $60) (Figure 4). For all the South Asian countries considered, workers' remittances are an important source of foreign exchange. In the early to mid 1980s, they amounted to almost double the value of Pakistan's merchandise exports, to three-quarters of Bangladesh's, and one-third of India's and Sri Lanka's (see Figure 5). Remittances represented almost 20 per cent of GDP in 1983 in Pakistan, but 5 per cent or less in the case of other South Asian countries (Figure 6). Measured on a regional basis, remittances represented 25 per cent of Kerala's GDP in 1980/81 (Nayyar 1989: 12).

Before the onset of out-migration to the Middle East, remittances to Bangladesh were unimportant, in spite of the large numbers of Bangladeshis settled in the United Kingdom. Between 1977 and 1986, the share of remittances officially arriving from the Middle East increased from less than 20 per cent to 82 per cent of total official remittances (based on data from the Foreign Exchange Department,

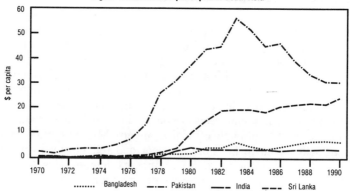

Figure 4. **Remittances per capita in South Asia**

Note: Official remittances only, except for Pakistan (ILO 1988) and Bangladesh (ILO 1988).
Sources: Calculated with data from World Bank, World Tables and ILO.

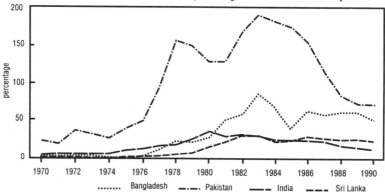

Figure 5. **Workers' remittances as a percentage of total merchandise exports**

Sources: Based on data from World Bank, World Tables, ILO (1988).

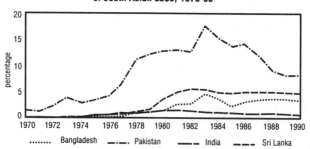

Figure 6. **Share of workers' remittances in gross domestic product of South Asian LECs, 1970-90**

Sources: Based on data from World Bank, World Tables 1990, ILO (1988).

Bangladesh Bank; cited from Mahmud 1989). The total share is most probably higher given that part of the Middle Eastern remittances (particularly those of professionals) are routed through Western financial centres (Mahmud 1989: 65). According to estimates by Nayyar (1989), remittances (from the sterling area) to India were predominantly from the United Kingdom up until the early 1970s. Afterwards remittances from the Middle East formed about two-thirds of the total amount during the period 1976-1977; the remaining one-third was divided into equal parts between the United Kingdom and Australia on the one hand and developing countries in East Africa and South Asia on the other.

The share of earned income which is saved and remitted varies with several factors, including a migrant's income and skill level, place of origin (urban or rural) and migration status (whether temporary or permanent). According to Kazi (1989), Pakistanis in the Middle East are target savers who migrate with the objective to accumulate a specific amount. On average they consume about 23 per cent of their monthly income while abroad (ILO/ARTEP 1987, Vol. II), remit about 46 per cent and save the difference. Professionals on average remit around 35 per cent of their income, semi-skilled workers 62.5 per cent if they come from rural, and 45.6 per cent if they come from urban regions, while unskilled workers from rural regions remit 54.4 per cent, and those from urban regions 46.6 per cent. The share of retained savings as distinct from remittances increases with income received abroad. Whereas Indian workers in the Gulf typically remit one-third to one-half of their income, highly educated Indians in the United States send home a much smaller share (Weiner 1985: 6). The value of the remittances by contrast could be larger in the case of permanent migrants since their salaries are higher than those of Middle Eastern migrants. In the case of Sri Lanka, a migrant of the higher income group sends about six times as much money home as an unskilled worker (ILO 1988: 9).

In Pakistan, Gilani *et al.* (1981) estimated that in the early 1980s 85 per cent of migrants used informal channels for remitting at least part of their earnings. The *Hundi* system is the most common among them (Kazi 1989). Here, the earned foreign exchange is transferred to the buyer in the host country, while the family at home receives the rupee counterpart. It offers more attractive exchange rates than on the official market and avoids administrative delays and formalities. Another part of the remittances is hand-carried and exchanged upon return. Also, sizeable amounts of consumer durables are transferred by returnees from abroad duty-free under the "Personal Baggage Scheme" or smuggled into the country, with the value of such goods estimated at 9-17 per cent of total home transfers. Bangladeshi migrants were found to send 25 per cent of their remittances through private intermediaries, friends and relatives (based on a survey conducted by Islam 1980).

Government Policies to Encourage Remittances Through Official Channels

A variety of measures have been adopted in South Asian countries to increase the total amount of remittances and to encourage migrants to send them through official channels. The Pakistani government considerably expanded the network of bank branches in the Middle East and in small towns and villages of Pakistan, and simplified banking procedures (Kazi 1989). Furthermore, the official exchange rate was made more attractive by delinking the rupee from the US dollar (Noman 1991: 77). Residents abroad were also allowed to open with banks in Pakistan transferable foreign currency accounts whose interest rates varied in line with international rates. The balance held in these accounts increased from $26 million in 1975 to $1 495 million in 1987 (State Bank of Pakistan; cited in Kazi 1989). Furthermore, in 1985, the government introduced Foreign Exchange Bearer certificates which can be cashed in foreign or domestic currency at any time; profits earned on these are free from income tax.

In Bangladesh, the main instrument to encourage the inflow of remittances through legal channels was the "Wage Earners' Scheme" (WES) introduced in 1974. It allows Bangladeshis living abroad to hold foreign currency accounts in domestic banks and to use them for importing specific goods, to travel abroad, or to sell them together with their special import licences at a market rate. In the late 1980s, the premium on foreign exchange sold under the WES as compared to foreign exchange from other sources was almost 10 per cent. The improvements of Bangladesh's offshore banking facilities have contributed to bring about a reversal from the situation where the black market rate of remitted foreign exchange was higher than under the WES scheme (Mahmud 1989). The anti-smuggling drive launched by the government of Bangladesh in 1986 is said to have increased the official flow of remittances, which increased from $50.7 million per month in November 1986 to $70.9 in March 1987 (Mahmud 1989). Informal remittances have diminished in importance as the banking links between Bangladesh and the Middle East have improved.

Although remittances in India have been important since the early 1950s, no explicit measures were taken to influence the inflow of remittances. As a result of a strict regime of import and exchange rate controls introduced in 1957, remittances of foreign exchange were channelled largely through unofficial brokers who used them for financing smuggling activities (Nayyar 1989). Also, over three decades, the import of consumer goods was discouraged, except for a few essential commodities such as foodgrains, edible oils and medicines. After the mid-1970s, official remittances increased due to several reasons. First, the numbers of migrants expanded enormously with the Middle East construction boom. Second, beginning in 1975/77, the government strongly enforced the laws against smuggling. Furthermore, over the period 1970-1984, India shifted from a regime of fixed exchange rates to one of managed floating and restrictions on imports were gradually removed. To encourage migrants to send their remittances through official channels, the government simplified banking procedures, extended its banking services abroad, and liberalised the foreign exchange regulations for non-resident Indians. All these measures helped to increase the flow of official remittances which in 1981 peaked at about $2.5 billion.

Government interventions to encourage official remittances have tended to favour the richer migrants. Persons of Indian origin living abroad are allowed to open external rupee and repatriable foreign currency non-resident accounts in US dollars or pounds sterling (Nayyar 1989). They are exempted from wealth tax on the deposits and the interest received on them. Furthermore, they receive higher interest rates than those given on comparable domestic deposits, and above those for comparable deposits in the capital markets of countries where non-resident Indians live. Between 1975/76, the net inflows on non-resident external rupee accounts increased from Rupees (Rs) 330 million to Rs 8 748 million, those on foreign currency non-resident accounts denominated in US dollars from Rs 66 million to Rs 12 885 million, and those on foreign currency non-resident accounts denominated in pounds sterling from Rs 9 million to Rs 344 million (Ministry of Finance, cited in Nayyar 1989: 110). The majority of persons who owned these accounts lived in the United States and the United Kingdom.

Analysis of Economic Impacts of Remittances

This section discusses the effect of remittances on sending country economies. It examines their impact on real exchange rates and on macro-aggregates such as real GDP and its sectoral components, and imports. A more complete presentation of results is contained in Knerr (1994). There is no quantitative estimation of the labour market impacts of out-migration, but the earlier discussion has suggested that they are rather small at national level, though localised impacts may be greater as may impacts on markets for certain types of skilled labour.

Spending Out of Remittances: The First Round

The impact of remittances on labour exporting South Asian economies is to a large extent determined by the way they are spent by migrants' families in the first round of expenditures. Thus, influencing that spending behaviour becomes a key policy objective.

Investment in land and housing are major spending categories in all countries considered. Kerala's migrants spend an estimated 31 per cent of their remittances for house construction, 19.3 per cent on the purchase of land, 7.3 per cent on jewellery, and 6.4 per cent on the education of their children. In Pakistan, almost two-thirds of migrants' remittances are used for consumption; another 22 per cent is invested in real estate, mostly construction or purchase of houses (based on data from Amjad 1989). The rest is largely used for industrial and commercial investment as returning migrants tend to open their own businesses. Although migrants' families spend part of their additional income on productive inputs like agricultural machinery, fertiliser, or repair services, non-farm activities in rural regions have not expanded as a result, largely because these goods are often produced in urban areas. Furthermore, the remittance-generated demand for labour increased more in urban sectors than in agriculture (de Kruijk and van Leeuwen 1985: 416).

Bangladesh's remittance-receiving households spend around 50 per cent of their income on consumption, half on food and drinks (Ali *et al.* 1981). The BIDS survey shows that migrants' families spend 22.3 per cent of their saved remittances on house building, 20.5 per cent on land purchases, and 6.3 per cent on business investment. The survey also shows that the family income of returned migrants tends to be lower than it was before migration due to a sharp decline of salary and wage income which is not compensated by increased income from other sources (like rents, interest or business income). Nevertheless, these families have maintained their higher standard of living, which would seem to suggest two conclusions: a) investment out of remittances does not lead to a long-term improvement of the family's income; and b) migrants' families live off their savings accumulated out of remittances.

Belonging to the lower income group, Sri Lanka's migrant families have a high propensity to spend their money on food. In 1985, food amounted to an estimated 57.6 per cent of their remittance expenditures. Out of the part which was saved, 14 per cent was spent on housing and 15.6 per cent on the purchase of land. Fixed deposits and business investment are allocated about 14 per cent each. One-third of remittances is estimated to be spent on imports (Rodrigo and Jayatissa 1989).

Governments have tried to influence migrants' spending behaviour through various instruments. The government of Pakistan has instituted facilities to direct remittances into more productive uses. For example, investments by overseas migrants can be effected within the framework of the Non-Repatriable Investment Scheme which allows imports of machinery at concessionary rates of duty. Investment by overseas Pakistanis within that scheme increased from Rs 157 million in 1977/78 to Rs 517 million in 1985/86. Migrants are also allowed to invest in export processing zones where machinery and raw materials can be imported duty-free, but this programme has not been successful in attracting migrants' funds. There are special import regulations for migrants who have been abroad for at least 2 years relating to motor vehicles and certain capital goods; also, they are permitted the duty-free importation of professional tools and equipment up to a value of Rs 5 000 (Kazi 1989). The government also provides incentives for the financial investment of remittances through programmes such as the Defence Saving Certificates and the Khaas Deposit Certificates which are issued to Pakistanis abroad against payment of foreign currency. These, however, have not been successful in attracting migrants' funds, largely as a result of lack of information, high rates of inflation, deduction of the *zakat*, and the long maturation period.

In India, by contrast, little is done to influence the use of remittances once they arrive in the country and are converted into rupees.

Remittances and Exchange Rates

Although it has been hypothesised that the real exchange rate is sensitive to remittances, there appears to be little empirical support for this relationship in South Asia[6]: in all countries, the real exchange rate shows a continuous upward trend independently of labour outflow or remittance inflow. In general, the exchange rate arrangements of LECs display considerably greater flexibility than those of other developing countries (based on IMF, Development of Exchange Rate Arrangements). All South Asian LECs have applied an exchange rate arrangement of managed floating as of the late 1980s, except for Bangladesh which maintained a dual exchange market, with an official rate pegged to a trade-weighted currency basket (based on IMF, Reports on Exchange Arrangements and Exchange Restrictions) but a flexible regime for workers' remittances within the WES. In all LECs there was a "black market" premium at least over a part of the period between 1970 and 1990 (IMF, Reports on Exchange Arrangements and Exchange Restrictions).

Response of Macro-Aggregates

Results of regressional[7] analysis indicates that in all South Asian LECs workers' remittances have had a significant positive effect on GDP growth. The example of India and Kerala state illustrates differences in impact between the national and regional levels. In Kerala, increasing international migration brought a rapid increase of per capita GNP, but per capita GDP in the state has grown at a slower rate than elsewhere in India (Nair 1988: 20). Moreover, in the districts with the highest incidence of migration, the growth rates of per capita domestic product are significantly below that of the whole state (Government of Kerala 1986: 22,28). One explanation may be that a substantial part of the additional demand generated by remittances has been met by imports from other regions. The out-migration of labour may also have been a supply-side factor limiting growth in local product.

The reaction of industrial production to remittance inflows is significantly more pronounced than that of manufactures alone, largely because the former includes the construction sector which receives a sizeable share of remittance expenditures. In Pakistan, for example, output in the construction sector increased at an average rate of 8.2 per cent per annum between 1976/77 and 1985/86, and the price index of building materials rose from 100 in 1975/76 to 217 in 1983/84 (against an increase of the general price index from 100 to 201) (Kazi 1988: 33). The service sector has also prospered during migration booms as trading and banking activities become increasingly important, though these branches also shrink rapidly once the boom is over. In Kerala state of India, the tertiary sector has experienced a substantial boom since the mid-1970s, mainly due to increasing demand for transport, trade, hotels and restaurants, banking and real estate. This expansion was the most pronounced in the districts with the highest incidence of migration[8]. The growth of the banking sector would have been even larger if a sizeable share of remittances had not been channelled into non-bank financial institutions (Nair 1988).

The agricultural sector in all the South Asian LECs has experienced growth effects from remittances considerably above the overall GDP growth effect. This is probably explained by the fact that agriculture faces a high income elasticity of demand in low-income South Asian countries and can draw on a large supply of cheap underemployed labour. Furthermore, there is a particularly high income elasticity of demand for the sector's non-tradeables, like fresh fruit, vegetables, and milk.

Imports also display a strong reaction to the inflow of remittances, and as a rule, show an elasticity which is more than twice that of domestic production, conforming to the expectations derived from theory. The import response is further enhanced by the growing trade liberalisation which has occurred during the migration boom period, perhaps partly because of reduced current account pressures. For example, the increased availability of remitted foreign exchange has induced the Pakistani government to liberalise imports, particularly of goods classified as non-essential (Burney 1989, Noman 1991: 88)[9]. Also, the government of India started to liberalise imports in the late 1970s, at a time when remittances were at their peak. Although no explicit trade policy measure has been taken in reaction to the inflow of remittances, without remittances it might have been difficult to sustain the pace of import liberalisation in the face of the balance-of-payments problems which surfaced and persisted during the first half of the 1980s (Nayyar 1989).

Conclusions

Since the early 1970s, the South Asian countries — India, Pakistan, Bangladesh and Sri Lanka — have been among the major labour exporting countries to the Middle East. While the outflow of labour appears to have had a marginal influence at the macro-level (except for Pakistan), the inflow of remittances has significantly influenced their economic development.

The preceding analysis suggests that labour export has generally stimulated economic growth in South Asia. As domestic resources could be mobilised to satisfy a share of the additional demand resulting from the migrants' remittances, particularly for non-tradeables, GDP has increased. Import demand has also grown with remittance inflows.

The effects of labour export on the domestic economy can be influenced by deliberate policy measures. To maximise the economic benefits of labour export, the policy response to a labour migration boom needs to focus on four issues: the process of out-migration, remittance inflows, remittance spending for consumption versus investment, and macroeconomic consequences of the out-migration process. In general, South Asian labour markets have responded flexibly to the outflow of workers, due to the high mobility of the domestic labour force and the active response of public education and training facilities.

A major objective in LEC's policy is to encourage migrants to send more remittances, particularly through official channels. Instruments to be used for that purpose are exchange rates, interest rates, and the development of the financial infrastructure. A devaluation of the domestic currency may increase official remittances, but the total amount may be only marginally affected: it may simply cause a shift from informal to official channels. Increasing interest rates may be more successful in this respect. Forms of co-operation with labour importing countries could also help increase the remitted share of migrants' income, but it is not always the case that the interests of labour importing countries coincide with those of LECs on this matter. While LECs would like to maximise the amount of remittances, labour importing countries may wish to hold migrant workers' financial savings within their domestic economy.

Given the low level of individual savings of migrants and their lack of entrepreneurial experience, it appears wiser to enhance migrants' financial investment rather than encourage them to put their investment into specific projects. Remittances deposited in banks can then be tapped by entrepreneurs for investment.

In order to avoid additional inflationary pressure, expansionary fiscal policy has to be reduced over the remittance boom, and money supply has to be controlled. Any policy which promotes higher domestic inflation would further weaken the competitiveness of domestically produced tradeables. While remittances can add to foreign exchange reserves, there is often a relatively high import propensity out of remittance income. Large remittance inflows may also encourage governments to proceed with import liberalisation.

Labour export is characterised by pronounced fluctuations. As private economic agents usually act in response to current situations, short-term price signals over boom periods may direct resources away from what would be the economy's long-run equilibrium. To avoid costly and time-consuming reallocations of resources, a far-sighted policy should try to maintain economic stability by an appropriate policy environment throughout the boom years. Other sources of foreign exchange should not be neglected over a remittance boom, and efforts to diversify exports should continue. Recapturing lost export markets by the re-establishment of marketing channels and the relearning of marketing know-how can be time-consuming and costly. Concerns about declining competitiveness of tradeables sectors due to "dutch disease-type" effects do not appear to be borne out by the analysis. In South Asian agriculture at least, there is little evidence of "dutch disease" symptoms, though the findings for manufacturing are more ambiguous.

The economic and political situation in (potential) host countries as well as in competing labour exporting countries should be closely monitored in any attempt by LECs to keep their out-migration comparative advantage. Countries that are most capable of diversifying the composition of their migrant outflows in terms of skills and countries of destination are the ones most likely to secure a niche in present and future foreign labour markets. Also, those LECs which have their labour export risk spread across different markets and skill categories are in a more favourable position to avoid wide fluctuations in remittance inflows.

For any effective migration planning, reliable data are required. Given the weaknesses of remittances-related data, more attention and work need to be given to appropriate data collection. Since the private household remains the main decision unit of out-migration, return migration, remittance inflow as well as first-round remittance spending, household surveys are likely to be an important data source. Extensive empirical micro-studies would also be necessary in any attempt to examine the micro-mechanisms by which the impact of labour export is transmitted to the rest of the economy. Once these mechanisms are understood there will be more scope for policies to maximise the benefits of migration both for the household and for the economy at large.

Notes

1. Contract migration includes wage and salary earners who are legally admitted for work in a foreign country for a specific period of time (Böhning 1984: 50).
2. The term *out-migrant* is used to express a person who leaves his country of origin; the term *in-migrant* a person who has moved to a country whose nationality he does not possess but without making any statement about the (expected) length of stay.
3. These packages refer to arrangements by which the successful bidder provides all the material and labour needed to carry out the project. Foreign workers employed in these projects often live in housing compounds provided by the company and are restricted in their movements and interaction with the country of employment. They are also obliged to leave as soon as the project is completed.
4. These results are based on a sample survey conducted in 1978-79 on 10 per cent of the officially recorded migrants.
5. Almost 30 per cent of the returnees with savings between 100 000 and 200 000 (Rupees) Rs were unemployed as compared to 17.5 per cent of those with savings of less than 25 000 Rs.
6. The method applied here for estimating real exchange rates purpose assumes that the countries considered effect all of their foreign trade with the United States, which of course is not the case but for the present purpose is considered as a satisfactory approximation. Estimation of the real effective exchange rate of a particular currency is a highly complex undertaking. Most often an indicator that measures the ratio of the price levels in the country considered to the weighted average of the price levels prevailing in its major trading partner countries is calculated for that purpose. Its accuracy is determined by the choice of the appropriate basket of goods to measure prices and price changes in each of these countries and the appropriate weighting of trading partners, which is particularly difficult if their trade shares vary considerably over time (see, e.g., Scherr 1989, and for more detail Maciejewski 1983).
7. See Knerr (1994) for details of the regression results.
8. These are the coastal districts Trichur, Malappuram, Kozikode, and Cannanore. The only exception is the capital Trivandrum where high rates of emigration coincide with comparatively high growth rates of the domestic product.
9. Migrants abroad may also trigger higher demand for exports from their home, especially for consumer goods. In Pakistan, for example, merchandise exports to the Middle East increased from 16 to 34 per cent of Pakistan's total exports between 1973 and 1983 largely due to the demand by Pakistani guestworkers for native goods such as rice and clothing. Such trade flows, however, remain marginal in comparison to remittance inflows (for India see, for example, Nayyar 1989:126; for Pakistan Noman 1991).

Bibliographical References

ABELLA, Manolo I. (1987), "Asian Labour Mobility", *The Pakistan Development Review* XXV (8).
AHMED, M. (1982), *Emigration and Scarce Skills in Pakistan*, Geneva.
ALI, Syed Ashraf *et al.* (1981), "Labour Migration from Bangladesh to the Middle East", World Bank Staff Working Paper Number 454, Washington.
ARNOLD, F. (1992), "The Contribution of Remittances to Economic and Social Development", in M. Kritz, L.L. Lim, and H. Slotnik, *International Migration Systems*, Oxford, pp. 205-220.
ATLAF, M.A. and OBAIDULLAH (1992), "The Spatial Pattern of International Labour Flows from and to Pakistan: A Preliminary Analysis", *Pakistan Development Review* 31(2), pp. 145-164.
BALTZLEN, Ch. (1994), "Agricultural Development in a Labour Exporting Economy. A Case Study of Kerala", Paper presented at the XXII International Conference of Agricultural Economists, Harare, August 22-29, 1994.
BANGLADESH BUREAU OF STATISTICS, *Statistical Yearbook of Bangladesh*, Dhaka, Various issues.
BANGLADESH INSTITUTE OF DEVELOPMENT STUDIES (BIDS) (1986), *Survey of Returned Migrants from the Middle East*, Dhaka.
BETZ, J. (1982), *Wirtschafts- und Entwicklungspolitik in Sri Lanka seit 1977*, Hamburg.
BÖHNING, W.R. (1984), *Studies in International Labour Migration*, London and Basingstoke.
BURNEY, N.A. (1989), "A Macro-Economic Analysis of the Impact of Workers' Remittances on Pakistan's Economy", in R. Amjad (Ed.), *To the Gulf and Back*, ILO/ARTEP, New Delhi.
DE KRUIJK, H. and M. VAN LEEUWEN, (1985), "Changes in Poverty and Income Inequality in Pakistan During the 1970s", *The Pakistan Development Review*, Vol. XXIV(3-4).
FEDERAL BUREAU OF STATISTICS PAKISTAN, *Statistical Yearbook of Pakistan*, Islamabad, Various issues.
GILANI, I., M. KHAN, and J. MANUWAR, (1981), "Labour Migration from Pakistan to the Middle East and its Impact on the Domestic Economy", A Report to the World Bank, South Asia Country Programs Department, Washington, D.C.
GOVERNMENT OF INDIA (1992), *Statistical Yearbook of India*, New Delhi, Various issues.

GOVERNMENT OF KERALA (1986), "Between 1970 and 1985, the number of motor vehicles in Kerala increased by nearly tenfold, that of three-wheelers by 25 times", *Economic Review*, State Planning Board, Trivandrum.

GOVERNMENT OF KERALA, Department of Economics and Statistics (1988), *Report of the Survey on the Utilization of Gulf Remittances in Kerala*, Trivandrum.

GOVERNMENT OF KERALA, State Planning Board (1990), *Economic Review 1990*, Thiruvananthapuram.

GOVERNMENT OF PAKISTAN, Ministry of Labour, Manpower and Overseas Pakistanis (Manpower and Overseas Pakistanis Division) (1990), *Report of the National Manpower Commission*, Islamabad.

GUISINGER, S. (1984), "The Impact of Temporary Workers' Migration on Pakistan", in S.J. Burki, and R. La Porte (Eds.), *Pakistan's Developing Priorities*, Oxford, Karachi.

ILO (1988), *International Labour Statistics*, 1988, Geneva.

ILO/ARTEP (1985), *Impact of Out and Return Migration on Domestic Employment in Sri Lanka: A Preliminary Analysis*, Geneva.

ILO/ARTEP (1987), *Impact of Out and Return Migration on Domestic Employment in Pakistan*, Volumes I to VII, New Delhi.

INTERNATIONAL LABOUR OFFICE (ILO)(1993), *World Labour Report*, Geneva.

INTERNATIONAL LABOUR ORGANIZATION (ILO)/United Nations Development Programme (UNDP) (1988) *Agenda for Policy*, Asian Migration Project, Geneva 1988.

INTERNATIONAL MONETARY FUND: *Development of Exchange Rates*, Washington, D.C., Various issues.

INTERNATIONAL MONETARY FUND (IMF), *International Financial Statistics Yearbook*, Washington, D.C., Various issues.

INTERNATIONAL MONETARY FUND (IMF), Report on Exchange Arrangements and Exchange Restrictions, Washington, D.C., Various issues.

IRFAN, M. and M.A. AHMED (1985), "Real Wages in Pakistan: Structure and Trends", *Pakistan Development Review*, Vol. XXIV, p. 428.

ISLAM, R. (1980), "Export of Manpower from Bangladesh to the Middle East Countries: The Impact of Remittance Money on Household Expenditure", mimeo, National Foundation for Research on Human Resource Development, Dhaka.

KAZI, S. (1988), "Domestic Impact of Remittances and Overseas Migration: Pakistan", ILO-UNDP Project, Working Paper No. 7, New Delhi.

KAZI, S. (1989), "Domestic Impact of Overseas Migration: Pakistan", in R. Amjad (Ed.), *To the Gulf and Back*, New Delhi.

KHAN, A.R. and J. E. LEE, (Eds.) (1984): *Poverty in Rural Asia*, Bangkok.

KHAN, Q.M. (1985), "A Model of Endowment-Constrained Demand for Food in an Agricultural Economy with Empirical Application to Bangladesh", *World Development* 13, pp. 1055-1066.

KIBRIA, M.G. and C.A. TISDELL (1985), "Productivity, Progress and Learning: The Case of Jute Spinning in Bangladesh", *World Development* 13, pp. 1151-1162.

KNERR, B. (1989), "Labour Emigration and Its Effects on the Economies of South Asia", *Internationales Asienforum, International Quarterly for Asian Studies* Vol. 20 (3-4): 263-293.

KNERR, B. (1990a), "Labour Export from South Asia: Another Case of the 'Dutch Disease'?", in Georgio Borsa (Ed.), *The Indian Ocean*, New Delhi, pp. 248-315.

KNERR, B. (1990b), "Effects of International Labour Migration on the Economic Growth of Bangladesh", in Marc Homström, (Ed.), *Work for Wages in South Asia*, New Delhi, Manohar, pp. 118-159.

KNERR, B. (1990c), "South Asian Countries as Competitors on the World Labour Market", in Clarke, C. et al. (Eds.), *South Asians Overseas: Contexts and Communities*, Oxford, pp. 173-196.

KNERR, B. (1992), "Agricultural Policies and Tropical Forest", in M. Bellamy, and B. Greenschields, (Eds.), *Issues in Agricultural Development, Sustainability and Cooperation*, Aldershot (UK) and Brookfield (USA).

KORALE, R.B.M. (1983), *Migration for Employment to the Middle East: Its Demographic and Socio-Economic Effects on Sri Lanka*, Ministry of Plan Implementation, Colombo.

LA PORTE, R. (1984), "The Ability of South and East Asia to Meet the Labour Demands of the Middle East and North Africa", *The Middle East Journal* 38 (4), pp. 699-711.

LING, L.M.-M. (1984), "East Asian Migration to the Middle East: Causes, Consequences and Considerations", *International Migration Review*, Vol. 18, pp. 19-36.

MACIEJEWSKI, Edouard B. (1983), "'Real' Effective Exchange Rate Indices: A Re-examination of the Major Conceptual and Methodological Issues", *International Monetary Fund Staff Papers*, Vol. 30 (3), pp. 491-539.

MAHMOOD, R.A. (1986), *Bangladeshi Labour Migration to the Middle East: Past Trends and Future Prospects* (mimeo), Dhaka, BIDS.

MAHMUD, W. (1988), "The Impact of Overseas Labour Migration on the Bangladesh Economy: A Macroeconomic Perspective", Asian Regional Programme on International Labour Migration, Working Paper No. 5, New Delhi.

MAHMUD, W. (1989), "The Impact of Overseas Labour Migration on the Bangladesh Economy", in Rashid Amjad, (Ed.), *To the Gulf and Back*, International Labour Office (ILO/ARTEP), New Delhi.

MARGA INSTITUTE (1986), *Migrant Workers to the Arab World*, Colombo.

MATHEWS, S. (1983), "Letter from Kerala", *Far Eastern Economic Review*.

MINISTRY OF PLAN IMPLEMENTATION (MPI) (1985), *Dimensions of Sri Lankan Return Migration*, Colombo.

NAIR, P.R.G. (1988), "Incidence, Impact and Implications of Migration to the Middle East from Kerala (India)", ILO-UNDP Project Working Paper No. 12, New Delhi.

NAIR, P.R.G. (1989) "Incidence, Impact and Implications of Migration to the Middle East from Kerala (India)" in R. Amjad (Ed.), *To the Gulf and Back*, New Delhi.

NAYYAR, D. (1987), "International Labour Migration from India: A Macro-Economic Analysis", Asian Employment Programme (IL0/ARTEP) Working Paper No. 3, New Delhi.

NAYYAR, D. (1989), "International Migration from India: A Macro-Economic Analysis, in R. Amjad (Ed.), *To the Gulf and Back*, Geneva.

NOMAN, Omar (1991), "The Impact of Migration on Pakistan's Economy and Society", in Hastings Donnan and Pinna Webner (Eds.), *Economy and Culture in Pakistan*, Basingstoke and London.

PAKISTAN CENSUS ORGANISATION, Census 1981.

PAPADEMETRIOU, Demetrios G. (1988), "International Migration in North America and Western Europe", in Charles Stahl (Ed.), *International Migration Today*, Vol. I, *Trends and Prospects*, UNESCO, Gembloux, Belgium.

RODRIGO, Ch. and R.A. JAYATISSA (1989), "Maximizing Benefits from Labour Migration: Sri Lanka", in R. Amjad, (Ed.), *To the Gulf and Back*, New Delhi.

SCHERR, Sara J. (1989), "Agriculture in an Export Boom Economy: A Comparative Analysis of Policy and Performance in Indonesia, Mexico and Nigeria", *World Development* 17(4), pp. 543-560.

SERAGELDIN, I. *et al.* (1983), *Manpower and International Migration in the Middle East and North Africa*, Oxford.

UNITED NATIONS DEVELOPMENT PROGRAMME (UNDP) (1993), *Human Development Report 1993*, New York, Oxford.

UNITED STATES (US) IMMIGRATION AND NATURALIZATION SERVICE (1979), *Annual Report*, Washington, D.C.

WEINER (1985), "International Migration and International Relations", *Population and Development Review*, p. 9.

WORLD BANK (1985), *Bangladesh, Economic and Social Development Prospects* (in four volumes), Washington, D.C.

PART IV

TRADE LIBERALISATION, ECONOMIC GROWTH AND MIGRATION HUMPS

Trade and Migration: the Case of NAFTA

by Philip Martin*

Summary

The North American Free Trade Agreement (NAFTA) represents the first time a free trade area has linked two countries whose primary historic linkage has been through labour migration. While the trade, investment and employment expansion engendered by the agreement could be expected in the long run to diminish migratory flows from Mexico to the United States, the short-run effect is likely to be a "migration hump", i.e. a temporary increase in migration above trend. Both supply-push and demand-pull factors — some but not all associated with NAFTA — appear to favour an increase in south-north migration, and the cross-border networks formed through past migration should facilitate increased short-term flows.

The major supply-push factor is likely to be the expected decline in the Mexican maize sector (and in the incomes of maize farmers) when confronted by cheaper US imports. A major demand-pull factor will be the continued expansion of labour-intensive crop production in the United States, notably fruit and vegetables, not only to meet local demand but possibly to export to Mexico. Demand for unskilled immigrant labour has spread beyond the sunbelt of California, Texas and Florida to the midwest and southeast, and beyond agriculture to construction and low-skill services. Also, the Immigration Reform and Control Act (IRCA) of 1986 resulted in a large surge in the number of legal Mexican immigrants, thereby expanding the network of cross-border family and other connections which should smooth paths for other would-be immigrants. Finally, in the short run, the steep devaluation of the Mexican peso could be expected to increase incentives to migrate, quite apart from any adverse effects on Mexican growth.

* Department of Economics, University of California-Davis

Introduction

The major linkage between the United States and Mexico during most of the 20th century has been migration of Mexican workers to US labour markets. This migration is increasingly controversial, as exemplified by the approval of Proposition 187 in California in November 1994[1]. Thus, one hoped-for effect of the North American Free Trade Agreement (NAFTA), which went into effect on 1 January 1994, is that the employment and wage growth it stimulates in Mexico will eventually reduce emigration pressures there.

Migration, however, played only a background role during the Congressional debate over whether NAFTA should be ratified[2]. This was primarily because the migration message from researchers could be used by both opponents and proponents of NAFTA. The consensus among experts was that NAFTA would contribute to an initial increase in Mexico-to-US migration, and decrease the cross border flow after a decade or more (Martin, 1993). NAFTA proponents, who took a long-run perspective, argued that the prospect of eventually reduced migration was an argument in favour of NAFTA, while some NAFTA opponents opposed the agreement because of the predicted short-run migration hump.

This paper traces the likely adjustment path of Mexico-to-US migration under NAFTA. Its major conclusion is that unilateral policies in both the United States and Mexico, plus NAFTA, are likely to have a hump effect on Mexico-to-US migration, first increasing and only later decreasing it. The major policy implication of this analysis is that the same economic and trade policies that make migration controls less necessary in the long run make them more necessary in the short run. In other words, reluctant countries of immigration that hope to reduce immigration by freeing up trade must prepare their publics not only for the potential loss of some industrial jobs; they must also prepare residents for temporarily larger migration. In the case of NAFTA, the migration hump seems to be a worthwhile price to pay to deal with one of the world's major migration linkages, but migration was handled badly in making the case for ratification[3].

Many observers expected Mexico-to-US migration to begin to decrease as soon as the North American Free Trade Agreement (NAFTA) was signed. Then Mexican President Carlos Salinas de Gortari explained the relationship between NAFTA and migration in this way: "Today, Mexicans have to migrate to where jobs are being created, the northern part of our country. With NAFTA, employment opportunities will move toward where the people live, reducing drastically migration, within the country and outside of the country." (quoted in the *San Diego Tribune*, November 14, 1993, 1)[4]. Just before the US Congressional vote on whether to ratify NAFTA, Attorney General Janet Reno echoed Salinas, asserting that "We will not reduce the flow of illegal immigration until these immigrants can find decent jobs at decent wages in Mexico" (quoted in the *San Diego Tribune*, November 14, 1993, 1).

The purpose of NAFTA is to promote the free flow of goods and capital and thereby to stimulate economic and job growth in Mexico, the United States, and Canada. Trade-stimulated economic growth should also reduce emigration from Mexico: the US Commission for the Study of International Migration and Cooperative Economic Development looked for "mutually beneficial, reciprocal trade and investment programmes" to reduce unauthorised migration from Mexico and concluded that "*expanded trade* between the sending countries and the United States *is the single most important remedy*" for unauthorised immigration (1990, p. xv, emphasis added).

However, the Commission warned that "the economic development process itself tends in the short to medium term to stimulate migration." Policies that accelerate economic growth, including privatisation, land reform, and freer trade, produce a migration hump, or temporarily greater migration, creating "a very real short-term versus long-term dilemma" for a country such as the United States that wants to use free trade agreements as one means to curb unauthorised immigration (US Commission, 1990, p. xvi). Accelerating development should eventually reduce unwanted migration, but "the development solution to unauthorised migration is measured in decades — even generations" (US Commission, 1990, p. xxxvi).

Migration humps, or temporary increases in emigration during a country's economic take-off, are not new phenomena. The 48 million Europeans who emigrated from Europe between 1850 and 1925 represented about one-eighth of Europe's population in 1900, suggesting that "large scale emigration was quite common during Europe's period of industrialisation" (Massey, 1988, p. 17). When southern European nations such as Italy and Spain industrialised and took the first steps toward integrating into what became the European Union (EU), they too were characterised by significant emigration pressures. However, economic gaps narrowed enough during the 6- to 10-year wait for labour mobility that, when Italians or Spaniards were permitted to search freely for jobs throughout the EU, few did (Staubhaar, 1988; 1992).

Migration humps are also visible in Asia. Korea, for example, sent over 200 000 migrant workers to the Middle East in 1982 but, by 1992, there were an estimated 100 000 foreign workers in the country and employer pleas for more (Park, 1994). Fast-growing countries such as Malaysia and Thailand both export and import unskilled, skilled, and professional labour. In Malaysia's case, Chinese Malaysians are construction workers in Chinese Taipei, and Indonesians immigrate to Malaysian construction sites for jobs.

Temporarily larger emigration — a migration hump — is a usual part of the process of economic development when industrialisation occurs in a country that satisfies one or more of three conditions: an emigration tradition, established networks that allow nationals to defy immigration controls and enter another country, or programmes for recruitment of migrant workers. Mexico satisfies the first two of these conditions, a result in part of past programmes that recruited Mexican workers for US jobs.

The volume of Mexico-to-US migration is significant. Mexico sent 3 million immigrants to the United States during the past 12 years, equivalent to 20 per cent of Mexico's net population growth, and 35 per cent of legal US immigration (Figure 1). Most of these Mexicans were "illegal aliens" before they became legal immigrants. When many of them were acknowledged to be legal immigrants in 1991, official immigration from Mexico topped immigration from all other countries.

NAFTA will provide a test case of how freer trade and investment can affect an established migration linkage. Mexico has adopted internal privatisation and deregulation policies, and joined multilateral organisations that promote open economies, such as GATT in 1986 and NAFTA and OECD in 1994. Although the two C's that shook Mexico in 1994 — the uprising in Chiapas and the assassination of PRI Presidential candidate Colosio — have led some observers to assert that "anything can happen" in Mexico, most believe that Mexico is committed to an open and market-oriented economy.

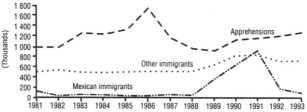

Figure 1. **Mexican, other immigrants and apprehensions, 1981-93**

While it is relatively easy to project a short-term increase in Mexico-to-US migration because of NAFTA, it is very hard to anticipate how much more migration there may be and how long any incremental migration due to NAFTA might persist. Nineteenth century European emigration involved over 10 per cent of the population, and persisted for decades. In the case of southern Europe and Asia, migration humps involved less than 10 per cent of the population and lasted less than two decades.

The uncertainties in projecting the Mexican migration hump emanate from the difficulty of projecting Mexico's economic growth path in the 1990s. Mexico has changed her economic policies, and the combination of NAFTA and a growing world economy may permit Mexico to experience rapid 1960s Italian-style or 1980s Korean-style growth. However, economic development in Mexico could evolve as it did in Puerto Rico, where investment from the US mainland created a handful of high-paying jobs, but did not stop US-bound migration.

The best analyses of NAFTA's likely effects caution that Mexico's economic growth prospects depend on many variables, including Mexico's ability to maintain stable fiscal and monetary policies and a continued expansion of world trade (Hufbauer and Schott, 1992, pp. 332-343). The current outlook is mixed: the January 1994 uprising in the southern state of Chiapas (Harvey *et al*, 1994) reminded everyone of the inequalities within the country, and the assassination of PRI Presidential candidate Colosio in March 1994 highlighted the fact that Mexico remains practically a one-party state.

Mexico's economy shrank during the last two quarters of 1993 and, by one estimate, over $8 billion left Mexico during the first quarter of 1994 because of recession and a possible devaluation. However, growth resumed in 1994, though the prospects for 1995 are clouded by the recent "peso crisis". The Mexican government expects Direct Foreign Investment (DFI) to continue increasing — it rose by 24 per cent in 1994 to $6.1 billion, but 85 per cent of the foreign investments in Mexico continue to pour into stocks and bonds, and such funds can exit the country quickly (as during the first few months of 1995).

If Mexico grows at 3 to 5 per cent annually during the rest of the 1990s, how will potential US-bound migrants respond? Nothing changed on January 1, 1994 for most Mexicans. However, more Mexicans can be expected to enter the United States as a result of faster labour displacement in rural Mexico, the continued opportunity to find jobs in the United States, and networks established over the past century that can bridge the border despite US immigration controls.

NAFTA, Labour, and Migration

NAFTA brought together three different countries in the world's largest free trade area. Canada and the United States have similar GNPs per capita, but their per capita GNP and population growth rates have diverged since 1985 — Canada has experienced very slow economic growth and relatively fast population growth compared to the United States. Mexico, in comparison to the United States, had the same real per capita GNP growth rate of 1.1 per cent per year, but its population grew at twice the US rate (see Table 1).

Table 1. **Canada, Mexico, and the United States (1992)**
GDP per Capita

	GNP ($ billion)	GNP Per Capita	Ratio US=1	Real Growth Rate (1985-92)	Population (million)	Population Growth Rate (1985-92)
Canada	566	20 320	0.9	0.3	27.8	1.4
Mexico	295	3 470	0.2	1.1	85	1.8
US	5 905	23 120	1.0	1.1	255.4	0.9
Total	6 766				368	

Source: The World Bank Atlas 1994.

In an unexpected move, Mexico's President Carlos Salinas de Gortari in May 1990 announced his support for a free trade agreement with the United States — reportedly after a tour of Europe convinced him that European capital was going to flow to Eastern Europe rather than to newly-opened Mexico. On September 21, 1990, Salinas formally requested negotiations, and President Bush notified Congress on September 25, 1990 that the United States intended to negotiate a free trade agreement with Mexico. On May 17-18, 1991, Congress failed to deny Bush the authority to negotiate a FTA with Mexico. Negotiations began on June 12, 1991, and the US Congress voted to approve NAFTA in November 1993.

NAFTA is based on four principles (Grayson, 1993, p. 39):

— The elimination of tariff and nontariff barriers to trade between Canada, Mexico, and the United States;

— Equal treatment in each country for all goods and services produced in North America;

— A commitment not to erect new obstacles to trade after NAFTA is signed;

— A commitment to extend to NAFTA partners any special trade preferences any of the three countries makes available to non-NAFTA countries.

According to Grayson (1993, p. 41), it was relatively easy to reach agreement on reducing tariff and nontariff barriers, on safeguards to deal with import surges, and on land transportation issues, such as the right of US drivers to deliver goods inside Mexico (and vice versa). However, the longest list of subjects was in the relatively difficult to agree on category: rules of origin, government procurement, energy subsidies, financial and insurance services, agriculture, investment, and automobiles.

NAFTA's Economic Effects

The major economic effect of NAFTA should be to stimulate the flow of investment, goods, and services across North American borders. There were more than 50 models that projected the effects of NAFTA on the economies and labour markets of Canada, Mexico, and the United States. Most emphasized that NAFTA would primarily affect the relationship between the United States and Mexico, because the United States and Canada are more similar economies that have had a free trade agreement since 1989. However, the economic effects of NAFTA in the United States were projected to be small, both because the Mexican economy is only 1/20 the size of the US economy and because tariffs are already low — the average US tariff on Mexican imports in 1991 was 4 per cent, and the average Mexican tariff on US imports was 10 per cent.

Most of the models that simulated the effects of NAFTA reached the conclusion that Mexico would be the agreement's major economic "winner." According to the US International Trade Commission:

— Trade between the three economies should rise, and this should increase the GDP of each country as firms are forced to compete harder and because costs of production may fall as firms produce for a larger market. According to the International Trade Commission, Mexico's real GDP could rise by 0.1 to 11.4 per cent because of NAFTA, and the US and Canadian GDPs might rise by up to 0.5 per cent.

— All three economies should gain jobs and see wages rise as a result of NAFTA. The ITC projected a 7 per cent employment gain due to NAFTA in Mexico and up to 1 per cent employment gains for the United States and Canada. Real wages in Mexico might rise 0.7 to 16.2 per cent because of NAFTA, but less than 0.5 per cent in the United States and Canada.

NAFTA should have these economic effects in Mexico because it is expected to accelerate the flow of foreign capital to Mexico, as foreign investors move labour-intensive operations there to obtain easy access to the North American market. Mexico could, in this development-with-foreign-investment scenario, run a trade deficit for years as foreign investors build up the country's productive capacity and infrastructure, much as the United States did in the late 19th century and South Korea did in the 1960s and 1970s.

NAFTA's Migration Effects

The major economic relationship between the United States and Mexico has been the bi-national labour market created when Mexican workers find US jobs. The number of additional Mexicans who find US jobs each year — 150 000 to 200 000 — and the number who work seasonally in the United States — 1 to 3 million — dwarf even the most optimistic estimates of job gains in Mexico due to NAFTA, such as the 60 000 additional Mexican jobs per year that Hufbauer and Schott have projected (1992, p. 57).

Both migration and NAFTA job projection numbers are "soft," so that trying to determine the effect of NAFTA on labour migration is, at best, a very inexact science. There are several types of Mexico-to-US migrants — legal immigrants, non-immigrants, and unauthorised migrants. History shows that people can be shuffled between these US categories by policy changes: "Operation Wetback" in 1954, for example, converted illegal aliens into legal non-immigrants (Braceros), while the end of the Bracero programme in 1964 was followed by a US policy that allowed US employers to issue offers of employment to Mexicans that enabled them to become permanent immigrants (Martin, 1993, Chapter 3). It makes more sense, in other words, to estimate the effects of an agreement such as NAFTA on the total flow of Mexicans to the United States rather than on various sub-categories of Mexican immigrants, since often-changing US policies direct the flow into different sub-categories (Box 1).

Box 1. Types of Mexico-to-US Migration

Mexico was sending about 10 per cent of the 600 000 immigrants to the United States in the mid-1980s. Mexico's share as well as total immigration jumped sharply in the early 1990s as a consequence of mid-1980s programmes that permitted some illegal aliens to become immigrants and revisions to the migration system in 1990.

The few migration provisions in NAFTA are similar to those of the US-Canadian Free Trade Agreement of 1988. They permit four categories of "business persons" to enter the United States, Canada, and Mexico on a reciprocal basis[5], but they limit the number of Mexican professionals allowed to work temporarily in the United States to 5 500 annually. Mexican professionals, unlike Canadians, receive NAFTA-TN visas only after their US employer (1) files a Labour Condition Attestation (LCA) with the US Department of Labour which certifies that the employer tried and failed to attract American workers at prevailing wages for the vacant job; (2) files a petition with the INS that demonstrates that the Mexican alien has professional qualifications, generally a BS degree or more; and (3) the alien then applies at a US consulate in Mexico for a TN temporary employment visa to work in the United States. US employers do not have to file LCAs for Canadian professionals, they do not require visas to enter the United States, and there is no numerical limit on how many may enter.

Illegal immigration has generally exceeded legal immigration from Mexico, but NAFTA does not include provisions that deal with the unauthorised entry of 1.5 to 2 million Mexicans annually, including 150 000 to 200 000 who are believed to settle every year in the United States[6].

Between 1982 and 1992, about 3 million Mexicans were recognised as legally present in the United States, making the flow of Mexicans to the United States the largest migration relationship in the world. Most of these Mexican immigrants were in the United States illegally, and then had their status regularised. About two-thirds of these Mexican immigrants are believed to be in the US labour force.

How will NAFTA affect the net annual addition of at least 200 000 Mexican workers to the US workforce? There are a variety of models and methodologies, and all agree that there will be substantial Mexico-to-US migration in the 1990s. Indeed, most of the migration models that consider NAFTA expect the agreement to *increase* the flow of Mexicans to the United States. This migration hump scenario anticipates that the free trade in agricultural products envisioned by NAFTA will displace Mexican farmers, who have a tradition of migrating to the United States.

The projections summarised in Table 2 mix together legal and illegal migration, gross and net migration flows, workers and dependents, migration due to NAFTA versus migration due to other factors, and different time periods. All suggest substantial Mexico-to-US migration in the 1990s.

The most widely-cited projection of NAFTA's effects on Mexico-to-US migration is that of Hinojosa and Robinson (1991a). Using a CGE model of the US and Mexican economies and labour markets, and then projecting how freer trade might affect Mexican agriculture, they estimate that NAFTA could displace about 1.4 million rural Mexicans, largely due to changes in Mexican farm policies and freer trade in agricultural products.

If jobs are not created for these displaced farmers in the areas where they live — and few observers expect a significant number of "real" jobs to be created in these rural areas — they are expected to migrate internally and externally. Hinojosa and Robinson project that 800 000 could stay in Mexico, and that 600 000 could migrate (illegally) to the United States. These 600 000 additional US-bound migrants — say 100 000 per year over 6 years — are presumably NAFTA-caused additions to the "normal" flow of legal and illegal Mexican worker arrivals.

Espenshade developed estimates of unauthorised Mexican migration based on apprehensions. The key assumption in his analysis is that the probability of being apprehended when a Mexican attempts illegal entry is 0.3. This suggests that on 7 of 10 occasions, an alien eludes the US Border Patrol — so that the relationship between the number of apprehensions and the undocumented flow is 0.3/0.7. Multiplying this ratio times the undocumented flow yields the number of apprehensions. Since apprehensions are known, the estimated undocumented flow is apprehensions times (7/3) or 2.33 (Acevedo and Espenshade, 1992, p. 739). Apprehensions in 1991 and 1992 were about 1.2 million annually, suggesting that there were 2.8 million gross or one-way illegal entries in those years[7].

The baseline level of illegal immigration — the flow in 1987-88 — was estimated by Espenshade to be 2 million annually[8]. At that time, the US unemployment rate for men was 1.6 times *higher* than the Mexican rate for urban workers who had lost formal sector jobs, and US wages were 7.2 times Mexican wages (Acevedo and Espenshade, 1992, p. 737). Espenshade asked what would happen to the estimated flow of illegal Mexican immigrants if wages in Mexico were to rise and/or unemployment to fall relative to US rates. For example, if the

Table 2. **Projections of Mexico-to-US Migration in the 1990s**

Source	Migration Projection	Period	Annual Worker Migration	Methodology	Reason for Migration
1. Demographic Models					
Garcia y Griego	200 500 - 500 000	1995-2000 (5 years)	n/a	Regional Demographic Model	Demography
World Bank	750 000 - 900 000 Mexico to US	1995-2000 (5 years)	n/a	Trend Projection	Demography
Acevedo and Espenshade (1992) (workers)	1.1 to 2.9 million gross undocumented Mexico to US flow	Annual flow	1.1 to 2.9 million	Change from estimated baseline flow due to changing wages and unemployment ratios	Response in base flow due to relative labour market changes
2. CGE Models					
Hinojosa-McCleery (1992) (workers)	Average stock of 0 to 5.5 million unauthorised Mexicans in the US	1986-2000	n/a	Dynamic CGE model	NAFTA and US and Mexican policies
Levy and van Wijnbergen (1992a) (workers)	700 000 displaced from agriculture due to trade liberalisation	1 to 9 years	78 000	Dynamic CGE (Mexico only)	NAFTA and other trade liberalisation policies
Robinson et al. (1991) (workers)	800 000 rural-urban migrants in Mexico; 600 000 migrants to US	1994-2000 (6 years)	100 000	Comparative Statics CGE	NAFTA and other Mexican policies
3. Other Projections					
Calva (1991)	15 million displaced from Mexican agriculture	1990-2000 (10-years)	n/a	Various	NAFTA and other Mexican policies
Tellez (1992)	Annual exit of 1 million from Mexican agriculture	1992-2002	n/a	Various	NAFTA and other Mexican policies

Source: See text.

Mexican unemployment rate fell 30 per cent relative to the US rate, Espenshade projected that unauthorised Mexican entries would fall by almost 10 per cent to 1.8 million annually[9]. A 50 per cent fall in the unemployment rate would reduce entries by 20 per cent to 1.6 million (Acevedo and Espenshade, 1992, p. 738).

Both Hinojosa and McCleery (1992) and Levy and van Wijnbergen (1992) focused on the likely effects of NAFTA on trade in maize (corn) and production and employment in Mexico's countryside — the "smoking gun" in the NAFTA and migration story. The basic facts are straightforward. Between 30 and 50 per cent of all days worked in rural Mexico are devoted to production of corn and beans. US farmers can produce both crops more cheaply than Mexican farmers — the US corn price of $95 per ton early in 1994 is less than half the Mexican price of $205 per ton. Liberalising trade in corn (as NAFTA does over 15 years) is expected to shift North America's corn production northward, at US prices throughout the continent since Iowa alone produces twice as much corn as Mexico. Mexican corn farmers discouraged by the prospect of lower corn prices, this argument runs, will have to leave their often remote villages, and well-trodden pathways will bring at least some to the United States.

Some have suggested that trade liberalisation in corn should be slowed in order to prevent a migration hump — what would be good for Iowa farmers, this argument runs, would be bad for unskilled workers in Los Angeles, so that Mexico, the primary beneficiary for NAFTA, would have to take US opposition to immigration into account when it modified its agricultural policies in anticipation of NAFTA. While there is some truth in the general point, the previous Mexican government was concerned about the total cost of corn subsidies that were benefiting only a fraction of the neediest corn farmers: in order to obtain the government-guaranteed corn price, the crop had to be delivered to a government agency — CONASUPO — and many corn growers were too far from a CONASUPO outlet, or produced corn only for their own subsistence, so that they did not benefit from what was proving to be an expensive subsidy.

The Salinas government took several steps that are expected to transform rural Mexico in the 1990s, complicating the search for a NAFTA effect on US-bound migration. First, in 1992 the Mexican Constitution was amended to permit the ejiodos that farm about 70 per cent of Mexico's crop land and half of its irrigated land in a communal fashion to sell or rent their parcels[10]. In 1993, Mexico began to switch from supporting farmers by buying their corn at high prices to providing them with direct income payments instead. Finally, Mexico has since 1987 been reducing subsidies for the electricity, water, fertiliser, and credit used by farmers.

These policy changes amount to a revolution in Mexican government policies toward the one-third of the population in rural areas. Their net effect will undoubtedly be to promote emigration from rural Mexico. Although no one knows how many people will leave rural Mexico during its expected "great migration" of the 1990s, many echo Luis Tellez, the former Undersecretary for Planning in Mexico's Ministry of Agriculture and Hydraulic Resources, who suggested on several occasions that Mexico's rural population might shrink by 1 million annually, that up to 15 million rural Mexicans may migrate "within a decade or two" (Golden, 1991, p. A1)[11]. This great migration should improve the allocation of Mexican resources — Tellez frequently reminds audiences that 27 per cent of the Mexican population depends on agriculture for a living, but this sector generates only 9 per cent of GDP, and for this reason includes two-thirds of Mexico's poor people[12].

In his final state-of-the-nation address in November 1994, Mexican President Salinas condemned the approval of Proposition 187 in California, a state law approved 59 to 41 per cent by voters on November 8 that, if implemented, would establish a state-run eligibility screen to prevent unauthorised aliens from attending public schools or receiving most health and other services. According to Salinas, the movement of Mexican workers to the US "is inevitable, and it is better to order and regulate it than to confront it with administrative measures that are not going to stop it because the force of the economies is greater."

Deputy Foreign Minister Rozenthal predicted that, as North America integrates economically under NAFTA, "immigration is going to be the No. 1 issue between the US and Mexico for the next several years." However, it is not clear whether the immigration issue is going to be dealt with by negotiating a bilateral foreign worker programme, attempting to slow displacing changes in Mexico, and/or toughening enforcement efforts in the United States.

Mexican President Zedillo has promised to step up efforts to protect Mexican citizens living in the United States. Each of Mexico's 53 consulates in the United States has a person who receives and investigates complaints that the rights of Mexican nationals in the US have been violated. It is not yet clear whether Mexico will push for a bilateral foreign worker programme.

Mexican Migration to the United States

Mexican migration to the United States has its roots in development patterns on both sides of the border that have evolved over the past century. The southwestern United States was a part of Mexico until 1847 when, as a result of war, the United States absorbed what are today states from Texas to California. The southwestern economy began to boom in the second half of the 19th century, and it developed an enormous appetite for unskilled workers willing to work for low wages. Many of these workers were needed only seasonally, and US farms, railroads, and mines became dependent on recently- arrived immigrants who were willing to accept intermittent employment at low wages. Business decisions were soon being made under the assumption that immigrant workers would be available when they were needed — and paid low wages for that time — helping to explain why US employers for decades resisted restrictions on Mexican immigration[13].

Immigrants altered prices in the southwestern economy in a manner that made US employers favour continuing immigration. A California farm spokesman in 1872 observed that hiring Chinese immigrants who housed themselves and then "melted away" when they were not needed made them "more efficient ... than Negro labour in the South (because) it (Chinese labour) is only employed when actually needed, and is, therefore, less expensive" than slavery (Quoted in Fuller, 1942, p. 19809)[14].

The subsidy implicit in low farm wages was soon reflected in higher land prices, giving farmers an incentive to preserve access to immigrant workers and thus maintain higher land prices. California farmers, for example, tried to have the Chinese Exclusion Act of 1882 repealed, noting that land was worth $200 to

$300 per acre in 1888 for fruit production, where the wages paid to Chinese workers were $1.00 to $1.25 per day. Land used to produce grain and hay, by contrast, was worth only $25 to $50 per acre, and the wage paid to white workers on these farms was $2.00 to $3.00 daily (Fuller, 1942, p. 19816).

Development patterns in Mexico contributed to the willingness of Mexicans to emigrate. The seven central states of Mexico — Nuevo Leon, Tamaulipas, Zacatecas, San Luis Potosi, Guanajuato, Jalisco, and Michoacan — contributed over half of all migrants to the United States for most of the 20th century (Cross and Sandos, 1981, p. xvi). In these states, the hacienda system relied on permanent and temporary workers to work on farm estates. During the Mexican Revolution (1913-1920), these states became the battleground between the central government in Mexico City and revolutionaries from Mexican states near the US border, and the fighting led most haciendas to reduce their employment of permanent and seasonal workers. As a result, many Mexicans left. Between 1910 and 1930, by one estimate, 20 per cent of the population left the region, including 1.5 million (10 per cent of Mexico's entire population) who migrated to the United States (Cross and Sandos, 1981, pp. 9-10).

In the spring of 1942, California farmers predicted that there would be labour shortages for the fall harvest, and they called for the importation of between 40 000 and 100 000 Mexican farm workers — Braceros — in September. Farmers won the right to import Braceros by arguing that crop losses caused by labour shortages would hamper the war effort, and 1 500 Mexican farm workers were brought to California in September 1942.

The Bracero programme brought 5 million rural Mexicans "legally" to the rural USA over two decades in an "unprecedented experiment in inter-American labour migration" (Craig, 1971, p. 51). Many Braceros returned year-after-year, so that an estimated 1 to 2 million individuals participated, but the Bracero programme also deepened the dependence of US farmers on a workforce with no other US job options, and institutionalised the dependence of many rural Mexicans on the US labour market. Over the 22 year life of the programme, there were more Mexican workers apprehended in the United States illegally than admitted as legal workers.

The major impact of Braceros on US workers was indirect. Braceros in the fields held down wages there, and a booming nonfarm economy offered higher wage urban jobs, so Mexican-Americans during the 1950s changed from a predominantly rural to a mostly urban population. The availability of Braceros permitted the southwestern states to become the garden states of the United States. In California, fruit and nut production rose 15 per cent during the 1950s, and vegetable production rose 50 per cent. New irrigation facilities expanded the acreage available to grow fruits and vegetables, the interstate highway system allowed produce to be shipped cheaply to eastern markets, and new plant varieties and packing technologies made California produce preferred to locally-grown fruits and vegetables in the eastern United States where most Americans lived.

The expansion of labour-intensive agriculture in California was not accompanied by higher farm wages. The US Department of Agriculture's average hourly farm wage rose 41 per cent — slightly more than the 35 per cent increase in consumer prices — from $.85 in 1950 to $1.20 in 1960. In contrast, average factory wages in California rose 63 per cent, from $1.60 per hour in 1950 to $2.60 in 1960, and factory jobs offered mandatory (unemployment insurance) and optional (health care) benefits that were not available to farm workers. Slowly rising farm wages and faster-rising factory wages drew American workers to factory jobs where there were no Braceros. As a result, the farm labour market became an immigrant-dominated institution, in which conditions in Mexico rather than the United States determined wages and worker availability.

Demand Pull, Supply Push, and Networks

Bracero recruitment and legal and illegal migration created a bi-national labour market that today binds rural Mexico and rural America. This section reviews the demand pull, supply push, and network factors that today govern cross-border migration, and then discusses the impact of NAFTA on each.

NAFTA should eventually reduce the need for Mexican workers in US agriculture by encouraging US farmers to follow their workers to Mexico. If NAFTA stimulates job creation in Mexico, there should also be less of a push to migrate to the United States. However, these reduced demand-pull and supply-push factors are unlikely to be felt for a decade or more, while the networks that link Mexico and the United States were strengthened during the 1980s.

Demand-Pull in the United States for Mexican Workers

During the 1980s, rural Mexicans were drawn into rural America in a demand-pull fashion due to the continued expansion of the subsector of US agriculture that produces fruits and nuts, vegetables and melons, and horticultural specialties (FVH) such as flowers and nursery products. Fruits and vegetables play a small but growing role in US agriculture. Farmers received an average $21 billion for the fruits and vegetables they sold between 1986 and 1990, or about one-fourth of the $80 billion value of all crops sold[15]. The major study of NAFTA's likely effects on US fruit and vegetable agriculture concluded that American agriculture was likely to gain more jobs from expanded markets in Mexico during the 1990s than would be lost to Mexico as production shifts there to take advantage of lower Mexican wages (Cook *et al.*, 1991).

US fruit and vegetable production increased dramatically during the 1970s and 1980s. There were several reasons. First, consumer preferences shifted toward fruits and vegetables. Second, the United States is a net exporter of fruits and vegetables, so that a devalued dollar after 1986 and income growth, especially in Asia, permitted US farmers to expand dramatically their exports, creating jobs for Mexican workers in the United States. Third, fruit and vegetable production has expanded fastest in the areas of the United States that have traditionally relied on Mexican workers — southwestern states such as California as well as Florida — and the labour market features there that lead to dependence on Mexican workers — such as hiring workers through contractors — began to spread to agriculture in other states and to the first nonfarm industries in which farm workers find jobs, such as construction and janitorial services.

US fruit and vegetable consumption should continue to increase in the 1990s. The question is whether and how fast the production of the fruits and vegetables that affluent consumers want will shift to Mexico. Mexico's primary competitive advantage is climate — Mexico can produce fresh vegetables during the winter months when most US production areas except Florida are not producing. But even if Mexico were completely to displace production in Florida, most fruit and vegetable production would remain in the United States, because two-thirds of the production occurs in the summer and fall, when neither Mexico nor Florida is producing significant quantities.

Some 2.5 million persons are hired farm workers in the United States sometime during a typical year. These workers are increasingly Mexican-born immigrants, and most arrived in the United States within the past 10 years. Neither American nor Mexican workers remain seasonal farm workers for a lifetime, so that, as both groups pass through a seasonal labour market that operates like a revolving door, the farm labour market acts as a US demand-pull magnet that encourages Mexico-to-US migration.

Data collected to implement the US Immigration Reform and Control Act (IRCA) of 1986 found that two-thirds of all farm workers in "seasonal agricultural services" (SAS) or crop agriculture[16] were immigrants from Mexico who have been in the United States for less than 10 years. The National Agricultural Workers Survey (NAWS) reported that most of these farm workers are married men who are poorly educated and who live with their families at their US work sites.

According to the NAWS, an average farm worker is employed by almost 2 US farm employers for half of the year, meaning that workers average less than 13 weeks of employment on any one farm. Farm workers averaged $4.85 for 37 hours of work per week in 1990 while they were doing farm work, and $180 weekly for 26 weeks generates annual farm earnings of $4 665, about 72 per cent of the $6 465 poverty-level income of an individual in 1990. Farm workers average another 10 weeks of unemployment searching for farm and nonfarm jobs.

Two trends seem important for assessing the impact of NAFTA on the demand-pull of jobs in rural America. First, immigrants are a larger share of recent farm workforce entrants than they are of the entire farm workforce, suggesting that new entrants tend to come from abroad. Second, Mexican immigrants appear to be spreading throughout US agriculture: the NAWS and other surveys suggest that an unintended consequence of IRCA's legalisation programmes has been to spread Mexican immigrants workers throughout US agriculture. Hispanic immigrants no longer arouse automatic suspicion in the midwest, south, and northeast, and they are rapidly replacing US citizen whites and blacks in the tobacco fields of North Carolina, replacing US citizen Puerto Ricans in New York and New Jersey, and replacing white teenagers in Iowa.

Mexican workers are also appearing in nonfarm jobs throughout the midwest, from meat packing to construction. This "Mexicanisation" of rural and middle America will help to ensure that the demand pull of US jobs persists for Mexicans in the 1990s.

Supply-Push in the 1990s

During the 1980s, rural Mexicans responded to the demand-pull of jobs in US agriculture for three interrelated reasons. The Mexican work force grew extraordinarily rapidly at a time when Mexican farmers faced a cost-price squeeze, making farming there less attractive, while Mexico's urban economy was offering almost no new "real" jobs to those pushed out of rural areas. Disillusioned and unemployed rural Mexicans flocked to the United States. A culture of migration took hold in many rural areas of Mexico; young men were practically expected to go north to earn money in the United States, making emigration a normal part of coming of age. As one ex-resident of central Mexico explained: "When a boy of 12 finishes primary school, he doesn't go on. He wants to go north. Everybody goes. Everybody wants to go." (quoted in *Sacramento Bee*, May 31, 1993, A1).

Mexico is the world's 11th most populous country, with an estimated mid-1994 population of 92 million that is increasing by 2.2 per cent annually[17]. The Mexican population is young — 38 per cent are younger than 15, versus 21-22 per cent in Canada and the United States. The Mexican economy offers about 10 million "real", or formal sector, jobs to a workforce of 30 million, and has been creating about 300 000 to 400 000 additional formal sector jobs annually.

A comparison of Mexican population and labour force trends highlights two points (Figure 2). First, Mexico has an extraordinarily low labour force participation rate: in most industrial countries, half of the total population is in the labour force, but in Mexico, less than one-third are employed or seeking work. Second, the Mexican labour force participation rate fell during the 1980s, as discouraged workers gave up the search for jobs that did not exist. Mexico added 10 to 15 million people in the 1960s and 1970s, but the Mexican labour force increased by only 2 million during the 1980s. It should be noted, however, that there is wide disagreement over the size of the Mexican labour force: the 1990 labour force was reported to be 24 million in the COP and 30 million by the Mexican Ministry of Labour.

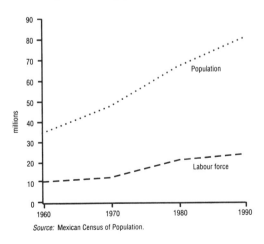

Figure 2. **Mexican population and labour force**

Source: Mexican Census of Population.

The Mexican employment problem has been described as a case of too many new labour force entrants, too much informal employment in the urban areas where most of the population lives, and too many poor farmers. Mexico will have about one million new job seekers each year during the 1990s, and to absorb them, Mexico's GDP must grow, by one estimate, at least 6 to 7 per cent annually (Cornelius, 1992a, p. 11). Mexico's GDP in 1990 was $238 billion, and a (real) 6 per cent growth rate would add $14.3 billion annually to GDP, implying that the cost in additional GDP to create each additional job in Mexico is $14 300. Such an economic growth rate would require very high levels of investment, including foreign investment.

Over the longer term, NAFTA should stimulate foreign investment and job creation in Mexico. But how many jobs will be created in rural Mexico, where two-thirds of Mexico's poor people — and three-fourths of Mexico's very poor people — live? The answer seems to be not as many as US critics of job losses fear and Mexicans hope.

US agribusiness in 1991 had a relatively small investment in Mexican agriculture: only $30 to $100 million, or less than California apricot farmers have invested in land to produce a very minor crop. There are several reasons why US agribusiness has avoided more direct investments in Mexico, but the most important is that low wages do not necessarily mean low production costs (*The Packer*, April 25, 1992, p. 1A). Indeed, after 5 years in Mexico, the second largest US vegetable grower ceased operations there with the observation that "we can even produce more efficiently for the Mexican market from the United States" (*Ag Alert*, July 14, 1993, p. 28).

Mexico in 1990 exported fruits and vegetables worth $900 million to the United States. Luis Tellez predicted that Mexican produce exports might reach $1.3 billion by 1998. How many jobs might an additional $400 million worth of produce exports create? Probably no more than 150 000: Mexico exported tomatoes worth $428 million in 1990, and tomato production created jobs from January through May for about 150 000 Mexican workers, suggesting that each $2 850 in tomato exports created one five-month seasonal job in Mexico.

Networks and Continuing Migration

A continued demand-pull in the US labour market, combined with rising supply-push pressures in rural Mexico, provide the two battery poles that can produce Mexico-to-US migration. All that is missing is a network – what demographers used to call "intervening variables" – the US contacts, immigration policies, and transportation and communications networks that bring Mexicans to the United States.

The networks that link rural Mexico to the United States have been forged over decades (Massey, Alarcon, and Durand, 1987). Mexico allowed its rural areas to become dependent on the United States labour market, and the United States in several instances was responsible for converting winding paths into freeways through which Mexicans could enter the United States. The Bracero programme planted the seed, and it proved to be naive to expect that, after 1 to 2 million

Mexicans had gained experience working seasonally in the United States, they would stop coming simply because the United States ended the programme through which such workers arrived legally.

It was well-known that there were strong Mexico-US migration networks in the early 1980s, but what was not appreciated was that the Immigration Reform and Control Act (IRCA) of 1986 would strengthen rather than weaken these networks. IRCA was supposed to close the back door through which rural Mexicans were illegally entering the United States, and enlist US employers in the immigration control effort by making them liable to fines and imprisonment if they knowingly hired unauthorised workers. But IRCA backfired, strengthening rather than weakening these networks because of massive fraud in the legalisation programme and flawed employer sanctions enforcement.

For rural Mexicans in the mid-1980s, IRCA and especially its Special Agricultural Worker (SAW) legalisation programme must have seemed a godsend, and many Mexicans took advantage of its easy route to legal US immigration status. Rural Mexicans did not immediately appreciate how easy it was to apply for the SAW programme.

There are only about 6 million adult males in rural Mexico, and over one-sixth of them eventually applied for the SAW programme[18], claiming that they had worked in US agriculture as illegal aliens in 1985-86. The INS soon became aware of the widespread "coaching" of alleged Mexican farm workers in border areas — "farm worker clothing" was rented by the hour and, after a 15 minute lesson in how grapes are picked and where Fresno, California, was located, the applicant entered the US port-of-entry office making claim to have done farmwork as an illegal alien in 1985-86. There was no penalty for falsely claiming to have worked and, as the lines lengthened in 1988, the INS was disapproving 9 out of 10 port-of-entry applicants.

SAW legalisation has made it easier rather than harder for rural Mexicans to find US jobs. The United States attempt to wipe the slate clean by legalising current workers and then dry up the illegal flow instead spawned a false document industry and encouraged the hiring of "falsely documented" workers through hard-to-police middlemen. The comparative advantage of these labour contractors was in many cases superior access to newly-arrived immigrant workers and a willingness to run the risk of labour and immigration enforcement.

In some rural villages, a majority of the adults are employed in the United States or in urban Mexico (Alarcon, 1992). Remittances may be one-fourth to three-fourths of a village's total income, and their spending accounts for much of the economic activity which takes place, such as building new or improved housing for the families that are fortunate enough to obtain remittances. More and more rural Mexicans seem to be following the adage "work in the United States, but live in Mexico," emphasizing that enjoyment at home is the reward for work abroad.

Could Mexican rural development policies and NAFTA reverse this culture of emigration? Surveys in emigration villages find that many rural Mexicans have given up on revitalising agriculture — only 12 per cent of 800 Mexican farmers surveyed in 1988-89 thought that agricultural improvements such as irrigation systems were their community's most important need, versus more than twice this percentage who wanted factories to come to their villages and 37 per cent who just wanted jobs (Cornelius, 1992b, p. 13). Emigration villages are often located too far from highways and railroads to justify locating factories in them, and since they currently are sending their young workers to distant labour markets, the workers available are not necessarily an attractive work force for potential factory operators.

Neither rural development nor NAFTA is likely to bring job-creating investments to these rural communities. A rural development strategy may be able to create micro industries that encourage some potential migrants to stay at home. But the most likely prospect is for new jobs to be created in places far removed from the emigration areas, so that young people will continue to migrate to find jobs. The question is whether they will stay in Mexico, perhaps by finding NAFTA-created jobs in Mexican factories or fields, or follow their networks to the United States.

The Migration Transition

Since NAFTA is unique in creating a free trade area between nations that have previously had primarily a migration linkage, there is little theory or experience to indicate the trajectory of the hoped-for migration transition. The most likely migration trajectory is analogous to the demographic transition. Just as a country's population temporarily grows faster as death rates fall before birth rates, and only later lower fertility slows population growth, so the displacement and disruption associated with opening and privatising the economy may encourage more people to emigrate, with job and wage growth slowing emigration only later.

The migration transition compares two scenarios. In the status quo scenario of a closed economy that has primarily migration linkages to the outside world, the level of migration depends on the gap between workforce and job growth. If too few jobs are created, the workforce is growing, and there are opportunities to emigrate, then there will be a rising level of emigration. If the workforce is not growing, as in much of Eastern Europe, then the status quo trajectory is likely to be flat.

The alternative open economy scenario produces the migration hump. In economies that have been creating too few jobs to absorb new labour force entrants, and where there are established international migration networks, the combination of displacement, disruption and, in some instances, more money in extremely poor areas can temporarily *increase* emigration above the previous trend. If viewed in a figure in which time is measured on the horizontal axis, and the number of migrants on the vertical axis, this temporary increase in emigration appears as a migration "hump."

The case for a migration hump is based on the expected behaviour of the demand-pull, supply-push, and network factors that govern migration. There are also theoretical reasons to expect trade and migration to be at least short-term complements (Martin and Taylor, 1995). The logic is that the establishment of networks that can move people across borders regardless of immigration controls, so that if there is some demand-pull in the form of available jobs, and then an increase in supply-push factors (e.g. as free trade under NAFTA displaces workers faster than additional investments create jobs for them), both potential and actual emigration increases.

Migration humps can take many forms. In the case of the southern European nations, most of the migration hump seemed to occur before 1973 — before 1968 in the case of Italy — and the migration that took place was the result of demand-pull, supply-push, and network factors. However, when demand-pull recruitment was largely halted in 1973, these countries had progressed past the peak of the hump, and there were enough opportunities to unite families — and to migrate seasonally in the case of Spain and Portugal — that the hump did not result in unwanted migration from southern to northern Europe.

Even if there are migration humps, the number of additional migrants may be small, especially relative to the amount of migration "saved" in the long run as a result of economic integration. Figure 3 illustrates this point for Mexico-to-US migration. As drawn, there is additional migration as a result of NAFTA for about 15 years, but this additional migration is a relatively small increment to an already significant flow — on the order of an additional 10 to 20 per cent of an average 300 000 immigrants annually. Second, the figure is drawn to show that, when viewed over 30 rather than 15 years, there is actually less migration with NAFTA, since C is larger than A.

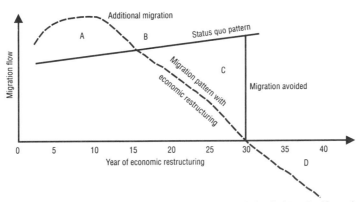

Figure 3. **The migration hump**

Source: Phillip Martin 1993, *Trade and Migration: NAFTA and Agriculture*, Institute for International Economics, Washington, D.C.

The migration hump, if a plausible hypothesis about what to expect from NAFTA, suggests that the same policies that make immigration controls less necessary in the long run make them more necessary in the short run. In the case of Mexico to US migration, the hump A is expected to be relatively short lived — less than 10 years — and the cross over point B is expected to be reached by 2005 (Martin, 1993; Bustamante, 1994). After that, predictions about the future evolution of Mexico to US migration are much more speculative, with some emphasizing the potential of foreign investment to create jobs in Mexico, and others noting that an overvalued currency and political instability continue to discourage long-term investments in Mexico.

Devaluation and Migration

Mexican migration to the United States is expected to increase as a result of the steep peso devaluation in December 1994 and the economic difficulties that precipitated the currency crisis. The US Treasury, for example, predicted a 30 per cent increase in illegal entries (or 430 000 additional) in 1995 if the United States did not extend Mexico $40 billion in loan guarantees. President Clinton argued that the Mexican bailout package would "help us to better protect our borders". The 1982 peso devaluation was followed by a 35 per cent increase in apprehensions in 1983, from 1 million to 1.3 million.

The INS Commissioner Doris Meissner and Edward Taylor of the University of California at Davis, a specialist on Mexican migration, predict that migration pressure will increase because the peso devaluation widens the wage gap between the US and Mexico from 6-7 to 1 to 10-12 to 1: Taylor's model, which links Mexican village economies to external labour markets, finds that a 30 per cent devaluation increases exits from Mexican villages by 25 per cent.

Not everyone agrees that the peso devaluation will increase unauthorised Mexico-to-US migration. Mexican migration expert Jorge Bustamante noted that the cost of being smuggled into the United States is set in dollars, and that some potential migrants may not be able to accumulate 30 per cent more to pay smugglers immediately. On the other hand, the increased value in Mexico of remittances from US migrants may make potential migrants better off unless inflation in Mexico offsets the effects of the devaluation.

There is general agreement that the migration effects of the peso devaluation will not become apparent until March or April 1995, when seasonal migrants seek US jobs. These migrants will have to elude a beefed-up Border Patrol to enter the United States illegally.

Emigration pressure and migration flows will also depend on economic prospects in Mexico and California, the destination of most illegal Mexican immigrants. On January 3, 1995, Mexican President Zedillo made a speech that laid out plans to deal with the economic crisis that caused the peso to lose over 30 per cent of its value in the last two weeks of 1994. The theme of the speech was sacrifice and austerity — wages and prices are to rise more slowly than inflation, the government will try to sell off more public enterprises, and government spending is to be cut. On January 17, 1995, the Zedillo government and the opposition parties signed a political reform agreement designed to minimise political unrest by ensuring honest elections, thus boosting the confidence of foreign investors.

A sluggish Mexican economy in 1995 could increase both internal migration to the northern border areas and emigration pressure. The Mexican economy is now expected to grow less than 1 per cent in 1995, inflation is projected to be 15 to 20 per cent, and some foreign investors may put at least a temporary stop to plans to build or expand factories and stores there. However, the lower wages and costs wrought by the peso devaluation should make Mexico more attractive to foreign investors. Indeed, there has already been some US interest in shifting to unused maquiladoras in the border areas plastics and other light assembly work to take advantage of Mexican wages and benefits that have fallen from $2 hourly to $1.50

(about half of these wage costs are payroll taxes and benefits). Since labour markets in Mexican border cities are fairly tight, such an expansion of maquiladora activity should attract internal migrants to the border. If the California and US border economies improve as expected in 1995, there could be more attempted migration across the border.

There is no doubt that Mexico will, over the next two decades, emerge as the low-cost manufacturing centre of North America. But no one knows exactly when and how this economic transformation will occur. At least 2 to 3 million of Mexico's 5 to 6 million farmers, plus their families, are likely to leave the land over the next two decades, but it is not clear whether foreign investment will create jobs for them in central Mexico or in border areas, or whether many will migrate to the United States.

Conclusions

US and Mexican Presidents embraced NAFTA as a means to accelerate economic growth in both countries by encouraging each nation to specialise in producing those goods in which it has a comparative advantage, and then to trade them without border barriers. For most of the 20th century, Mexico's comparative advantage in the North American economy has been to export unskilled workers. NAFTA, it is hoped, can speed up the substitution of labour-intensive goods and services for people exports from Mexico, and eventually reduce Mexican migration to the United States. Economic growth and development, which are accelerated by freer trade and investment, are a proven path to reducing migration in the long run.

NAFTA will not provide, of course, a pure test of the effects of freer trade on an established pattern of migration. Mexico has unilaterally adopted policies that opened its economy, and made internal reforms that will promote long-run growth but tend to drain people from the countryside. Simultaneously, the United States, with its legalisation programmes and ineffective enforcement of immigration laws during the 1980s, made it easier rather than harder for Mexicans to work in the United States.

Is there a way to open an economy and accelerate economic and job growth with only a small migration hump? The answer is a qualified yes. In the longer term, Mexico could reduce internal and external migration by strengthening the institutions that distribute broadly the benefits of development. Asian NIEs achieved both fast growth and an equitable distribution of that growth by not allowing rural-urban earnings differences to get too large. Mexico, by contrast, has a very unequal distribution of income.

In the short term, the United States and Mexico could co-operate on immigration control. In no other place do citizens of one nation mass openly awaiting their chance to enter another illegally. Mexican law prohibits Mexican citizens from leaving the country except at authorised ports, so Mexican citizens attempting illegal entry into the United States are also breaking Mexican law. It seems likely that migration considerations will enter into future trade and investment negotiations.

Notes

1. Proposition 187, approved by California voters on November 8, 1994, by a margin of 59 to 41, is a state law that establishes a state-run eligibility system that, if implemented, aims to prevent unauthorised aliens from attending public schools or receiving most health and social services.
2. There were dozens of hearings on whether NAFTA should be approved by the US Congress, but only one devoted specifically to how NAFTA would affect Mexico-to-US migration. During the November 3, 1993 hearing before the House Judiciary Subcommittee on International Law, Immigration and Refugees, Chairman Romano Mazzoli (D-Ky) repeatedly asked Administration officials why they had not reached an agreement with Mexico on additional steps to control illegal immigration. They responded with variations on the statement of Deputy United States Trade Representative Rufus Yerxa: "NAFTA does not explicitly address the issue of illegal immigration, but in the long run, it is one of our best bets to reducing illegal immigration."
3. In the opinion of most observers, President Bush handled the job displacement and environmental issues badly by not acknowledging them, implying that they would be minor bumps in a growing economy. President Clinton paid more attention to employment and environmental issues, but he too had no short-term proposals to cope with the migration hump. More or less independently of NAFTA, Attorney General Reno announced a package of immigration control proposals in February 1994.
4. According to press reports, Mexico used three arguments to convince Americans to support NAFTA: it will create jobs in the United States, it will help Mexico to enforce its environmental laws, and it will reduce illegal Mexican migration. In March 1992, it was reported that Mexico's promise of decreased migration seemed most appealing to Americans.
5. These four categories are business visitors, who enter the United States on B-1 visas, traders (E-1) and investors (E-2), intra-company transferees (L visas), and certain professionals who receive TN visas under NAFTA. Only the B-1 and L visas were available to Mexicans before NAFTA.
6. There is no precise measure of the annual influx or settlement of Mexican immigrants. Espenshade (1991) estimates the gross inflow of unauthorised Mexicans at 2 million annually, with 10 per cent settling in the United States. A GAO panel in February 1992 concluded that the gross inflow of illegal aliens from all countries was about 2 million annually, three-fourths of whom come from Mexico, and that 10 per cent settle in the United States.
7. Espenshade (1990) developed a model that predicted gross unauthorised migration on the basis of Mexico's 15 to 34 year-old population, seasonal agricultural worker (SAW)

8. applications, US/Mexico wage and unemployment ratios, and enforcement and seasonality variables. This model lays the basis for the relationship between apprehensions and the undocumented flow between 1986 and 1988.

8. The apprehension-gross flow relationship gives approximate results. In 1987 and 1988, there were 1.1 and 1 million apprehensions, respectively. Applying the 7/3 ratio to them would produce estimated undocumented inflows of 2.3 to 2.6 million, versus a post-IRCA flow reported to be 2.1 million (1992, p. 736).

9. This model may not fully capture rural Mexican and rural US variables. For example, the Mexican unemployment rate used – 3 to 4 per cent in 1987-88 – reflects that of urban workers in the largest cities who were separated from formal employment relationships, even though only 35 to 40 per cent of the Mexican workforce has such employment relationships. The United States unemployment rate does not accurately reflect conditions in seasonal agriculture, where many illegal Mexican workers find their first jobs.

10. Ejidos are semi-communal farms created to fulfil the Mexican government's revolutionary era promise of land for the peasants. In most cases, individuals farmed a plot of land that was theirs to work and pass on to children, but not to rent or sell. In 1993, it was estimated that 3.1 million farmers, and a total 18 million of Mexico's 92 million people live, work or depend upon the ejidos.

11. Tellez converted this to a labour displacement figure in May 1992, when he predicted that over 1.4 million farmers and workers would be displaced by 2002 due to freer trade and land reforms. Tellez projected that the farm workforce would fall from 26 per cent in 1992 (7.18 of 30 million) to 16 per cent by 2002 (6.4 of 40 million). Cited in Cornelius, 1992a, p. 6.

12. In 1990, the World Bank reported that Mexico had 86.2 million people and a GDP of $238 billion, for a per capita GDP of $2 490. However, the 23 million rural Mexicans must divide $21 billion among themselves, giving them an average per capita GDP of less than $1 000, while the 63 million urban Mexicans divide $217 billion, giving them an average per capita GDP of $3 400. *World Development Report*, 1992, pp. 222-223.

13. Varden Fuller argued that the structure of California agriculture—its system of large farms dependent on seasonal workers — developed because (immigrant) workers without other US job options were usually available. In his words, the assumption was "that with no particular effort on the part of the employer, a farm labour force would emerge when needed, do its work, and then disappear — accepting the terms and conditions offered, without question." (Fuller, 1942, p. vii).

14. The merits of slavery versus seasonal farm workers were debated extensively, with seasonal workers usually found to be cheaper because: (1) no capital outlay was required to purchase them; (2) they boarded themselves while employed and reproduced abroad; (3) they were available when needed but they were paid only for the time they were actually employed; and (4) at the end of the season they "moved on, relieving (the) employer of any burden or responsibility for his (workers) welfare during the slack season" (Fuller, p. 19824).

15. In 1959, the Census of Agriculture reported that the value of US fruit and nut, vegetable and melon, and horticultural specialty (FVH) production was $2.7 billion, or 9 per cent of the total $30 billion of US farm sales. By 1980, FVH sales as estimated by USDA totalled $18 billion, or 13 per cent of farm cash receipts. They jumped by 65 per cent during the 1980s to $30 billion in 1990, making these mostly labour-intensive commodities worth about one-sixth of total farm sales. It should be noted that USDA has several farm sales series; the 1987 Census of Agriculture reported that FVH sales were $17.6 billion, or 13 per cent of farm cash receipts.

16. The National Agricultural Workers Survey (NAWS) covers SAS agriculture, which by regulation and court decision expanded to include most of US crop agriculture. IRCA states that SAS is to be defined by commodity (perishable) and activity (field work), so that those legalised under the SAW programme had to have been illegal aliens who performed or supervised field work in 1985-86 related to planting, cultural practices, cultivating, growing, and harvesting fruits and vegetables of every kind and "other perishable commodities."

    The definition of "perishable commodity" was stretched first by USDA and then by courts to include virtually all plants grown for human food (except sugar cane) and many nonedible plants, such as cotton, Christmas trees, cut flowers, sod grass, and Spanish reeds. Field workers include all of the paid hand- or machine-operator workers involved with these SAS commodities, the supervisors of field workers and equipment operators, mechanics who repair machinery, and pilots who spray crops. This means that even e.g. an illegal Central American refugee paid to work 90 days in a church's vegetable garden could qualify as a SAW applicant. The youngest SAW approved was a 3 year old illegal alien child who helped his parents to bunch onions in 1985-86.

17. These data are from the Population Reference Bureau's World Population Data Sheet for 1994. There is considerable uncertainty about Mexico's population, largely because the 1990 Census of Population found 6 million fewer Mexicans than expected.

18. A small but unknown number of SAW applicants were from urban Mexico.

Bibliographical References

ACEVEDO, Dolores and Thomas ESPENSHADE (1992), "Implications of a NAFTA for Mexican Migration into the United States", *Population and Development Review* 18(4): 729-744.
ASCENCIO, Fernando (1993), *Bringing it Back Home: Remittances to Mexico from Migrant Workers in the United States*, La Jolla, California: University of California at San Diego Center for US-Mexican Studies.
BANAMEX, *Review of the Mexican Economy*, Mexico City, Monthly.
BÖHNING, W. R. (1984), *Studies in International Labour Migration*, London: Macmillan.
BORJAS, George J. (1990), *Friends or Strangers: The Impact of Immigrants on the U.S. Economy*, New York: Basic Books.
BRIGGS, Vernon, Jr. (1992), *Mass Immigration and the National Interest*, M.E. Sharpe: Armonk, NY.
BUSTAMANTE, Jorge (1994), "Projections of Mexican Migration to the United States," presentation to Migration Dialogue seminar, November 20, 1994, San Diego, CA.
BUSTAMANTE, Jorge, Clark REYNOLDS, and Raul HINOJOSA-OJEDA (Eds.) (1992), *U.S. Mexican Relations: Labour Market Interdependence*, Stanford, CA: Stanford University Press.
CALVA, Jose Luis (1992), *Probables Efectos de un Tratado de Libre Comercio en el Campo Mexico*, Mexico: Fontamara.
CARDENAS, Cuauhtemoc (1992), Speech to the World Affairs Council in San Francisco, February.
COALE, Ansley (1978), "Population Growth and Economic Development: The Case of Mexico", *Foreign Affairs*, 56(2): 415-429.
CONGRESSIONAL RESEARCH SERVICE (1980), *Temporary Worker Programmes: Background and Issues*, Prepared for the Senate Committee on the Judiciary.
CONGRESSIONAL RESEARCH SERVICE (1993), *A North American Free Trade Agreement and Immigration*, Publication 93-62EPW, Washington, D.C.: The Library of Congress.
COOK, Roberta, Carlos BENITO, James MATSON, David RUNSTEN, Kenneth SHWEDEL, and Timothy TAYLOR (1991), "Fruit and Vegetable Issues" in *NAFTA: Effects on Agriculture*, Vol. 4, Park Ridge, Il: American Farm Bureau Foundation.
CORNELIUS, Wayne (1992a), "The Politics and Economics of Reforming the Ejido Sector in Mexico: An Overview and Research Agenda", *LASA Forum*, XXIII(3): 3-10.

CORNELIUS, Wayne (1992b), "From Sojourners to Settlers: The Changing Profile of Mexican Immigration to the United States" in Jorge Bustamante, Clark Reynolds, and Raul Hinojosa-Ojeda (Eds.) *U.S. Mexican Relations: Labour Market Interdependence*, Stanford, CA: Stanford University Press.

COUNCIL OF ECONOMIC ADVISORS (1986), "The Economic Effects of Immigration", Economic Report of the President, Washington: Council of Economic Advisors, pp. 213-234.

CRAIG, Richard B. (1971), *The Bracero Program: Interest Groups and Foreign Policy*, Austin: University of Texas Press.

CROSS, Harry and James SANDOS (1981), *Across the Border: Rural Development in Mexico and Recent Migration to the United States*, Berkeley: Institute of Governmental Studies, University of California.

DÁVILA, Alberto and Rogelio SAENZ (1990), "The Effect of Maquiladora Employment on the Monthly Flow of Mexican Undocumented Immigration to the United States, 1978-1982", *International Migration Review*, 24(1): 96-107.

DURAND, Jorge and Douglas S. MASSEY (1992), "Mexican Migration to the United States", *Latin American Research Review*, 27(2): 3-42.

ESPENSHADE, Thomas (1990), "Undocumented Migration to the United States: Evidence from a Repeated Trials Model," in Frank D. Bean, Barry Edmonston, and Jeffrey S. Passel, Eds., *Undocumented Migration to the United States: IRCA and the Experience of the 1980s*, Washington, D.C.: The Urban Institute Press, pp.111-158.

ESPENSHADE, Thomas (1991), "Responsiveness of the Mexico-U.S. Flow of Undocumented Migrants to Relative Improvements in the Mexican Economy", Mimeo.

FAUX, Jeff and Thea LEE (1992), *The Effect of George Bush's NAFTA on American Workers: Ladder Up or Ladder Down?*, Washington DC: Economic Policy Institute.

FULLER, Varden (1942), *The Supply of Agricultural Labour as a Factor in the Evolution of Farm Organization in California*, Unpublished Ph.D. dissertation, U.C. Berkeley, 1939, Reprinted in *Violations of Free Speech and the Rights of Labour Education and Labour Committee*, Washington: Senate Education and Labour Committee), pp. 19778-19894.

GARCIA Y GRIEGO, Manuel (1981), "The Importation of Mexican Contract Labourers to the United States, 1942-1964: Antecedents, Operation, and Legacy", La Jolla, CA: Programme in US-Mexican Studies, U.C. San Diego, Working Paper 11.

GARCIA Y GRIEGO, Manuel (1989), "The Mexican Labour Supply, 1990-2010," in Wayne Cornelius and Jorge A. Bustamante (Eds.), *Mexican Migration to the United States: Origins, Consequences and Policy Options*, La Jolla: UCSD Center for US-Mexican Studies.

GOLDEN, Tim (1991), "The Dream of Land Dies Hard in Mexico", *New York Times*, November 27, p. A1.

GOLDEN, Tim (1992), "Mexican President Seeks to Address Clinton's Concerns: Salinas Calls for Efforts to Ease Curbs on Mexicans Moving Across Border into U.S.", *New York Times*, November 21, p. A1.

GRAYSON, George (1993), *The North American Free Trade Agreement*, New York: Foreign Policy Association.

HARVEY, Neil, Luis Hernandez NAVARRO, and Jeffrey RUBIN (1994), *Rebellion In Chiapas: Rural Reforms, Campesino Radicalism, and the Limits To Salinismo*, La Jolla, CA: Center for US-Mexican Studies, University of California, San Diego.

HIEMENZ, Ulrich and K. W. SCHATZ (1979), Trade in place of migration : an employment-oriented study with special reference to the Federal Republic of Germany, Spain, and Turkey, Geneva : International Labour Office.

HINOJOSA-OJEDA, Raul, and Robert McCLEERY (1992), "U.S.-Mexico Interdependence, Social Pacts and Policy Perspectives: A Computable General Equilibrium Approach", in Jorge Bustamante, Clark Reynolds, and Raul Hinojosa-Ojeda, (Eds.), *U.S. Mexican Relations: Labour Market Interdependence*, Stanford, CA: Stanford University Press.

HINOJOSA-OJEDA, Raul, and Sherman ROBINSON (1991a), "Alternative Scenarios of U.S.–Mexico Integration: A Computable General Equilibrium Approach", Department of Agricultural and Resource Economics, University of California, Berkeley, Working Paper No. 609.

HINOJOSA-OJEDA, Raul, and Sherman ROBINSON (1991b), "Labour Issues in a North American Free Trade Area", in Nora Lustig, Barry Bosworth, and Robert Lawrence (Eds.), *North American Free Trade: Assessing the Impact*, Washington, D.C.: The Brookings Institution.

HINOJOSA-OJEDA, Raul, Sherman ROBINSON, and Geotz WOLFF (1991), "The Impact of a North American Free Trade Agreement on California: A Summary of Key Research Findings", University of California, Los Angeles: Lewis Center for Regional Policy Studies, Working Paper No. 3.

HOLLIFIELD, James (1992), *Immigrants, Markets, and States: the Political Economy of Immigration in Postwar Europe and the U.S.*, Cambridge: Harvard.

HUFBAUER, Gary and Jeffrey SCHOTT (1992), *North American Free Trade: Issues and Recommendations*, Washington: Institute for International Economics.

LEVY, Santiago and Sweder VAN WIJNBERGEN (1992), "Mexico and the Free Trade Agreement between Mexico and the United States", *The World Bank Economic Review*, 4(3): 481-502.

LUSTING, Nora (1992), *Mexico: The Remaking of an Economy*, (Washington, Brookings Institution).

MARTIN, P. (1993), Trade and Migration: NAFTA and Agriculture, Institute for International Economics, Washington, D.C.

MARTIN, Philip and J. Edward TAYLOR (1995), "The Anatomy of a Migration Hump," forthcoming in J. Edward Taylor, Ed., *Development Strategy, Employment and Migration*, OECD, Paris.

MASSEY, Douglas S. (1988), "Economic Development and International Migration in Comparative Perspective", *Population and Development Review*, 14(3):383-413.

MASSEY, Douglas, Rafael ALARCON, Jorge DURAND, and Humberto GONZALES (1987), *Return to Aztlan: The Social Process of International Migration from Western Mexico*, (Berkeley, CA: University of California Press).

MASSEY, Douglas, Katherine DONATO, and Zai LIANG (1990), "Effects of the Immigration Reform and Control Act of 1986: Preliminary Data from Mexico" in Bean, Frank, Barry Edmonston, and Jeffrey Passel (Eds), *Undocumented Migration to the United States: IRCA and the Experience of the 1980s*, Washington: The Urban Institute Press, pp. 183-210.

MASSEY, Douglas S., Joaquin ARANGO, Graeme HUGO, Ali KOUAOUCI, Adela PELLIGRINO, and J. Edward TAYLOR (1993), "Theories of International Migration: A Review and Appraisal", *Population and Development Review*, 19(3): 431-466.

MOLYNEUX, Guy (1994), "Unified Opinion Leaders Best a Reluctant Public", *The Public Perspective*, 5(2).

PARK, Y. (1994), "The Turning Point in International Labour Migration and Economic Development in Korea", in Asian and Pacific Migration Journal, Vol.3, No.1

PAPADEMETRIOU, Demetrios and Philip MARTIN (Eds), (1991), *The Unsettled Relationship: Labour Migration and Economic Development*, Westport, CT: Greenwood Press.

PENNINX, Rinus (1982), "A Critical Review of Theory and Practice: The Case of Turkey", *International Migration Review*, 16: 781-818.

PRESIDENT'S COMMISSION ON MIGRATORY LABOUR (1951), *Migratory Labour In American Agriculture*, Washington: U.S. Government Printing Office.

REYNOLDS, Clark (1992), "Will a Free Trade Agreement Lead to Wage Convergence? Implications for Mexico and the United States", in Jorge Bustamante, Clark Reynolds, and Raul Hinojosa-Ojeda (Eds.), *U.S. Mexican Relations: Labour Market Interdependence*, Stanford, CA: Stanford University Press.

ROBINSON, Sherman, Mary E. BURFISHER, Raul HINOJOSA-OJEDA, and Karen E. THIERFELDER (1991), "Agricultural Policies and Migration in a U.S.-Mexico Free Trade Area: A Computable General Equilibrium Analysis", Department of Agricultural and Resource Economics, University of California, Berkeley, Working Paper No. 617.

ROTHMAN, Erik and Thomas ESPENSHADE (1992), "Fiscal Impacts of Immigration to the United States", *Population Index* 58(3): 381-415.

SANDERSON, Steven (Ed) (1985), *The Americas in the New International Division of Labour*, New York: Holmes and Meier.

SCHOEPFLE, Gregory and Jorge PEREZ-LOPEZ, (1989), "Export Assembly Operations in Mexico and the Caribbean", *Journal of Inter-American Studies*, Vol. 31, No. 4.

SELIGSON, Mitchell and Edward WILLIAMS (1981), *Maquiladoras and Migration: A Study of Workers in the Mexican-United States Border Industrialization Program*, Austin: University of Texas.

SKLAIR, Leslie (1989), *Assembling for Development: The Maquila Industry in Mexico and the United States*, Boston and London: Unwin Hyman, pp. 164-66.

STRAUBHAAR, Thomas (1988), *On the Economics of International Labour Migration*, Bern: Haupt.

STRAUBHAAR, Thomas (1992), "Allocational and Distributional Aspects of Future Immigration to Western Europe", *International Migration Review*, 26(2): 462-483.

TAYLOR, J. Edward (1992), "Remittances and Inequality Reconsidered: Direct, Indirect, and Intertemporal Effects", *Journal of Policy Modeling* 14: 187-208.

THOMPSON, Gary and Philip MARTIN (1989), *The Potential Effects of Labor Intensive Agriculture in Mexico on U.S.-Mexico Migration*, US Commission for the Study of Agricultural Workers, Working Paper 11.

TURNHAM, David (1993), *Employment and Development: A New Review of the Evidence*, OECD, Paris.

US COMMISSION FOR THE STUDY OF INTERNATIONAL MIGRATION AND COOPERATIVE ECONOMIC DEVELOPMENT (1990), *Unauthorized Migration: An Economic Development Response*, Washington, D.C.

US COMMISSION ON AGRICULTURAL WORKERS (1992), Final Report, Washington, D.C.: US Government Printing Office.

US DEPARTMENT OF AGRICULTURE (1992), *Agriculture in a North American Free Trade Agreement*, Washington: USDA, Foreign Agricultural Economic Report Number 246.

WEINTRAUB, Sidney (1984), *Free Trade between Mexico and the United States*, Washington, DC: The Brookings Institution.

WEINTRAUB, Sidney (1990), *A Marriage of Convenience: Relations between Mexico and the United States*, New York: Oxford University Press.

WEINTRAUB, Sidney (1992), "North American Free Trade and the European Situation Compared", *International Migration Review*, 26: 2(506-524).

WORLD BANK (1992), World Development Report, 1992, Washinton, D.C.

YUNEZ-NAUDE, Antonio (1991), "Towards a Free Trade Agreement Between Mexico and the U.S.A.: Effects on Mexican Primary, Non-Mineral Sectors", unpublished paper, Centro de Estudios Económicos, El Colegio de México.

MAIN SALES OUTLETS OF OECD PUBLICATIONS
PRINCIPAUX POINTS DE VENTE DES PUBLICATIONS DE L'OCDE

ARGENTINA – ARGENTINE
Carlos Hirsch S.R.L.
Galería Güemes, Florida 165, 4° Piso
1333 Buenos Aires   Tel. (1) 331.1787 y 331.2391
Telefax: (1) 331.1787

AUSTRALIA – AUSTRALIE
D.A. Information Services
648 Whitehorse Road, P.O.B 163
Mitcham, Victoria 3132   Tel. (03) 9210.7777
Telefax: (03) 9210.7788

AUSTRIA – AUTRICHE
Gerold & Co.
Graben 31
Wien I   Tel. (0222) 533.50.14
Telefax: (0222) 512.47.31.29

BELGIUM – BELGIQUE
Jean De Lannoy
Avenue du Roi 202 Koningslaan
B-1060 Bruxelles   Tel. (02) 538.51.69/538.08.41
Telefax: (02) 538.08.41

CANADA
Renouf Publishing Company Ltd.
1294 Algoma Road
Ottawa, ON K1B 3W8   Tel. (613) 741.4333
Telefax: (613) 741.5439
Stores:
61 Sparks Street
Ottawa, ON K1P 5R1   Tel. (613) 238.8985
12 Adelaide Street West
Toronto, ON M5H 1L6   Tel. (416) 363.3171
Telefax: (416)363.59.63

Les Éditions La Liberté Inc.
3020 Chemin Sainte-Foy
Sainte-Foy, PQ G1X 3V6   Tel. (418) 658.3763
Telefax: (418) 658.3763

Federal Publications Inc.
165 University Avenue, Suite 701
Toronto, ON M5H 3B8   Tel. (416) 860.1611
Telefax: (416) 860.1608

Les Publications Fédérales
1185 Université
Montréal, QC H3B 3A7   Tel. (514) 954.1633
Telefax: (514) 954.1635

CHINA – CHINE
China National Publications Import
Export Corporation (CNPIEC)
16 Gongti E. Road, Chaoyang District
P.O. Box 88 or 50
Beijing 100704 PR   Tel. (01) 506.6688
Telefax: (01) 506.3101

CHINESE TAIPEI – TAIPEI CHINOIS
Good Faith Worldwide Int'l. Co. Ltd.
9th Floor, No. 118, Sec. 2
Chung Hsiao E. Road
Taipei   Tel. (02) 391.7396/391.7397
Telefax: (02) 394.9176

**CZECH REPUBLIC –
RÉPUBLIQUE TCHÈQUE**
Artia Pegas Press Ltd.
Narodni Trida 25
POB 825
111 21 Praha 1   Tel. (2) 242 246 04
Telefax: (2) 242 278 72

DENMARK – DANEMARK
Munksgaard Book and Subscription Service
35, Nørre Søgade, P.O. Box 2148
DK-1016 København K   Tel. (33) 12.85.70
Telefax: (33) 12.93.87

EGYPT – ÉGYPTE
Middle East Observer
41 Sherif Street
Cairo   Tel. 392.6919
Telefax: 360-6804

FINLAND – FINLANDE
Akateeminen Kirjakauppa
Keskuskatu 1, P.O. Box 128
00100 Helsinki

Subscription Services/Agence d'abonnements :
P.O. Box 23
00371 Helsinki   Tel. (358 0) 121 4416
Telefax: (358 0) 121.4450

FRANCE
OECD/OCDE
Mail Orders/Commandes par correspondance :
2, rue André-Pascal
75775 Paris Cedex 16   Tel. (33-1) 45.24.82.00
Telefax: (33-1) 49.10.42.76
Telex: 640048 OCDE
Internet: Compte.PUBSINQ @ oecd.org

Orders via Minitel, France only/
Commandes par Minitel, France exclusivement :
36 15 OCDE

OECD Bookshop/Librairie de l'OCDE :
33, rue Octave-Feuillet
75016 Paris   Tel. (33-1) 45.24.81.81
(33-1) 45.24.81.67

Dawson
B.P. 40
91121 Palaiseau Cedex   Tel. 69.10.47.00
Telefax : 64.54.83.26

Documentation Française
29, quai Voltaire
75007 Paris   Tel. 40.15.70.00

Economica
49, rue Héricart
75015 Paris   Tel. 45.78.12.92
Telefax : 40.58.15.70

Gibert Jeune (Droit-Économie)
6, place Saint-Michel
75006 Paris   Tel. 43.25.91.19

Librairie du Commerce International
10, avenue d'Iéna
75016 Paris   Tel. 40.73.34.60

Librairie Dunod
Université Paris-Dauphine
Place du Maréchal-de-Lattre-de-Tassigny
75016 Paris   Tel. 44.05.40.13

Librairie Lavoisier
11, rue Lavoisier
75008 Paris   Tel. 42.65.39.95

Librairie des Sciences Politiques
30, rue Saint-Guillaume
75007 Paris   Tel. 45.48.36.02

P.U.F.
49, boulevard Saint-Michel
75005 Paris   Tel. 43.25.83.40

Librairie de l'Université
12a, rue Nazareth
13100 Aix-en-Provence   Tel. (16) 42.26.18.08

Documentation Française
165, rue Garibaldi
69003 Lyon   Tel. (16) 78.63.32.23

Librairie Decitre
29, place Bellecour
69002 Lyon   Tel. (16) 72.40.54.54

Librairie Sauramps
Le Triangle
34967 Montpellier Cedex 2   Tel. (16) 67.58.85.15
Tekefax: (16) 67.58.27.36

A la Sorbonne Actual
23, rue de l'Hôtel-des-Postes
06000 Nice   Tel. (16) 93.13.77.75
Telefax: (16) 93.80.75.69

GERMANY – ALLEMAGNE
OECD Publications and Information Centre
August-Bebel-Allee 6
D-53175 Bonn   Tel. (0228) 959.120
Telefax: (0228) 959.12.17

GREECE – GRÈCE
Librairie Kauffmann
Mavrokordatou 9
106 78 Athens   Tel. (01) 32.55.321
Telefax: (01) 32.30.320

HONG-KONG
Swindon Book Co. Ltd.
Astoria Bldg. 3F
34 Ashley Road, Tsimshatsui
Kowloon, Hong Kong   Tel. 2376.2062
Telefax: 2376.0685

HUNGARY – HONGRIE
Euro Info Service
Margitsziget, Európa Ház
1138 Budapest   Tel. (1) 111.62.16
Telefax: (1) 111.60.61

ICELAND – ISLANDE
Mál Mog Menning
Laugavegi 18, Póstholf 392
121 Reykjavik   Tel. (1) 552.4240
Telefax: (1) 562.3523

INDIA – INDE
Oxford Book and Stationery Co.
Scindia House
New Delhi 110001   Tel. (11) 331.5896/5308
Telefax: (11) 332.5993

17 Park Street
Calcutta 700016   Tel. 240832

INDONESIA – INDONÉSIE
Pdii-Lipi
P.O. Box 4298
Jakarta 12042   Tel. (21) 573.34.67
Telefax: (21) 573.34.67

IRELAND – IRLANDE
Government Supplies Agency
Publications Section
4/5 Harcourt Road
Dublin 2   Tel. 661.31.11
Telefax: 475.27.60

ISRAEL – ISRAËL
Praedicta
5 Shatner Street
P.O. Box 34030
Jerusalem 91430   Tel. (2) 52.84.90/1/2
Telefax: (2) 52.84.93

R.O.Y. International
P.O. Box 13056
Tel Aviv 61130   Tel. (3) 546 1423
Telefax: (3) 546 1442

Palestinian Authority/Middle East:
INDEX Information Services
P.O.B. 19502
Jerusalem   Tel. (2) 27.12.19
Telefax: (2) 27.16.34

ITALY – ITALIE
Libreria Commissionaria Sansoni
Via Duca di Calabria 1/1
50125 Firenze   Tel. (055) 64.54.15
Telefax: (055) 64.12.57

Via Bartolini 29
20155 Milano   Tel. (02) 36.50.83

Editrice e Libreria Herder
Piazza Montecitorio 120
00186 Roma   Tel. 679.46.28
                           Telefax: 678.47.51

Libreria Hoepli
Via Hoepli 5
20121 Milano   Tel. (02) 86.54.46
                      Telefax: (02) 805.28.86

Libreria Scientifica
Dott. Lucio de Biasio 'Aeiou'
Via Coronelli, 6
20146 Milano   Tel. (02) 48.95.45.52
                     Telefax: (02) 48.95.45.48

JAPAN – JAPON
OECD Publications and Information Centre
Landic Akasaka Building
2-3-4 Akasaka, Minato-ku
Tokyo 107   Tel. (81.3) 3586.2016
                     Telefax: (81.3) 3584.7929

KOREA – CORÉE
Kyobo Book Centre Co. Ltd.
P.O. Box 1658, Kwang Hwa Moon
Seoul   Tel. 730.78.91
                         Telefax: 735.00.30

MALAYSIA – MALAISIE
University of Malaya Bookshop
University of Malaya
P.O. Box 1127, Jalan Pantai Baru
59700 Kuala Lumpur
Malaysia   Tel. 756.5000/756.5425
                         Telefax: 756.3246

MEXICO – MEXIQUE
OECD Publications and Information Centre
Edificio INFOTEC
Av. San Fernando no. 37
Col. Toriello Guerra
Tlalpan C.P. 14050
Mexico D.F.
           Tel. (525) 606 00 11 Extension 100
               Fax : (525) 606 13 07

Revistas y Periodicos Internacionales S.A. de C.V.
Florencia 57 - 1004
Mexico, D.F. 06600   Tel. 207.81.00
                          Telefax: 208.39.79

NETHERLANDS – PAYS-BAS
SDU Uitgeverij Plantijnstraat
Externe Fondsen
Postbus 20014
2500 EA's-Gravenhage   Tel. (070) 37.89.880
Voor bestellingen: Telefax: (070) 34.75.778

**NEW ZEALAND –
NOUVELLE-ZÉLANDE**
GPLegislation Services
P.O. Box 12418
Thorndon, Wellington   Tel. (04) 496.5655
                     Telefax: (04) 496.5698

NORWAY – NORVÈGE
NIC INFO A/S
Bertrand Narvesens vei 2
P.O. Box 6512 Etterstad
0606 Oslo 6   Tel. (022) 57.33.00
                     Telefax: (022) 68.19.01

PAKISTAN
Mirza Book Agency
65 Shahrah Quaid-E-Azam
Lahore 54000   Tel. (42) 353.601
                        Telefax: (42) 231.730

PHILIPPINE – PHILIPPINES
International Booksource Center Inc.
Rm 179/920 Cityland 10 Condo Tower 2
HV dela Costa Ext cor Valero St.
Makati Metro Manila   Tel. (632) 817 9676
                    Telefax : (632) 817 1741

POLAND – POLOGNE
Ars Polona
00-950 Warszawa
Krakowskie Przedmieście 7   Tel. (22) 264760
                        Telefax : (22) 268673

PORTUGAL
Livraria Portugal
Rua do Carmo 70-74
Apart. 2681
1200 Lisboa   Tel. (01) 347.49.82/5
                    Telefax: (01) 347.02.64

SINGAPORE – SINGAPOUR
Gower Asia Pacific Pte Ltd.
Golden Wheel Building
41, Kallang Pudding Road, No. 04-03
Singapore 1334   Tel. 741.5166
                        Telefax: 742.9356

SPAIN – ESPAGNE
Mundi-Prensa Libros S.A.
Castelló 37, Apartado 1223
Madrid 28001   Tel. (91) 431.33.99
                     Telefax: (91) 575.39.98

Mundi-Prensa Barcelona
Consell de Cent No. 391
08009 – Barcelona   Tel. (93) 488.34.92
                     Telefax: (93) 487.76.59

Llibreria de la Generalitat
Palau Moja
Rambla dels Estudis, 118
08002 – Barcelona
         (Subscripcions) Tel. (93) 318.80.12
          (Publicacions) Tel. (93) 302.67.23
                    Telefax: (93) 412.18.54

SRI LANKA
Centre for Policy Research
c/o Colombo Agencies Ltd.
No. 300-304, Galle Road
Colombo 3   Tel. (1) 574240, 573551-2
                Telefax: (1) 575394, 510711

SWEDEN – SUÈDE
CE Fritzes AB
S-106 47 Stockholm   Tel. (08) 690.90.90
                    Telefax: (08) 20.50.21

Subscription Agency/Agence d'abonnements :
Wennergren-Williams Info AB
P.O. Box 1305
171 25 Solna   Tel. (08) 705.97.50
                     Telefax: (08) 27.00.71

SWITZERLAND – SUISSE
Maditec S.A. (Books and Periodicals - Livres
et périodiques)
Chemin des Palettes 4
Case postale 266
1020 Renens VD 1   Tel. (021) 635.08.65
                     Telefax: (021) 635.07.80

Librairie Payot S.A.
4, place Pépinet
CP 3212
1002 Lausanne   Tel. (021) 320.25.11
                    Telefax: (021) 320.25.14

Librairie Unilivres
6, rue de Candolle
1205 Genève   Tel. (022) 320.26.23
                    Telefax: (022) 329.73.18

Subscription Agency/Agence d'abonnements :
Dynapresse Marketing S.A.
38 avenue Vibert
1227 Carouge   Tel. (022) 308.07.89
                    Telefax: (022) 308.07.99

See also – Voir aussi :
OECD Publications and Information Centre
August-Bebel-Allee 6
D-53175 Bonn (Germany)   Tel. (0228) 959.120
                    Telefax: (0228) 959.12.17

THAILAND – THAÏLANDE
Suksit Siam Co. Ltd.
113, 115 Fuang Nakhon Rd.
Opp. Wat Rajbopith
Bangkok 10200   Tel. (662) 225.9531/2
                   Telefax: (662) 222.5188

TUNISIA – TUNISIE
Grande Librairie Spécialisée
Fendri Ali
Avenue Haffouz Imm El-Intilaka
Bloc B 1 Sfax 3000   Tel. (216-4) 296 855
                   Telefax: (216-4) 298.270

TURKEY – TURQUIE
Kültür Yayınları Is-Türk Ltd. Sti.
Atatürk Bulvari No. 191/Kat 13
Kavaklidere/Ankara
                Tel. (312) 428.11.40 Ext. 2458
                   Telefax: (312) 417 24 90
Dolmabahce Cad. No. 29
Besiktas/Istanbul   Tel. (212) 260 7188

UNITED KINGDOM – ROYAUME-UNI
HMSO
Gen. enquiries   Tel. (171) 873 8242
Postal orders only:
P.O. Box 276, London SW8 5DT
Personal Callers HMSO Bookshop
49 High Holborn, London WC1V 6HB
                       Telefax: (171) 873 8416
Branches at: Belfast, Birmingham, Bristol,
Edinburgh, Manchester

UNITED STATES – ÉTATS-UNIS
OECD Publications and Information Center
2001 L Street N.W., Suite 650
Washington, D.C. 20036-4922   Tel. (202) 785.6323
                      Telefax: (202) 785.0350

Subscriptions to OECD periodicals may also be placed through main subscription agencies.

Les abonnements aux publications périodiques de l'OCDE peuvent être souscrits auprès des principales agences d'abonnement.

Orders and inquiries from countries where Distributors have not yet been appointed should be sent to: OECD Publications Service, 2, rue André-Pascal, 75775 Paris Cedex 16, France.

Les commandes provenant de pays où l'OCDE n'a pas encore désigné de distributeur peuvent être adressées à : OCDE, Service des Publications, 2, rue André-Pascal, 75775 Paris Cedex 16, France.

1-1996

OECD PUBLICATIONS, 2, rue André-Pascal, 75775 PARIS CEDEX 16
PRINTED IN FRANCE
(41 96 01 1) ISBN 92-64-14790-X – No. 48589 1996